Fundamentals of Computer Graphics

Fundamentals of Computer Graphics

Zoey Clark

WILLFORD **P**RESS

www.willfordpress.com

Published by Willford Press,
118-35 Queens Blvd., Suite 400,
Forest Hills, NY 11375, USA

ISBN: 978-1-64728-027-7

Cataloging-in-Publication Data

Fundamentals of computer graphics / Zoey Clark.
    p. cm.
Includes bibliographical references and index.
ISBN 978-1-64728-027-7
1. Computer graphics. 2. Computer art. 3. Image processing--Digital techniques.
4. New media art. I. Clark, Zoey.
T385 .F86 2022
006.6--dc23

For information on all Willford Press publications
visit our website at www.willfordpress.com

Table of Contents

Preface

This book has been written, keeping in view that students want more practical information. Thus, my aim has been to make it as comprehensive as possible for the readers. I would like to extend my thanks to my family and co-workers for their knowledge, support and encouragement all along.

The discipline which focuses on generating images with the aid of computers is known as computer graphics. It is also responsible for processing image data which has been received from the physical world. The images within computer graphics are broadly divided into two-dimensional images and three-dimensional images. The two dimensional images are further classified into raster graphics and vector graphics. Three-dimensional graphics use a three dimensional representation of geometric data. It makes use of a diverse array of sciences such as physics, perception, optics and geometry. Some of the different types of media where computer graphics are extensively used are advertising, animation, video games and movies. This textbook provides comprehensive insights into the field of computer graphics. The topics included herein on this field are of utmost significance and bound to provide incredible insights to readers. The book is appropriate for students seeking detailed information in this area as well as for experts.

A brief description of the chapters is provided below for further understanding:

Chapter – Introduction

The pictures and films that are created using computers are known as computer graphics. The main types of computer graphics are raster graphics and vector graphics. This chapter has been carefully written to provide an easy understanding of the different types and applications of computer graphics.

Chapter – Key Concepts in Computer Graphics

Some of the basic concepts of computer graphics are soft-body dynamics, sprite, reflection, specular highlight, physically based animation, procedural textures, rendering equation, etc. This chapter closely examines these key concepts of computer graphics to provide an extensive understanding of the subject.

Chapter – Computer Graphics: Hardware and Software

Graphics hardware are the different types of hardware components that are essential to quickly render 3D objects as pixels on the computer screen. The program which enables a person to manipulate images on a computer is known as graphics software. The topics elaborated in this chapter will help in gaining a better perspective about the diverse types of hardware and software used in computer graphics.

Chapter – Techniques and Methods in Computer Graphics

Various types of techniques and methods used in computer graphics include ray tracing, texture filtering, visualization, fluid animation, multiview projection, shaders, 3D modeling, reflection mapping, normal mapping, bump mapping, texture mapping and displacement mapping. The diverse applications of these techniques and methods in computer graphics have been thoroughly discussed in this chapter.

Chapter – 3D Projection

Any method of mapping three-dimensional points on a two-dimensional plane is known as 3D projection. Some of the most common types of projection are parallel projection, orthographic projection, oblique projection, isometric projections and perspective projection. This chapter closely examines these types of 3D projection to provide an extensive understanding of the subject.

Zoey Clark

1

Introduction

The pictures and films that are created using computers are known as computer graphics. The main types of computer graphics are raster graphics and vector graphics. This chapter has been carefully written to provide an easy understanding of the different types and applications of computer graphics.

Computer Graphics

Computer graphics is an art of drawing pictures, lines, charts, etc using computers with the help of programming. Computer graphics is made up of number of pixels. Pixel is the smallest graphical picture or unit represented on the computer screen. Basically there are two types of computer graphics namely.

Interactive Computer Graphics: Interactive Computer Graphics involves a two way communication between computer and user. Here the observer is given some control over the image by providing him with an input device for example the video game controller of the ping pong game. This helps him to signal his request to the computer.

The computer on receiving signals from the input device can modify the displayed picture appropriately. To the user it appears that the picture is changing instantaneously in response to his commands. He can give a series of commands, each one generating a graphical response from the computer. In this way he maintains a conversation, or dialogue, with the computer.

Interactive computer graphics affects our lives in a number of indirect ways. For example, it helps to train the pilots of our airplanes. We can create a flight simulator which may help the pilots to get trained not in a real aircraft but on the grounds at the control of the flight simulator. The flight simulator is a mock up of an aircraft flight deck, containing all the usual controls and surrounded by screens on which we have the projected computer generated views of the terrain visible on take off and landing.

Flight simulators have many advantages over the real aircrafts for training purposes, including fuel savings, safety, and the ability to familiarize the trainee with a large number of the world's airports.

Non Interactive Computer Graphics: In non interactive computer graphics otherwise known as passive computer graphics. it is the computer graphics in which user does not have any kind of control over the image. Image is merely the product of static stored program and will work according to the instructions given in the program linearly. The image is totally under the control of program instructions not under the user. Example: screen savers.

Raster Graphics

Raster graphics, also called bitmap graphics is a type of digital image that uses tiny rectangular pixels, or picture elements, arranged in a grid formation to represent an image. Because the format can support a wide range of colours and depict subtle graduated tones, it is well-suited for displaying continuous-tone images such as photographs or shaded drawings, along with other detailed images.

Raster graphics has origins in television technology, with images constructed much like the pictures on a television screen. A raster graphic is made up of a collection of tiny, uniformly sized pixels, which are arranged in a two-dimensional grid made up of columns and rows. Each pixel contains one or more bits of information, depending on the degree of detail in the image. For example, a black-and-white image contains only one bit per pixel (a binary bit can be in one of two states; thus, a single bit can represent white or black); an image with shading and colour commonly contains 24 bits of information per pixel—with 2^{24}, or more than 16 million, possible states per pixel. Known as "truecolor," 24-bit colour can realistically depict colour images. The number of bits stored in each pixel is known as the colour depth. The number of pixels, called resolution, affects how much detail can be depicted in an image. Resolution is often expressed as the number of pixels in a column times the number of pixels in a row (for example, 800×600).

Detailed images often result in large file sizes, although file size can be managed through data compression. Compression can be either lossy (meaning that some data is discarded) or lossless (no data is lost). Popular raster file formats include GIF (graphics interchange format) and JPEG (joint photographic experts group), which are lossy formats, and BMP (Windows bitmap) and TIFF (tagged image file format), which are lossless.

Although raster graphics saw some use in the 1970s and '80s, it was mostly limited to expensive graphics workstations (i.e., high-end computers that were specially optimized for working with graphics). As the graphics capability of personal computers improved in the 1990s, raster graphics became widely used. Images produced from optical scanners and digital cameras are raster graphics, as are most images on the Internet. A commonly used graphics program for working with raster images is Adobe Photoshop.

Vector Graphics

Vector graphics is the creation of digital images through a sequence of commands or mathematical statements that place lines and shapes in a given two-dimensional or three-dimensional space. In physics, a *vector* is a representation of both a quantity and a direction at the same time. In vector graphics, the file that results from a graphic artist's work is created and saved as a sequence of vector statements. For example, instead of containing a bit in the file for each bit of a line drawing, a vector graphic file describes a series of points to be connected. One result is a much smaller file.

At some point, a vector image is converted into a raster graphics image, which maps bits directly to a display space (and is sometimes called a bitmap). The vector image can be converted to a raster image file prior to its display so that it can be ported between systems.

A vector file is sometimes called a geometric file. Most images created with tools such as Adobe Illustrator and CorelDraw are in the form of vector image files. Vector image files are easier to modify than raster image files (which can, however, sometimes be reconverted to vector files for further refinement).

Animation images are also usually created as vector files. For example, Shockwave's Flash product lets you create 2-D and 3-D animations that are sent to a requestor as a vector file and then rasterized "on the fly" as they arrive.

Vector vs. Raster Graphics

The main difference between vector and raster graphics is that raster graphics are composed of pixels, while vector graphics are composed of paths. A raster graphic, such as a gif or jpeg, is an array of pixels of various colors, which together form an image.

Raster Graphics	Vector Graphics
They are composed of pixel.	They are composed of paths.
In Raster graphics , refresh process is independent of the complexity of the image	Vector displayed flicker when the number of primitives in the image become too large.
Graphics primitives are specified in terms of end point and must be scan converted into corresponding pixel.	Scan conversation is not required
Raster graphics can draw mathematical curves. Polygons and boundaries of curved primitives only by pixel approximation.	Vector graphics draw continuous and smooth lines.
Raster graphics cost less.	Vector graphics cost more as compared to raster Graphics
They occupy more space which depends on image quality.	The occupy less space.
File extension:. BMP,.TIF,.GIF,.JPG	File extension:. SVG,.EPS,.PDF,.Al,.DXF

Applications of Computer Graphics

Computer graphics are very useful. Today almost every computer can do some graphics, and people have even come to expect to control their computer through icons and pictures rather than just by typing.

Computer-generated imagery is used for movie making, video game and computer program development, scientific modeling, and design for catalogs and other commercial art. Some people even make computer graphics as art. We can classify applications of computer graphics into four main areas:

- Display of information,

- Design,

- User interfaces,

- Simulation.

According to these four areas there are several types of applications which are used in today's world. These are,

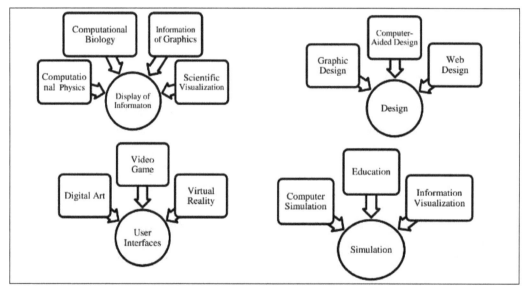

Application of Computer Graphics.

- Computational Biology: Computational biology is an interdisciplinary field that applies the techniques of computer science, applied mathematics and statistics to address biological problems. The main focus lies on developing mathematical modeling and computational simulation techniques.

- Computational Physics: Computational physics is the study and implementation of numerical algorithm to solve problems in physics for which a quantitative theory already exists. It is often regarded as a sub discipline of theoretical physics but some consider it an intermediate branch between theoretical and experimental physics.

- Information of Graphics: Information graphics or information graphics are visual representations of information, data or knowledge. These graphics are used where complex information needs to be explained quickly and clearly, such as in signs, maps, journalism, technical writing, and education. They are also used extensively as tools by computer scientists, mathematicians, and statisticians to ease the process of developing and communicating conceptual information.

- Scientific Visualization: Scientific visualization is a branch of science, concerned with the visualization of three dimensional phenomena, such as architectural, meteorological, medical, biological systems. Scientific visualization focuses on the use of computer graphics to create visual images which aid in understanding of complex, often massive numerical representation of scientific concepts or results.

- Graphic Design: The term graphic design can refer to a number of artistic and professional disciplines which focus on visual communication and presentation. Various methods are used to create and combine symbols, images and/or words to create a visual representation of ideas and messages. Graphic design often refers to both the process (designing) by which the communication is created and the products (designs) which are generated.

- Computer-aided Design: Computer-aided design (CAD) is the use of computer technology for the design of objects, real or virtual. The design of geometric models for object shapes, in particular, is often called computer-aided geometric design (CAGD). CAD may be used to design curves and figures in two-dimensional ("2D") space; or curves, surfaces, or solids in three-dimensional ("3D") objects. CAD is also widely used to produce computer animation for special effects in movies, advertising, technical manuals.

- Web Design: Web design is the skill of designing presentations of content usually hypertext or hypermedia that is delivered to an end-user through the World Wide Web, by way of a Web browser. The process of designing Web pages, Web sites, Web applications or multimedia for the Web may utilize multiple disciplines, such as animation, authoring, communication design, corporate identity, graphic design, human-computer interaction, information architecture, interaction design, marketing, photography, search engine optimization and typography.

- Digital Art: Digital art most commonly refers to art created on a computer in digital form. On other hand, is a term applied to contemporary art that uses the methods of mass production or digital media. The impact of digital technology has transformed traditional activities such as painting, drawing and sculpture, while new forms, such as net art, digital installation art, and virtual reality, have been recognized artistic practices.

- Video Games: A video game is an electronic game that involves interaction with a user interface to generate visual feedback on a raster display device. The electronic systems used to play video games are known as platforms. This platform creates through graphics.

- Virtual Reality: Virtual reality (VR) is a technology which allows a user to interact with a computer-simulated environment. The simulated environment can be similar to the real world, for example, simulations for pilot or combat training, or it can differ significantly from reality, as in VR games. It is currently very difficult to create a high-fidelity virtual reality experience, due largely to technical limitations on processing power, image resolution and communication bandwidth. Virtual Reality is often used to describe a wide variety of applications, commonly associated with its immersive, highly visual, 3D environments.

- Computer Simulation: A computer simulation, a computer model or a computational model is a computer program, or network of computers, that attempts to simulate an abstract model of a particular system.

- Education: A computer simulation, a computer model or a computational model is a computer program, or network of computers, that attempts to simulate an abstract model of a particular system. Computer simulations have become a useful part of mathematical modeling of many natural systems in physics (computational physics), chemistry and biology, human systems in economics, psychology, and social science and in the process of engineering new technology, to gain insight into the operation of those systems, or to observe their behavior.

- Information Visualization: Information visualization is the study of the visual representation of large-scale collections of non-numerical information, such as files and lines of code in software systems, and the use of graphical techniques to help people understand and analyze data.

The computer-generated images we see on television and in movies have advanced to the point that they are almost indistinguishable from real-world images. Computer graphics become a power field for the production of pictures. There are no areas in which graphical displays can't be used to some advantages, so it is not surprising to find the use of computer graphics so widespread.

Computer Animation

Animation is the process of designing, drawing, making layouts and preparation of photographic sequences which are integrated in the multimedia and gaming products. Animation involves the exploitation and management of still images to generate the illusion of movement. A person who creates animations is called animator. He / she use various computer technologies to capture the still images and then to animate these in desired sequence.

Multimedia is the term used to represent combination of visual and audio materials gathered from various resources and then added into one single combination. A multimedia product can be sets of texts, graphic arts, sounds, animations and videos. Precisely, term multimedia is used to refer visual and audio materials into a single common presentation which can be played in a computer including CD ROM or digital video, internet or web technology, streaming audio or video and data projection system etc.

Modern entertainment industry i.e. film and television has gained new heights because of advances in animation, graphics and multimedia. Television advertisements, cartoons serials, presentation and model designs - all use animation and multimedia techniques.

- Traditional animation (cel animation or hand-drawn animation),

- Stop motion animation (Claymation, Cut-outs),

- Motion Graphics (Typography, Animated logo).

Types of Animation

- Computer Animation,

- 2D animation,

- 3D animation.

Importance of Computer Graphics and Animation

Computer graphics and animation have left an undeniable mark on the entertainment industry. Pioneers in the field of CGI have struggled to bring highly detailed realism and beauty to their work. Events, scenes and characters are being brought to life without the use of hokey rubber suits or stilted animatronics. As computer graphics and animation continue to evolve, the limits on what is possible in entertainment continue to dissipate.

Fantasy and Science Fiction

Sci-fi and fantasy films have been greatly altered by the evolution of CGI. Tolkien's "The Lord of The Rings" creatures and locations were made possible through the use of computer-generated effects. The "Star Wars" prequels also made heavy use of CGI to create worlds that would be impossible to make in model or in a studio.

Video Games

Computer graphics have also assisted video games in growing to match and then eclipse almost all forms of popular entertainment in terms of sales. While computer graphics-based games started as primitive dots and lines across the screen, they have evolved into compelling virtual worlds. Games such as "Grand Theft Auto," "Oblivion" and "Fallout 3" have earned record-breaking sales for ensnaring players in impossibly detailed virtual lives.

Weaknesses

While these advances in technology have allowed film, television and video game makers to create worlds undreamed of, there are those who worry about it's overuse. Film critics such as Roger Ebert have pointed out the flatness of dialogue given back actors trapped in a world of blue screens. Effects for effects sake have also become a problem for many critics who worry that style is preferred to substance.

References

- What-is-computer-graphics-explain-interactive-and-non-interactive, basic-of-computer-graphics, computer graphics: ecomputernotes.com, Retrieved 9 May, 2019

- Raster-graphics, technology: britannica.com, Retrieved 8 August , 2019

- Vector-vs-raster-graphics: geeksforgeeks.org, Retrieved 28 April, 2019

- Application-computer-graphics-niropam-das, pulse: linkedin.com, Retrieved 19 May, 2019

- What-is-animation, animation: indiaeducation.net, Retrieved 3 August, 2019

- Importance-of-computer-graphics-animation: itstillworks.com, Retrieved 23 June, 2019

2
Key Concepts in Computer Graphics

Some of the basic concepts of computer graphics are soft-body dynamics, sprite, reflection, specular highlight, physically based animation, procedural textures, rendering equation, etc. This chapter closely examines these key concepts of computer graphics to provide an extensive understanding of the subject.

WebGL Graphics Pipeline

To render 3D graphics, we have to follow a sequence of steps. These steps are known as graphics pipeline or rendering pipeline.

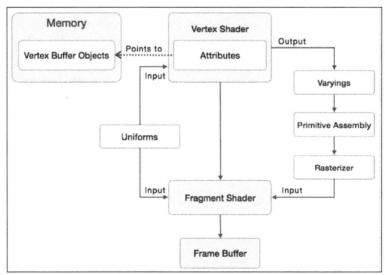

WebGL graphics pipeline.

JavaScript

While developing WebGL applications, we write Shader language code to communicate with the GPU. JavaScript is used to write the control code of the program, which includes the following actions:

- Initialize WebGL – JavaScript is used to initialize the WebGL context.

- Create arrays – We create JavaScript arrays to hold the data of the geometry.

- Buffer objects – We create buffer objects (vertex and index) by passing the arrays as parameters.

- Shaders – We create, compile, and link the shaders using JavaScript.

- Attributes – We can create attributes, enable them, and associate them with buffer objects using JavaScript.

- Uniforms – We can also associate the uniforms using JavaScript.

- Transformation matrix – Using JavaScript, we can create transformation matrix.

Initially we create the data for the required geometry and pass them to the shaders in the form of buffers. The attribute variable of the shader language points to the buffer objects, which are passed as inputs to the vertex shader.

Vertex Shader

When we start the rendering process by invoking the methods drawElements() and drawArray(), the vertex shader is executed for each vertex provided in the vertex buffer object. It calculates the position of each vertex of a primitive polygon and stores it in the varying gl_position. It also calculates the other attributes such as color, texture coordinates, and vertices that are normally associated with a vertex.

Primitive Assembly

After calculating the position and other details of each vertex, the next phase is the primitive assembly stage. Here the triangles are assembled and passed to the rasterizer.

Rasterization

In the rasterization step, the pixels in the final image of the primitive are determined. It has two steps:

- Culling – Initially the orientation (is it front or back facing?) of the polygon is determined. All those triangles with improper orientation that are not visible in view area are discarded. This process is called culling.

- Clipping – If a triangle is partly outside the view area, then the part outside the view area is removed. This process is known as clipping.

Fragment Shader

The fragment shader gets:

- Data from the vertex shader in varying variables.

- Primitives from the rasterization stage.

- Calculates the color values for each pixel between the vertices.

The fragment shader stores the color values of every pixel in each fragment. These color values can be accessed during fragment operations.

Fragment Operations

Fragment operations are carried out after determining the color of each pixel in the primitive. These fragment operations may include the following:

- Depth,

- Color buffer blend,

- Dithering.

Once all the fragments are processed, a 2D image is formed and displayed on the screen. The frame buffer is the final destination of the rendering pipeline.

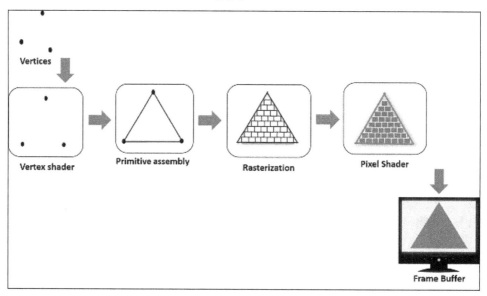

Frame Buffer

Frame buffer is a portion of graphics memory that hold the scene data. This buffer contains details such as width and height of the surface (in pixels), color of each pixel, and depth and stencil buffers.

Soft-body Dynamics

Soft-body dynamics is a field of computer graphics that focuses on visually realistic physical simulations of the motion and properties of deformable objects (or *soft bodies*). The applications are mostly in video games and films. Unlike in simulation of rigid bodies, the shape of soft bodies can change, meaning that the relative distance of two points on the object is not fixed. While the relative distances of points are not fixed, the body is expected to retain its shape to some degree (unlike a fluid). The scope of soft body dynamics is quite broad, including simulation of soft organic materials such as muscle, fat, hair and vegetation, as well as other deformable materials such as clothing and fabric. Generally, these methods only provide visually plausible emulations rather than accurate scientific/engineering simulations, though there is some crossover with scientific methods, particularly in the case of finite element simulations. Several physics engines currently provide software for soft-body simulation.

Deformable Solids

The simulation of volumetric solid soft bodies can be realised by using a variety of approaches.

Spring/Mass Models

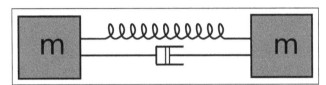

Two nodes as mass points connected by a
parallel circuit of a spring and a damper.

In this approach, the body is modeled as a set of point masses (nodes) connected by ideal weightless elastic springs obeying some variant of Hooke's law. The nodes may either derive from the edges of a two-dimensional polygonal mesh representation of the surface of the object, or from a three-dimensional network of nodes and edges modeling the internal structure of the object (or even a one-dimensional system of links, if for example a rope or hair strand is being simulated). Additional springs between nodes can be added, or the force law of the springs modified, to achieve desired effects. Applying Newton's second law to the point masses including the forces applied by the springs and any external forces (due to contact, gravity, air resistance, wind, and so on) gives a system of differential equations for the motion of the nodes, which is solved by standard numerical schemes for solving ODEs. Rendering of a three-dimensional mass-spring lattice is often done using free-form deformation, in which the rendered mesh is embedded in the lattice and distorted to conform to the shape of the lattice as it evolves. Assuming all point masses equal to zero one can obtain the Stretched grid method aimed at several engineering problems solution relative to the elastic grid behavior. These are sometimes known as mass-spring-damper models. In pressurized soft bodies spring-mass model is combined with a pressure force based on the ideal gas law.

Finite Element Simulation

This is a more physically accurate approach, which uses the widely used finite element method to solve the partial differential equations which govern the dynamics of an elastic material. The body is modeled as a three-dimensional elastic continuum by breaking it into a large number of solid elements which fit together, and solving for the stresses and strains in each element using a model of the material. The elements are typically tetrahedral, the nodes being the vertices of the tetrahedra (relatively simple methods exist to *tetrahedralize* a three dimensional region bounded by a polygon mesh into tetrahedra, similarly to how a two-dimensional polygon may be *triangulated* into triangles). The strain (which measures the local deformation of the points of the material from their rest state) is quantified by the strain tensor ϵ. The stress (which measures the local forces per-unit area in all directions acting on the material) is quantified by the Cauchy stress tensor σ. Given the current local strain, the local stress can be computed via the generalized form of Hooke's law: $\sigma = C\varepsilon$, where C is the "elasticity tensor" which encodes the material properties (parametrized in linear elasticity for an isotropic material by the Poisson ratio and Young's modulus).

The equation of motion of the element nodes is obtained by integrating the stress field over each element and relating this, via Newton's second law, to the node accelerations.

Pixelux (developers of the Digital Molecular Matter system) use a finite-element-based approach for their soft bodies, using a tetrahedral mesh and converting the stress tensor directly into node forces. Rendering is done via a form of free-form deformation.

Energy Minimization Methods

This approach is motivated by variational principles and the physics of surfaces, which dictate that a constrained surface will assume the shape which minimizes the total energy of deformation (analogous to a soap bubble). Expressing the energy of a surface in terms of its local deformation (the energy is due to a combination of stretching and bending), the local force on the surface is given by differentiating the energy with respect to position, yielding an equation of motion which can be solved in the standard ways.

Shape Matching

In this scheme, penalty forces or constraints are applied to the model to drive it towards its original shape (i.e. the material behaves as if it has shape memory). To conserve momentum the rotation of the body must be estimated properly, for example via polar decomposition. To approximate finite element simulation, shape matching can be applied to three dimensional lattices and multiple shape matching constraints blended.

Rigid-body based Deformation

Deformation can also be handled by a traditional rigid-body physics engine, modeling the soft-body motion using a network of multiple rigid bodies connected by constraints, and using (for example) matrix-palette skinning to generate a surface mesh for rendering. This is the approach used for deformable objects in Havok Destruction.

Cloth Simulation

In the context of computer graphics, *cloth simulation* refers to the simulation of soft bodies in the form of two dimensional continuum elastic membranes, that is, for this purpose, the actual structure of real cloth on the yarn level can be ignored (though modeling cloth on the yarn level has been tried). Via rendering effects, this can produce a visually plausible emulation of textiles and clothing, used in a variety of contexts in video games, animation, and film. It can also be used to simulate two dimensional sheets of materials other than textiles, such as deformable metal panels or vegetation. In video games it is often used to enhance the realism of clothed characters, which otherwise would be entirely animated.

Cloth simulators are generally based on mass-spring models, but a distinction must be made between force-based and position-based solvers.

Force-based Cloth

The mass-spring model (obtained from a polygonal mesh representation of the cloth) determines the internal spring forces acting on the nodes at each timestep (in combination with gravity and applied forces). Newton's second law gives equations of motion which can be solved via standard ODE solvers. To create high resolution cloth with a realistic stiffness is not possible however with simple explicit solvers (such as forward Euler integration), unless the timestep is made too small for interactive applications (since as is well known, explicit integrators are numerically unstable for sufficiently stiff systems). Therefore, implicit solvers must be used, requiring solution of a large sparse matrix system (via e.g. the conjugate gradient method), which itself may also be difficult to achieve at interactive frame rates. An alternative is to use an explicit method with low stiffness, with *ad hoc* methods to avoid instability and excessive stretching (e.g. strain limiting corrections).

Position-based Dynamics

To avoid needing to do an expensive implicit solution of a system of ODEs, many real-time cloth simulators (notably PhysX, Havok Cloth, and Maya nCloth) use *position based dynamics* (PBD), an approach based on constraint relaxation. The mass-spring model is converted into a system of constraints, which demands that the distance between the connected nodes be equal to the initial distance. This system is solved sequentially and iteratively, by directly moving nodes to satisfy each constraint, until sufficiently stiff cloth is obtained. This is similar to a Gauss-Seidel solution of the implicit matrix system for the mass-spring model. Care must be taken though to solve the constraints in the same sequence each timestep, to avoid spurious oscillations, and to make sure that the constraints do not violate linear and angular momentum conservation. Additional position constraints can be applied, for example to keep the nodes within desired regions of space (sufficiently close to an animated model for example), or to maintain the body's overall shape via shape matching.

Collision Detection for Deformable Objects

Realistic interaction of simulated soft objects with their environment may be important for obtaining visually realistic results. Cloth self-intersection is important in some applications for acceptably realistic simulated garments. This is challenging to achieve at interactive frame rates, particularly in the case of detecting and resolving self collisions and mutual collisions between two or more deformable objects.

Collision detection may be discrete/a posteriori (meaning objects are advanced in time through a pre-determined interval, and then any penetrations detected and resolved), or continuous/a priori (objects are advanced only until a collision occurs, and the collision is handled before proceeding). The former is easier to implement and faster, but leads to failure to detect collisions (or detection of spurious collisions) if objects move fast enough. Real-time systems generally have to use discrete collision detection, with other ad hoc ways to avoid failing to detect collisions.

Detection of collisions between cloth and environmental objects with a well defined "inside" is straightforward since the system can detect unambiguously whether the cloth mesh vertices and faces are intersecting the body and resolve them accordingly. If a well defined "inside" does not exist (e.g. in the case of collision with a mesh which does not form a closed boundary), an "inside" may be constructed via extrusion. Mutual- or self-collisions of soft bodies defined by tetrahedra is straightforward, since it reduces to detection of collisions between solid tetrahedra.

However, detection of collisions between two polygonal cloths (or collision of a cloth with itself) via discrete collision detection is much more difficult, since there is no unambiguous way to locally detect after a timestep whether a cloth node which has penetrated is on the "wrong" side or not. Solutions involve either using the history of the cloth motion to determine if an intersection event has occurred, or doing a global analysis of the cloth state to detect and resolve self-intersections. Pixar has presented a method which uses a global topological analysis of mesh intersections in configuration space to detect and resolve self-interpenetration of cloth. Currently, this is generally too computationally expensive for real-time cloth systems.

To do collision detection efficiently, primitives which are certainly not colliding must be identified as soon as possible and discarded from consideration to avoid wasting time. To do this, some form of spatial subdivision scheme is essential, to avoid a brute force test of $O\left[n^2\right]$ primitive collisions. Approaches used include:

- Bounding volume hierarchies (AABB trees, OBB trees, sphere trees).

- Grids, either uniform (using hashing for memory efficiency) or hierarchical (e.g. Octree, kd-tree).

- Coherence-exploiting schemes, such as sweep and prune with insertion sort, or tree-tree collisions with front tracking.

- Hybrid methods involving a combination of various of these schemes, e.g. a coarse AABB tree plus sweep-and-prune with coherence between colliding leaves.

Other Applications

Other effects which may be simulated via the methods of soft-body dynamics are:

- Destructible materials: fracture of brittle solids, cutting of soft bodies, and tearing of cloth. The finite element method is especially suited to modelling fracture as it includes a realistic model of the distribution of internal stresses in the material, which physically is what determines when fracture occurs, according to fracture mechanics.

- Plasticity (permanent deformation) and melting.

- Simulated hair, fur, and feathers.

- Simulated organs for biomedical applications.

Simulating fluids in the context of computer graphics would not normally be considered soft-body dynamics, which is usually restricted to mean simulation of materials which have a tendency to retain their shape and form. In contrast, a fluid assumes the shape of whatever vessel contains it, as the particles are bound together by relatively weak forces.

2D Computer Graphics

2D computer graphics is the computer-based generation of digital images—mostly from two-dimensional models (such as 2D geometric models, text, and digital images) and by techniques specific to them. The word may stand for the branch of computer science that comprises such techniques or for the models themselves.

Raster graphic sprites (left) and masks (right).

2D computer graphics are mainly used in applications that were originally developed upon traditional printing and drawing technologies, such as typography, cartography, technical drawing, advertising, etc. In those applications, the two-dimensional image is not just a representation of a real-world object, but an independent artifact with added semantic value; two-dimensional models are therefore preferred, because they give more direct control of the image than 3D computer graphics (whose approach is more akin to photography than to typography).

In many domains, such as desktop publishing, engineering, and business, a description of a document based on 2D computer graphics techniques can be much smaller than the corresponding digital image—often by a factor of 1/1000 or more. This representation is also more flexible since it can be rendered at different resolutions to suit different output devices. For these reasons, documents and illustrations are often stored or transmitted as 2D graphic files.

2D computer graphics started in the 1950s, based on vector graphics devices. These were largely supplanted by raster-based devices in the following decades. The PostScript language and the X Window System protocol were landmark developments in the field.

2D Graphics Techniques

2D graphics models may combine geometric models (also called vector graphics), digital images (also called raster graphics), text to be typeset (defined by content, font style and size, color, position, and orientation), mathematical functions and equations, and more. These components can be modified and manipulated by two-dimensional geometric transformations such as translation, rotation, scaling. In object-oriented graphics, the image is described indirectly by an object endowed with a self-rendering method—a procedure which assigns colors to the image pixels by an arbitrary algorithm. Complex models can be built by combining simpler objects, in the paradigms of object-oriented programming.

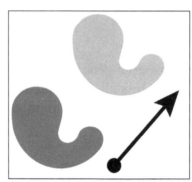

A translation moves every point of a figure or a space
by the same amount in a given direction.

In Euclidean geometry, a translation moves every point a constant distance in a specified direction. A translation can be described as a rigid motion: other rigid motions include rotations and reflections. A translation can also be interpreted as the addition of a constant vector to every point, or as shifting the origin of the coordinate system. A translation operator is an operator T_δ such that

$$T_\delta f(v) = f(v + \delta).$$

If v is a fixed vector, then the translation T_v will work as $T_v(p) = p + v$.

If T is a translation, then the image of a subset A under the function T is the translate of A by T. The translate of A by T_v is often written A + v.

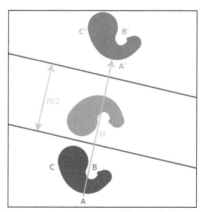

A reflection against an axis followed by a reflection
against a second axis parallel to the first one results
in a total motion which is a translation.

In a Euclidean space, any translation is an isometry. The set of all translations forms the translation group T, which is isomorphic to the space itself, and a normal subgroup of Euclidean group $E(n)$. The quotient group of $E(n)$ by T is isomorphic to the orthogonal group $O(n)$:

$$E(n) / T \cong O(n).$$

Translation

Since a translation is an affine transformation but not a linear transformation, homogeneous coordinates are normally used to represent the translation operator by a matrix and thus to make it linear. Thus we write the 3-dimensional vector $w = (w_x, w_y, w_z)$ using 4 homogeneous coordinates as $w = (w_x, w_y, w_z, 1)$.

To translate an object by a vector v, each homogeneous vector p (written in homogeneous coordinates) would need to be multiplied by this translation matrix:

$$T_v = \begin{bmatrix} 1 & 0 & 0 & v_x \\ 0 & 1 & 0 & v_y \\ 0 & 0 & 1 & v_z \\ 0 & 0 & 0 & 1 \end{bmatrix}$$

As shown below, the multiplication will give the expected result:

$$T_v\, p = \begin{bmatrix} 1 & 0 & 0 & v_x \\ 0 & 1 & 0 & v_y \\ 0 & 0 & 1 & v_z \\ 0 & 0 & 0 & 1 \end{bmatrix} \begin{bmatrix} p_x \\ p_y \\ p_z \\ 1 \end{bmatrix} = \begin{bmatrix} p_x + v_x \\ p_y + v_y \\ p_z + v_z \\ 1 \end{bmatrix} = p + v$$

The inverse of a translation matrix can be obtained by reversing the direction of the vector:

$$T_v^{-1} = T_{-v}.$$

Similarly, the product of translation matrices is given by adding the vectors:

$$T_u T_v = T_{u+v}.$$

Because addition of vectors is commutative, multiplication of translation matrices is therefore also commutative (unlike multiplication of arbitrary matrices).

Rotation

In linear algebra, a rotation matrix is a matrix that is used to perform a rotation in Euclidean space:

$$R = \begin{bmatrix} \cos\theta & -\sin\theta \\ \sin\theta & \cos\theta \end{bmatrix}$$

rotates points in the xy-Cartesian plane counterclockwise through an angle θ about the origin of the Cartesian coordinate system. To perform the rotation using a rotation matrix R, the position of each point must be represented by a column vector v, containing the coordinates of the point. A rotated vector is obtained by using the matrix multiplication Rv. Since matrix multiplication has no effect on the zero vector (i.e., on the coordinates of the origin), rotation matrices can only be used to describe rotations about the origin of the coordinate system.

Rotation matrices provide a simple algebraic description of such rotations, and are used extensively for computations in geometry, physics, and computer graphics. In 2-dimensional space, a rotation can be simply described by an angle θ of rotation, but it can be also represented by the 4 entries of a rotation matrix with 2 rows and 2 columns. In 3-dimensional space, every rotation can be interpreted as a rotation by a given angle about a single fixed axis of rotation and hence it can be simply described by an angle and a vector with 3 entries. However, it can also be represented by the 9 entries of a rotation matrix with 3 rows and 3 columns. The notion of rotation is not commonly used in dimensions higher than 3; there is a notion of a rotational displacement, which can be represented by a matrix, but no associated single axis or angle.

Rotation matrices are square matrices, with real entries. More specifically they can be characterized as orthogonal matrices with determinant 1:

$$R^T = R^{-1}, \det R = 1..$$

The set of all such matrices of size n forms a group, known as the special orthogonal group SO(n).

In Two Dimensions

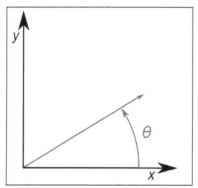

A counterclockwise rotation of a vector through angle θ.
The vector is initially aligned with the x-axis.

In two dimensions every rotation matrix has the following form:

$$R(\theta) = \begin{bmatrix} \cos\theta & -\sin\theta \\ \sin\theta & \cos\theta \end{bmatrix}.$$

This rotates column vectors by means of the following matrix multiplication:

$$\begin{bmatrix} x' \\ y' \end{bmatrix} = \begin{bmatrix} \cos\theta & -\sin\theta \\ \sin\theta & \cos\theta \end{bmatrix}\begin{bmatrix} x \\ y \end{bmatrix}.$$

So the coordinates (x',y') of the point (x,y) after rotation are:

$$x' = x\cos\theta - y\sin\theta,$$
$$y' = x\sin\theta + y\cos\theta.$$

The direction of vector rotation is counterclockwise if θ is positive (e.g. 90°), and clockwise if θ is negative (e.g. -90°).

$$R(-\theta) = \begin{bmatrix} \cos\theta & \sin\theta \\ -\sin\theta & \cos\theta \end{bmatrix}.$$

Non-standard Orientation of the Coordinate System

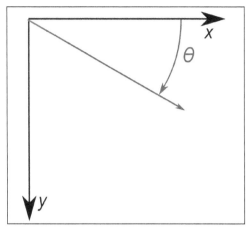

A rotation through angle θ with non-standard axes.

If a standard right-handed Cartesian coordinate system is used, with the x axis to the right and the y axis up, the rotation R(θ) is counterclockwise. If a left-handed Cartesian coordinate system is used, with x directed to the right but y directed down, R(θ) is clockwise. Such non-standard orientations are rarely used in mathematics but are common in 2D computer graphics, which often have the origin in the top left corner and the y-axis down the screen or page.

Common Rotations

Particularly useful are the matrices for 90° and 180° rotations:

$$R(90^\circ) = \begin{bmatrix} 0 & -1 \\ 1 & 0 \end{bmatrix} \text{ (90° counterclockwise rotation)}$$

$$R(180^\circ) = \begin{bmatrix} -1 & 0 \\ 0 & -1 \end{bmatrix} \text{ (180° rotation in either direction – a half-turn)}$$

$$(270^\circ) = \begin{bmatrix} 0 & 1 \\ -1 & 0 \end{bmatrix} \text{ (270° counterclockwise rotation, the same as a 90° clockwise rotation)}$$

In Euclidean geometry, uniform scaling (isotropic scaling, homogeneous dilation, homothety) is a linear transformation that enlarges (increases) or shrinks (diminishes) objects by a scale factor that is the same in all directions. The result of uniform scaling is similar (in the geometric sense) to the original. A scale factor of 1 is normally allowed, so that congruent shapes are also classed as similar. (Some school text books specifically exclude this possibility, just as some exclude squares from being rectangles or circles from being ellipses.)

More general is scaling with a separate scale factor for each axis direction. Non-uniform scaling (anisotropic scaling, inhomogeneous dilation) is obtained when at least one of the scaling factors is different from the others; a special case is directional scaling or stretching (in one direction). Non-uniform scaling changes the shape of the object; e.g. a square may change into a rectangle, or into a parallelogram if the sides of the square are not parallel to the scaling axes (the angles between lines parallel to the axes are preserved, but not all angles).

Scaling

A scaling can be represented by a scaling matrix. To scale an object by a vector $v = (v_x, v_y, v_z)$, each point $p = (p_x, p_y, p_z)$ would need to be multiplied with this scaling matrix:

$$S_v = \begin{bmatrix} v_x & 0 & 0 \\ 0 & v_y & 0 \\ 0 & 0 & v_z \end{bmatrix}.$$

As shown below, the multiplication will give the expected result:

$$S_v p = \begin{bmatrix} v_x & 0 & 0 \\ 0 & v_y & 0 \\ 0 & 0 & v_z \end{bmatrix} \begin{bmatrix} p_x \\ p_y \\ p_z \end{bmatrix} = \begin{bmatrix} v_x p_x \\ v_y p_y \\ v_z p_z \end{bmatrix}.$$

Such a scaling changes the diameter of an object by a factor between the scale factors, the area by a factor between the smallest and the largest product of two scale factors, and the volume by the product of all three.

The scaling is uniform if and only if the scaling factors are equal ($v_x = v_y = v_z$). If all except one of the scale factors are equal to 1, we have directional scaling.

In the case where $v_x = v_y = v_z = k$, the scaling is also called an enlargement or dilation by a factor k, increasing the area by a factor of k^2 and the volume by a factor of k^3.

A scaling in the most general sense is any affine transformation with a diagonalizable matrix. It includes the case that the three directions of scaling are not perpendicular. It includes also the case that one or more scale factors are equal to zero (projection), and the case of one or more negative scale factors. The latter corresponds to a combination of scaling proper and a kind of reflection: along lines in a particular direction we take the reflection in the point of intersection with a plane that need not be perpendicular; therefore it is more general than ordinary reflection in the plane.

Using Homogeneous Coordinates

In projective geometry, often used in computer graphics, points are represented using homogeneous coordinates. To scale an object by a vector $v = (v_x, v_y, v_z)$, each homogeneous coordinate vector $p = (p_x, p_y, p_z, 1)$ would need to be multiplied with this projective transformation matrix:

$$S_v = \begin{bmatrix} v_x & 0 & 0 & 0 \\ 0 & v_y & 0 & 0 \\ 0 & 0 & v_z & 0 \\ 0 & 0 & 0 & 1 \end{bmatrix}.$$

As shown below, the multiplication will give the expected result:

$$S_v p = \begin{bmatrix} v_x & 0 & 0 & 0 \\ 0 & v_y & 0 & 0 \\ 0 & 0 & v_z & 0 \\ 0 & 0 & 0 & 1 \end{bmatrix} \begin{bmatrix} p_x \\ p_y \\ p_z \\ 1 \end{bmatrix} = \begin{bmatrix} v_x p_x \\ v_y p_y \\ v_z p_z \\ 1 \end{bmatrix}.$$

Since the last component of a homogeneous coordinate can be viewed as the denominator of the other three components, a uniform scaling by a common factor s (uniform scaling) can be accomplished by using this scaling matrix:

$$S_v = \begin{bmatrix} 1 & 0 & 0 & 0 \\ 0 & 1 & 0 & 0 \\ 0 & 0 & 1 & 0 \\ 0 & 0 & 0 & \dfrac{1}{s} \end{bmatrix}.$$

For each vector $p = (p_x, p_y, p_z, 1)$ we would have:

$$S_v p = \begin{bmatrix} 1 & 0 & 0 & 0 \\ 0 & 1 & 0 & 0 \\ 0 & 0 & 1 & 0 \\ 0 & 0 & 0 & \dfrac{1}{s} \end{bmatrix} \begin{bmatrix} p_x \\ p_y \\ p_z \\ 1 \end{bmatrix} = \begin{bmatrix} p_x \\ p_y \\ p_z \\ \dfrac{1}{s} \end{bmatrix}$$

which would be homogenized to:

$$\begin{bmatrix} sp_x \\ sp_y \\ sp_z \\ 1 \end{bmatrix}.$$

Direct Painting

A convenient way to create a complex image is to start with a blank "canvas" raster map (an array of pixels, also known as a bitmap) filled with some uniform background color and then "draw", "paint" or "paste" simple patches of color onto it, in an appropriate order. In particular the canvas may be the frame buffer for a computer display.

Some programs will set the pixel colors directly, but most will rely on some 2D graphics library or the machine's graphics card, which usually implement the following operations:

- Paste a given image at a specified offset onto the canvas;

- Write a string of characters with a specified font, at a given position and angle;

- Paint a simple geometric shape, such as a triangle defined by three corners, or a circle with given center and radius;

- Draw a line segment, arc, or simple curve with a *virtual pen* of given width.

Extended Color Models

Text, shapes and lines are rendered with a client-specified color. Many libraries and cards provide color gradients, which are handy for the generation of smoothly-varying backgrounds, shadow effects, etc. The pixel colors can also be taken from a texture, e.g. a digital image (thus emulating rub-on screentones and the fabled *checker paint* which used to be available only in cartoons).

Painting a pixel with a given color usually replaces its previous color. However, many systems support painting with transparent and translucent colors, which only modify the previous pixel values. The two colors may also be combined in more complex ways, e.g. by computing their bitwise exclusive or. This technique is known as inverting color or color inversion, and is often used in graphical user interfaces for highlighting, rubber-band drawing, and other volatile painting—since re-painting the same shapes with the same color will restore the original pixel values.

Layers

A 2D animated character composited
with 3D backgrounds using layers.

The models used in 2D computer graphics usually do not provide for three-dimensional shapes, or three-dimensional optical phenomena such as lighting, shadows, reflection, refraction, etc. However, they usually can model multiple layers (conceptually of ink, paper, or film; opaque, translucent, or transparent—stacked in a specific order. The ordering is usually defined by a single number (the layer's depth, or distance from the viewer).

Layered models are sometimes called "$2\frac{1}{2}$-D computer graphics". They make it possible to mimic traditional drafting and printing techniques based on film and paper, such as cutting and pasting; and allow the user to edit any layer without affecting the others. For these reasons, they are used in most graphics editors. Layered models also allow better spatial anti-aliasing of complex drawings and provide a sound model for certain techniques such as mitered joints and the even-odd rule.

Layered models are also used to allow the user to suppress unwanted information when viewing or printing a document, e.g. roads or railways from a map, certain process layers from an integrated circuit diagram, or hand annotations from a business letter.

In a layer-based model, the target image is produced by "painting" or "pasting" each layer, in order of decreasing depth, on the virtual canvas. Conceptually, each layer is first rendered on its own, yielding a digital image with the desired resolution which is then painted over the canvas, pixel by pixel. Fully transparent parts of a layer need not be rendered, of course. The rendering and painting may be done in parallel, i.e., each layer pixel may be painted on the canvas as soon as it is produced by the rendering procedure.

Layers that consist of complex geometric objects (such as text or polylines) may be broken down into simpler elements (characters or line segments, respectively), which are then painted as separate layers, in some order. However, this solution may create undesirable aliasing artifacts wherever two elements overlap the same pixel.

2D Graphics Hardware

Modern computer graphics card displays almost overwhelmingly use raster techniques, dividing the screen into a rectangular grid of pixels, due to the relatively low cost of raster-based video hardware as compared with vector graphic hardware. Most graphic hardware has internal support for blitting operations or sprite drawing. A co-processor dedicated to blitting is known as a Blitter chip.

2D Graphics Software

Many graphical user interfaces (GUIs), including macOS, Microsoft Windows, or the X Window System, are primarily based on 2D graphical concepts. Such software provides a visual environment for interacting with the computer, and commonly includes some form of window manager to aid the user in conceptually distinguishing between different applications. The user interface within individual software applications is typically 2D in nature as well, due in part to the fact that most common input devices, such as the mouse, are constrained to two dimensions of movement.

2D graphics are very important in the control peripherals such as printers, plotters, sheet cutting machines, etc. They were also used in most early video games; and are still used for card and board games such as solitaire, chess, mahjongg, etc.

2D graphics editors or drawing programs are application-level software for the creation of images, diagrams and illustrations by direct manipulation (through the mouse, graphics tablet, or similar device) of 2D computer graphics primitives. These editors generally provide geometric primitives as well as digital images; and some even support procedural models. The illustration is usually represented internally as a layered model, often with a hierarchical structure to make editing more convenient. These editors generally output graphics files where the layers and primitives are separately preserved in their original form. MacDraw, introduced in 1984 with the Macintosh line of computers, was an early example of this class; recent examples are the commercial products Adobe Illustrator and CorelDRAW, and the free editors such as xfig or Inkscape. There are also many 2D graphics editors specialized for certain types of drawings such as electrical, electronic and VLSI diagrams, topographic maps, computer fonts, etc.

Image editors are specialized for the manipulation of digital images, mainly by means of free-hand drawing/painting and signal processing operations. They typically use a direct-painting paradigm, where the user controls virtual pens, brushes, and other free-hand artistic instruments to apply paint to a virtual canvas. Some image editors support a multiple-layer model; however, in order to support signal-processing operations like blurring each layer is normally represented as a digital image. Therefore, any geometric primitives that are provided by the editor are immediately converted to pixels and painted onto the canvas. The name raster graphics editor is sometimes used to contrast this approach to that of general editors which also handle vector graphics. One of the first popular image editors was Apple's MacPaint, companion to MacDraw. Modern examples are the free GIMP editor, and the commercial products Photoshop and Paint Shop Pro. This class too includes many specialized editors — for medicine, remote sensing, digital photography, etc.

Developmental Animation

With the resurgence of 2D animation, free and proprietary software packages have become widely available for amateurs and professional animators. The principal issue with 2D animation is labor requirements. With software like RETAS UbiArt Framework and Adobe After Effects, coloring and compositing can be done in less time.

Various approaches have been developed to aid and speed up the process of digital 2D animation. For example, by generating vector artwork in a tool like Adobe Flash an artist may employ software-driven automatic coloring and in-betweening.

Programs like blender allow the user to do either 3D animation, 2D animation or combine both in its software allowing experimentation with multiple forms of animation.

3D Computer Graphics

3D computer graphics, or three-dimensional computer graphics (in contrast to 2D computer graphics), are graphics that use a three-dimensional representation of geometric data (often Cartesian) that is stored in the computer for the purposes of performing calculations and rendering 2D images. The resulting images may be stored for viewing later (possibly as an animation) or displayed in real time.

3D computer graphics rely on many of the same algorithms as 2D computer vector graphics in the wire-frame model and 2D computer raster graphics in the final rendered display. In computer graphics software, 2D applications may use 3D techniques to achieve effects such as lighting, and, similarly, 3D may use some 2D rendering techniques.

The objects in 3D computer graphics are often referred to as 3D models. Unlike the rendered image, a model's data is contained within a graphical data file. A 3D model is a mathematical representation of any three-dimensional object; a model is not technically a graphic until it is displayed. A model can be displayed visually as a two-dimensional image through a process called 3D rendering, or it can be used in non-graphical computer simulations and calculations. With 3D printing, models are rendered into an actual 3D physical representation of themselves, with some limitations as to how accurately the physical model can match the virtual model.

3D computer graphics creation falls into three basic phases:

1. 3D modeling – The process of forming a computer model of an object's shape.

2. Layout and animation – The placement and movement of objects within a scene.

3. 3D rendering – The computer calculations that, based on light placement, surface types, and other qualities, generate the image.

Modeling

The model describes the process of forming the shape of an object. The two most common sources of 3D models are those that an artist or engineer originates on the computer with some kind of 3D modeling tool, and models scanned into a computer from real-world objects. Models can also be produced procedurally or via physical simulation. Basically, a 3D model is formed from points called vertices (or vertexes) that define the shape and form polygons. A polygon is an area formed from at least three vertexes (a triangle). A polygon of n points is an n-gon. The overall integrity of the model and its suitability to use in animation depend on the structure of the polygons.

Materials and Textures

Materials and textures are properties that the render engine uses to render the model, in an unbiased render engine like blender cycles, one can give the model materials to tell the engine how to treat light when it hits the surface. Textures are used to give the material color using a color or albedo map, or give the surface features using a bump or normal map. It can be also used to deform the model itself using a displacement map.

Layout and Animation

Before rendering into an image, objects must be laid out in a scene. This defines spatial relationships between objects, including location and size. Animation refers to the temporal description of an object (i.e., how it moves and deforms over time. Popular methods include keyframing, inverse kinematics, and motion capture). These techniques are often used in combination. As with animation, physical simulation also specifies motion.

Rendering

Rendering converts a model into an image either by simulating light transport to get photo-realistic images, or by applying an art style as in non-photorealistic rendering. The two basic operations in realistic rendering are transport (how much light gets from one place to another) and scattering (how surfaces interact with light). This step is usually performed using 3D computer graphics software or a 3D graphics API. Altering the scene into a suitable form for rendering also involves 3D projection, which displays a three-dimensional image in two dimensions. Although 3D modeling and CAD software may perform 3D rendering as well (e.g. Autodesk 3ds Max or Blender), exclusive 3D rendering software also exists.

Examples of 3D rendering

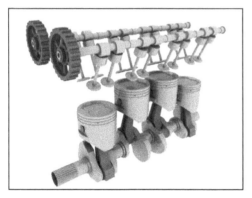

A 3D rendering with ray tracing and ambient occlusion using Blender and YafaRay.

A 3d model of a Dunkerque-class battleship rendered with flat shading.

Experience Curiosity, a real-time web application which leverages 3D rendering capabilities of browsers (WebGL).

Software

3D computer graphics software produces computer-generated imagery (CGI) through 3D modeling and 3D rendering or produces 3D models for analytic, scientific and industrial purposes.

Modeling

3D modeling software is a class of 3D computer graphics software used to produce 3D models. Individual programs of this class are called modeling applications or modelers.

3D modelers allow users to create and alter models via their 3D mesh. Users can add, subtract, stretch and otherwise change the mesh to their desire. Models can be viewed from a variety of angles, usually simultaneously. Models can be rotated and the view can be zoomed in and out.

3D modelers can export their models to files, which can then be imported into other applications as long as the metadata are compatible. Many modelers allow importers and exporters to be plugged-in, so they can read and write data in the native formats of other applications.

Most 3D modelers contain a number of related features, such as ray tracers and other rendering alternatives and texture mapping facilities. Some also contain features that support or allow animation of models. Some may be able to generate full-motion video of a series of rendered scenes (i.e. animation).

Computer-aided Design (CAD)

Computer aided design software may employ the same fundamental 3D modeling techniques that 3D modeling software use but their goal differs. They are used in computer-aided engineering, computer-aided manufacturing, Finite element analysis, product lifecycle management, 3D printing and computer-aided architectural design.

Complementary Tools

After producing video, studios then edit or composite the video using programs such as Adobe Premiere Pro or Final Cut Pro at the mid-level, or Autodesk Combustion, Digital Fusion, Shake at the high-end. Match moving software is commonly used to match live video with computer-generated video, keeping the two in sync as the camera moves.

Use of real-time computer graphics engines to create a cinematic production is called machinima.

Communities

There are a multitude of websites designed to help, educate and support 3D graphic artists. Some are managed by software developers and content providers, but there are standalone sites as well. These communities allow for members to seek advice, post tutorials, provide product reviews or post examples of their own work.

Distinction from Photorealistic 2D Graphics

Not all computer graphics that appear 3D are based on a wireframe model. 2D computer graphics with 3D photorealistic effects are often achieved without wireframe modeling and are sometimes indistinguishable in the final form. Some graphic art software includes filters that can be applied to 2D vector graphics or 2D raster graphics on transparent layers. Visual artists may also copy or visualize 3D effects and manually render photorealistic effects without the use of filters.

Pseudo-3D and True 3D

Some video games use restricted projections of three-dimensional environments, such as isometric graphics or virtual cameras with fixed angles, either as a way to improve performance of the game engine, or for stylistic and gameplay concerns. Such games are said to use pseudo-3D graphics. By contrast, games using 3D computer graphics without such restrictions are said to use *true 3D*.

Sprite

In computer graphics, a sprite is a two-dimensional image or animation that is integrated into a larger scene. Initially used to describe graphical objects handled separately of the memory bitmap of a video display, the term has since been applied more loosely to refer to various manner of graphical overlays.

Originally, sprites were a method of integrating unrelated bitmaps so that they appeared to be part of the normal bitmap on a screen, such as creating an animated character that can be moved on a screen without altering the data defining the overall screen. Such sprites can be created by either circuitry or software. In circuitry, a sprite is a hardware construct that employs custom DMA channels to integrate visual elements with the main screen in that it super-imposes two discrete video sources. Software can simulate this through specialized rendering methods.

As three-dimensional graphics became more prevalent, the term was used to describe a technique whereby flat images are seamlessly integrated into complicated three-dimensional scenes.

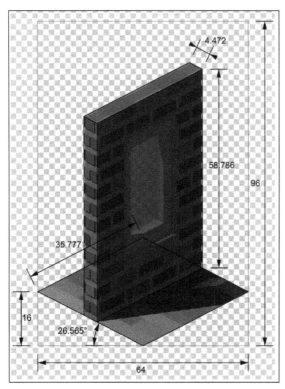

2D coordinates of an isometric sprite.

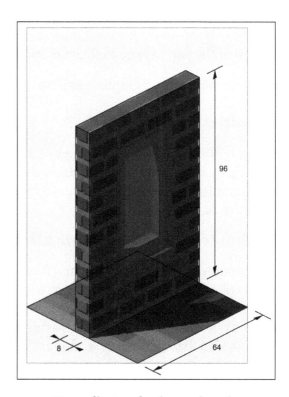

3D coordinates of an isometric sprite.

The use of read-only memory in arcade games from around 1974 allowed the widespread use of sprites. Taito released some of the earliest known video games with sprites that year, including Basketball, a sports game that represented four basketball players and two baskets as sprite images, and Speed Race, a racing video game that represented cars as sprite images, which could collide with each other and vertically scroll across a race track. The following year, they released Western Gun, a run and gun multi-directional shooter that was the earliest known video game to visually represent game characters as sprites, as well as the first to depict a gun on screen.

In the mid-1970s, Signetics devised the first video/graphics processors capable of generating sprite graphics. The Signetics 2636 video processors were first used in the 1976 Radofin 1292 Advanced Programmable Video System.

The Atari VCS, released in 1977, featured a hardware sprite implementation wherein five graphical objects could be moved independently of the game playfield. The VCS's sprites, called players and missiles, were constructed from a single row of pixels that displayed on a scan line; to produce a two-dimensional shape, the sprite's single-row bitmap was altered from by software from one scanline to the next.

The Atari 400 and 800 home computers of 1979 featured similar, but more elaborate circuitry, capable of moving eight Player/Missile objects. This more advanced version allowed a two-dimensional bitmap several pixels wide, and as tall as the screen. To simulate vertical motion, the sprite's bitmap had to be moved up and down incrementally in memory.

The Elektor TV Games Computer was an early microcomputer capable of generating sprite graphics, which Signetics referred to as "objects".

The term "sprite", a Greek fairy, was coined by one of the definers of the Texas Instruments 9918(A) video display processor (VDP). By this time, sprites had advanced to the point where complete two-dimensional shapes could be moved around the screen horizontally and vertically with minimal software overhead.

During most of the 1980s, hardware speed was in the low, single-digit megahertz and memory was measured in kilobytes. Beside CISC processors, all chips are hardwired. Sprites are rare in most video hardware today.

The CPU would instruct the external chips to fetch source images and integrate them into the main screen using direct memory access channels. Calling up external hardware, instead of using the processor alone, greatly improved graphics performance. Because the processor was not occupied by the simple task of transferring data from one place to another, software could run faster; and because the hardware provided certain innate abilities, programs were also smaller.

Hardware Sprites

In early video gaming, sprites were a method of integrating unrelated bitmaps so that they appear to be part of a single bitmap on a screen.

Many early graphics chips had true spriting use capabilities in which the sprite images were integrated into the screen, often with priority control with respect to the background graphics, at the time the video signal was being generated by the graphics chip. This improved performance greatly since the sprite data did not need to be copied into the video memory in order to appear on the screen, and further since this spared the programmer of the task of having to save and restore the underlying graphics, something which otherwise was needed if the programmer chose to progressively update.

The sprite engine is a hardware implementation of scanline rendering. For each scanline the appropriate scanlines of the sprites are first copied (the number of pixels is limited by the memory bandwidth and the length of the horizontal retrace) into very fast, small, multiple (limiting the # of sprites on a line), and costly caches (the size of which limit the horizontal width) and as the pixels are sent to the screen, these caches are combined with each other and the background. It may be larger than the screen and is usually tiled, where the tile map is cached, but the tile set is not. For every pixel, every sprite unit signals its presence onto its line on a bus, so every other unit can notice a collision with it. Some sprite engines can automatically reload their "sprite units" from a display list. The sprite engine has synergy with the palette. To save registers, the height of the sprite, the location of the texture, and the zoom factors are often limited. On systems where the word size is the same as the texel there is no penalty for doing unaligned reads needed for rotation. This leads to the limitations of the known implementations.

Many third party graphics cards offered sprite capabilities. Sprite engines often scale badly, starting to flicker as the number of sprites increases above the number of sprite units, or uses more and more silicon as the designer of the chip implements more units and bigger caches.

Sprites by Software

Many popular home computers of the 1980s lack any support for sprites by hardware. The animated characters, bullets, pointing cursors, etc. for videogames (mainly) were rendered exclusively with the CPU by software, as part of the screen video memory in itself. Hence the term software sprites.

Mainly, two distinct techniques were used to render the sprites by software, depending on the display hardware characteristics:

- Binary image masks, mainly for systems with bitmapped video frame buffers. It employs the use of an additional binary *mask* for every sprite displayed to create transparent areas within a sprite.

- Transparent color, mainly for systems with indexed color displays. This method defines a particular color index (typically index '0' or index '255') with a palletted display mode as a 'transparent color' which the blitter ignores when blitting the sprite to video memory or the screen.

Sprites by CSS

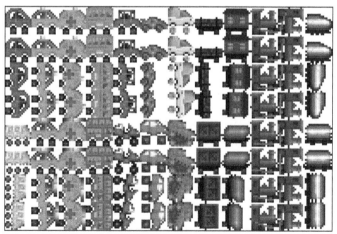

Example of a sprite sheet.

To reduce the number of requests the browser makes to the server, some web designers combine numerous small images or icons into a larger image called a sprite sheet. CSS is used to select the parts of the composite image to display at different points in the page. If a page has 10 1 kB images, they can be combined into one 10 kB image, downloaded with a single HTTP request, and then positioned with CSS. Reducing the number of HTTP requests can make a Web page load much faster. In this usage, the sprite sheet format that had been developed for use in game and animation engines is being applied to static images.

Move to 3D

Prior to the popularizing of true 3D graphics in the late 1990s, many 2D games attempted to imitate the look of three-dimensionality with a variety of sprite production methods. These included:

- Rotoscoping: The filmed performances of live actors were sometimes used for creating sprites, most famously in the case of Prince of Persia which added a relative element of realism to a platform game. The method was used in a number of other fighting games, mostly in the mid 1990s.

- Claymation or the use of posable models which were used for characters that could not be portrayed by actors. Famous early examples include Goro of Mortal Kombat and various enemies from Doom. Used to a greater extent in games like Clay Fighter.

- Pre-rendered CGI models: Introduced by Rise of the Robots and made famous by Donkey Kong Country, and later used to a great extent in PC real-time strategy and role-playing video game games prior to the move to true 3D. Since computers of the day could not run complex 3D graphics, footage of pre-rendered three-dimensional character models were often used which created a (relative) illusion of 3D.

More often sprite now refers to a partially transparent two dimensional animation that is mapped onto a special plane in a 3D scene. Unlike a texture map, the sprite plane is always perpendicular to the axis emanating from the camera. The image can be scaled to simulate perspective, rotated two dimensionally, overlapped with other objects, and be occluded, but it can only be viewed from a single angle. This rendering method is also referred to as billboarding.

Sprites create an effective illusion when:

- The image inside the sprite already depicts a three dimensional object;

- The animation is constantly changing or depicts rotation;

- The sprite exists only shortly;

- The depicted object has a similar appearance from many common viewing angles (such as something spherical);

- The perspective of the object from the viewer cannot possibly change fast enough for the viewer to discern a difference from true 3D geometry, as in the case of object a long distance away from the viewer in 3D space.

- The viewer accepts that the depicted object only has one perspective (such as small plants or leaves).

When the illusion works, viewers will not notice that the sprite is flat and always faces them. Often sprites are used to depict phenomena such as fire, smoke, small objects, small plants (like blades of grass), or special symbols (like "1-Up"), or object of any size where the angle of view does not appreciably change with respect to the rectilinear projection of the object (usually from a long distance). The sprite illusion can be exposed in video games by quickly changing the position of the camera while keeping the sprite in the center of the view. Sprites are also used extensively in particle effects and commonly represented pickups in early 3D games especially.

An example of extensive usage of sprites to create the illusion is the game The Elder Scrolls IV: Oblivion, whose main graphical feature was the ability to display hundreds, if not thousands of animated trees on-screen at one time. Closer inspection of those trees reveals that the leaves are in fact sprites, and rotate along with the position of the user. The tree rendering package used by Oblivion uses sprites to create the appearance of a high number of leaves. However, this fact is only revealed when the player actually examines the trees up-close, and rotates the camera.

Sprites have also occasionally been used as a special-effects tool in movies. One such example is the fire breathing Balrog in The Lord of the Rings: The Fellowship of the Ring; the effects designers utilized sprites to simulate fire emanating from the surface of the demon. Small bursts of fire were filmed in front of a black background and made transparent using a luma key. Many bursts were then attached to the surface of the animated Balrog model and mixed with simulated smoke and heat waves to create the illusion of a monster made from fire.

The term "sprite" is often confused with low resolution 2D graphics drawn on a computer, also known as pixel art. However, sprite graphics (bitmaps) can be created from any imaginable source, including prerendered CGI, dynamic 3D graphics, vector art, and even text. Likewise, pixel art is created for many purposes other than as a sprite, such as video game backgrounds, textures, icons, websites, display art, comics, and t-shirts. With the advancement in computer graphics and improved power and resolution, actual pixel art sprites are becoming increasingly infrequent outside of handheld game systems and cell phones.

Application

Sprites are typically used for characters and other moving objects in video games. They have also been used for mouse pointers and for writing letters to the screen. For on-screen moving objects larger than one sprite's extent, sprites may sometimes be scaled and/or combined.

Billboarding is one term used to describe the use of sprites in a 3D environment. In the same way that a billboard is positioned to face drivers on a highway, the 3D sprite always faces the camera. There is both a performance advantage and an aesthetic advantage to using billboarding. Most 3D rendering engines can process "3D sprites" much faster than other types of 3D objects. So it is possible to gain an overall performance improvement by substituting sprites for some objects that might normally be modeled using texture mapped polygons. Aesthetically sprites are sometimes desirable because it can be difficult for polygons to realistically reproduce phenomena such as fire. In such situations, sprites provide a more attractive illusion.

Sprites are also made and used by various online digital artists, usually to train their ability to make more complicated images using different computer programs or just for the fun of it. "Sprite Artists" will either create their own "Custom" sprites, or use & edit pre-existing sprites (Usually made by other artists or "ripped" from a video game or other media) in order to create art, comics, or animations.

Physically based Animation

Physically based animation is an area of interest within computer graphics concerned with the simulation of physically plausible behaviors at interactive rates. Advances in physically based animation are often motivated by the need to include complex, physically inspired behaviors in video games, interactive simulations, and movies. Although off-line simulation methods exist to solve most all of the problems studied in physically-based animation, these methods are intended for applications that necessitate physical accuracy and slow, detailed computations. In contrast to methods common in offline simulation, techniques in physically based animation are concerned with physical plausibility, numerical stability, and visual appeal over physical accuracy. Physically based animation is often limited to loose approximations of physical behaviors because of the strict time constraints imposed by interactive applications. The target frame rate for interactive applications such as games and simulations is often 25-60 hertz, with only a small fraction of the time allotted to an individual frame remaining for physical simulation. Simplified models of physical behaviors are generally preferred if they are more efficient, easier to accelerate (through pre-computation, clever data structures, or SIMD/GPGPU), or satisfy desirable mathematical properties (such as unconditional stability or volume conservation when a soft body undergoes deformation). Fine details are not important when the overriding goal of a visualization is aesthetic appeal or the maintenance of player immersion since these details are often difficult for humans to notice or are otherwise impossible to distinguish at human scales.

Physically based animation is now common in movies and video games, and many techniques were pioneered during the development of early special effects scenes and game engines. Star Trek II: The Wrath of Khan famously used particle systems in the Genesis explosion scene to create the visual effect of a flaming shockwave engulfing a planet. Despite being released before physics engines were a common feature in games, System Shock incorporated rigid body physics in its engine and was widely considered innovative for this feature and the novel sense of interaction it afforded players. Valve later developed Half-Life and used rigid body physics to create environmental puzzles for the player, such as obstacles that could not be reached without stacking boxes. Half-Life 2 featured a more advanced physics engine that incorporated constrained systems such as pulleys or levers with more environmental puzzles to showcase these features. Physics engines are now much more common in games, and their frequent appearance has motivated research in physically based animation by companies such as Nvidia.

Physically based Animation in Games and Simulations

Physically based animation is common in games and simulations where users have the expectation of interaction with the environment. Physics engines such as Havok, PhysX, and Bullet exist as separately developed products to be licensed and included in games. In games such as Angry Birds or World of Goo, physically based animation is itself the primary game mechanic and players are expected to interact with or create physically simulated systems in order to achieve goals. Aspects of physics puzzle games exist in many games that belong to other genres but feature physically based simulation. Allowing physical interaction with the environment through physically based animation promotes non-linear solutions to puzzles by players, and can sometimes results in solutions to problems presented in games that were not deliberately included by level designers.

Simulations used for purposes other than entertainment, such as military simulations, also make use of physically based animation to portray realistic situations and maintain the immersion of users. Many techniques in physically based animation are designed with GPGPU implementations in mind or can otherwise be extended to benefit from graphics hardware, which can be used to make physically based simulations fast enough for gaming. GPU time is often reserved for rendering, however, and frequent data transfers between the host and device can easily become a bottleneck to performance.

Physically based Animation in Movies

Simulations can be performed offline (as in apart from when they are viewed) in the development of special effects for movies. Speed is therefore not strictly a necessity in the production of special effects but is still desirable for reasonably responsive feedback and because the hardware required for slower methods is more expensive. However, physically based animation is still preferred because slower, more accurate methods can be costly and limiting. The physical accuracy of small details in a special effect are not meaningful to their visual appeal, restrict the amount of control that artists and directors can exert over behavior, and increase the monetary cost and time required to achieve results. It is necessary to be able to dictate the high level behavior of physically inspired effects in movies in order to achieve a desired artistic direction, but scripting physical behaviors on the level of small details can be unfeasible when fluids, smoke, or many individual objects are involved. Physically based animation generally affords more artist control over the appearance of simulated results and is also more convenient when desired effects might bend or defy physics.

Rigid Body Simulation

Simplified rigid body physics is relatively cheap and easy to implement, which is why it appeared in interactive games and simulations earlier than most other techniques. Rigid bodies are assumed to undergo no deformation during simulation so that rigid body motion between time steps can be described as a translation and rotation, traditionally using affine transformations stored as 4x4 matrices. Alternatively, quaternions can be used to store rotations and vectors can be used to store the objects offset from the origin. The most computationally expensive aspects of rigid body dynamics are collision detection, correcting interpenetration between bodies and the environment, and handling resting contact. Rigid bodies are commonly simulated iteratively, with back-tracking to correct error using smaller timesteps. Resting contact between multiple rigid bodies (as is the case when rigid bodies fall into piles or are stacked) can be particularly difficult to handle efficiently and may require complex contact and shock propagation graphs in order to resolve using impulse-based methods. When simulating large numbers of rigid bodies, simplified geometries or convex hulls are often used to represent their boundaries for the purpose of collision detection and response (since this is generally the bottleneck in simulation).

Soft Body Simulation

Soft bodies can easily be implemented using spring-mesh systems. Spring mesh systems are composed of individually simulated particles that are attracted to each other by simulated spring forces and experience resistance from simulated dampeners. Arbitrary geometries can be more easily simulated by applying spring and dampener forces to the nodes of a lattice and deforming the object with the lattice.

However, explicit solutions to these systems are not very numerically stable and are extremely difficult to control the behavior of through spring parameters. Techniques that allow for physically plausible and visually appealing soft bodies, are numerically stable, and can be configured well by artists were prohibitively expensive in early gaming history, which is why soft bodies were not as common as rigid bodies. Integration using Runge-Kutta methods can be used to increase the numerical stability of unstable techniques such as spring meshes or finer time steps can be used for simulation (although this is more costly and cannot make spring meshes stable for arbitrarily large forces). Techniques such as shape matching and position based dynamics address these problems with interactive games and simulations in mind. Position based dynamics is used in mainstream game engines such as Bullet (software), Havok, and PhysX. Unconditional stability and ease of configuration are particularly desirable properties of soft body simulations that can be difficult to achieve with spring-mesh systems, although they are still often used in games because of their simplicity and speed.

Fluid Simulation

Computational fluid dynamics can be expensive, and interactions between multiple fluid bodies or with external objects/forces can require complex logic to evaluate. Fluid simulation is generally achieved in video games by simulating only the height of bodies of water to create the effect of waves, ripples, or other surface features. For relatively free bodies of liquid, Lagrangian or semi-Lagrangian methods are often used to speed up the simulation by treating particles as finite elements of fluid (or carriers of physical properties) and approximating the Navier-Stokes equations . It is uncommon to simulate bodies of fluid in games, although surface features may be simulated using similar methods and fluid simulations may be used to generate textures or height-fields to render water in real-time without real-time simulation (this is commonly done for large bodies of water in games). Fluid simulations can be computed using commodity graphics hardware through GPG-PU, and height fields can be efficiently computed that result in wave-like behavior using Lattice Boltzmann methods. Alternatively, surface features and waves can be simulated as particles and a height field generated from the simulated particles in real-time. This also allows for efficient two way interaction between the fluid and floating objects.

Particle Systems

Particle systems are an extremely popular technique for creating visual effects in movies and games because of their ease of implementation, efficiency, extensibility, and artist control. The update cycle of particle systems usually consists of the three phases: generation, simulation, and extinction. These phases respectively consist of the introduction of new particles, simulating them through the next timestep, and removing particles that have exceeded their life-span. The physical and visual attributes of particles are usually randomized on generation with the range and distribution of attributes controlled by the artist. Particle systems can further be made to generate particle systems themselves to create more complex and dynamic effects, and their high-level behavior can be choreographed through a framework of operators as in the canonical Sims paper. Early games that rendered systems of particles suffered from clipping artifacts when particles partially intersected geometry in the environment, and this artifact was especially noticeable for large particles (which were often used to stand in for smoke). Soft particles address these artifacts through careful shading and manipulation of the transparency of particles, such that particles become more transparent as they approach surfaces.

Flocking

In physically based animation, flocking refers to a technique that models the complex behavior of birds, schools of fish, and swarms of insects using virtual forces. These virtual forces simulate the tendency for flocks to center their velocities, avoid collisions and crowding, and move toward the group. In these simulations, individual members of the flock (sometimes called boids, short for bird-oid) act without collaboration using only information about the position and velocity of their peers to create the illusion of synchronized, group behavior efficiently. Flocking can be used to efficiently approximate the behavior of crowds of humans as well, and methods based on flocking are often used for crowds of NPCs in gaming. Unreal and Half-Life were among the first games to implement flocking, which was used to model the behavior of birds and flying creatures present in outdoor levels.

Physically based Character Animation

Characters in games and simulations are traditionally animated through methods such as keyframing that define animations through compositions of smaller, static motions sequenced to convey more complex behavior. Visually, these static methods cannot easily convey complex interactions with the environment and make life like character motion difficult to accomplish. Techniques in physically based character animation achieve dynamic animations that respond to user interaction, external events, and the environment by optimizing motions toward specified goals given physically based constraints such as energy minimization. The adoption of physically based character animation, as opposed to more static methods, has been slow in the gaming industry due to the increased cost and complexity associated with its use. Physically based character animation has been used in the Skate (video game) series of video games, and in the independently developed first-person shooter StarForge.

Reflection

Reflection in computer graphics is used to emulate reflective objects like mirrors and shiny surfaces.

Ray traced model demonstrating specular reflection.

Reflection is accomplished in a ray trace renderer by following a ray from the eye to the mirror and then calculating where it bounces from, and continuing the process until no surface is found, or a non-reflective surface is found. Reflection on a shiny surface like wood or tile can add to the photorealistic effects of a 3D rendering.

- Polished - A polished reflection is an undisturbed reflection, like a mirror or chrome.

- Blurry - A blurry reflection means that tiny random bumps on the surface of the material cause the reflection to be blurry.

- Metallic - A reflection is metallic if the highlights and reflections retain the color of the reflective object.

- Glossy - This term can be misused. Sometimes, it is a setting which is the opposite of blurry (e.g. when "glossiness" has a low value, the reflection is blurry). However, some people use the term "glossy reflection" as a synonym for "blurred reflection". Glossy used in this context means that the reflection is actually blurred.

Example:

- Polished or Mirror Reflection

Mirror on wall rendered with 100% reflection.

Mirrors are usually almost 100% reflective.

- Metallic Reflection

The large sphere on the left is blue with its reflection marked
as metallic. The large sphere on the right is the same color but
does not have the metallic property selected.

Normal (nonmetallic) objects reflect light and colors in the original color of the object being reflected. Metallic objects reflect lights and colors altered by the color of the metallic object itself.

- Blurry Reflection

The large sphere on the left has sharpness set to 100%. The sphere
on the right has sharpness set to 50% which creates a blurry reflection.

Many materials are imperfect reflectors, where the reflections are blurred to various degrees due to surface roughness that scatters the rays of the reflections.

- Glossy Reflection

Fully glossy reflection, shows highlights from light sources, but does not show a clear reflection from objects

The sphere on the left has normal, metallic reflection. The sphere on the right
has the same parameters, except that the reflection is marked as "glossy".

Procedural Textures

In computer graphics, a procedural texture is a texture created using a mathematical description (i.e. an algorithm) rather than directly stored data. The advantage of this approach is low storage cost, unlimited texture resolution and easy texture mapping. These kinds of textures are often used to model surface or volumetric representations of natural elements such as wood, marble, granite, metal, stone, and others.

Procedurally generated tiling textures.

Usually, the natural look of the rendered result is achieved by the usage of fractal noise and turbulence functions. These functions are used as a numerical representation of the "randomness" found in nature.

Solid Texturing

Solid texturing is a process where the texture generating function is evaluated over R^3 at each visible surface point of the model so the resulting material properties (like color, shininess or normal) depends only on their 3D position, not their parametrized 2D surface position like in traditional 2D texture mapping. Consequently, solid textures are unaffected by distortions of the surface parameter space, such as you might see near the poles of a sphere. Also, continuity between the surface parameterization of adjacent patches isn't a concern either. Solid textures will remain consistent and have features of constant size regardless of distortions in the surface coordinate systems. Initially these functions were based on simple combination of procedural noise functions like Simplex noise or Perlin noise. Currently a vast arsenal of techniques are available, ranging from structured regular texture (like a brick wall), to structured irregular textures (like a stonewall), to purely stochastic textures.

Cellular Texturing

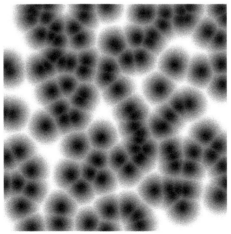

Cellular Texture.

Cellular texturing differs from the majority of other procedural texture generating techniques as it does not depend on noise functions as its basis, although it is often used to complement the technique. Cellular textures are based on feature points which are scattered over a three-dimensional space. These points are then used to split up the space into small, randomly tiled regions called cells. These cells often look like "lizard scales", "pebbles", or "flagstones". Even though these regions are discrete, the cellular basis function itself is continuous and can be evaluated anywhere in space. Worley noise is a common type of cellular texture.

Genetic Textures

Genetic texture generation is an experimental approach to generate textures. It is an automated process guided by a human moderator. The flow of control usually has a computer generate a set of texture candidates. From these, a user picks a selection. The computer then generates another set of textures by mutating and crossing over elements of the user selected textures. The process continues until a suitable texture for the user is generated. As the outcome is difficult to control, this method is typically used only for experimental or abstract textures.

Self-organizing Textures

Starting from a simple white noise, self-organization processes can lead to structured patterns while preserving some randomness. Reaction-diffusion systems are one way of generating such textures. Realistic textures can be generated by simulating complex chemical reactions within fluids. These systems may show behaviors similar to real processes (Morphogenesis) found in nature, such as animal markings (shells, fish, wild cats).

Image Plane

In computer graphics, especially three-dimensional (3D) graphics, the term "image plane" is used to indicate the conceptual plane that represents the actual display screen through which a user views a virtual 3D scene. The plane is not usually an actual geometric object in a 3D scene, but instead is usually a collection of target coordinates or dimensions that are used during the rasterization process so the final output can be displayed as intended on the physical screen. The term also can loosely be used in other ways, including to indicate a geometric plane within a 3D scene that has an image texture attached to it, or to describe a single slice that is geometrically identified as a plane within a larger volumetric object, such as a single frame from a completed magnetic resonance imaging (MRI) scan.

An image plane within a 3D scene can have several purposes. The location of the image plane can be used to help determine which objects within a scene require processing and which can be ignored. This can be easily done because objects on one side of the image plane are technically behind the viewer, will not be displayed and, thus, can be ignored.

If a scene is rendered using classic ray tracing, then light is followed from the virtual eyes of the viewers into a scene and then from the surface of an object to the defined light source. The image plane gives the location of the viewer in the scene and is used to help calculate how the rays scatter and how they should be rendered. If the plane is defined only as a shape that extends infinitely in two of the three axial directions, then it also is the basis for the viewport, which is a rectangular area within the plane that matches the aspect ratio of the display screen and can be used for some per-pixel operations.

When used in the context of 3D modeling, an image plane can be a geometric primitive that has an image texture attached to it. These are commonly used to represent a sky, background or floor in a scene. In some modeling programs, the image plane is an object in the scene that represents the angle at which a scene will be rendered, sometimes also called the camera.

In volume rendering in which an object has some type of content within its boundaries, an image plane is a slice of that volume. This can be visualized with an MRI scan in which several planes are compressed to form a complete 3D object. Each of the slices can be isolated and viewed by itself as a planar image.

Rendering Equation

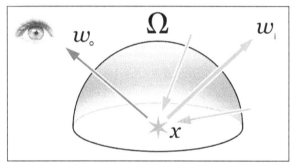

The rendering equation describes the total amount of light emitted from a point x along a particular viewing direction, given a function for incoming light and a BRDF.

In computer graphics, the rendering equation is an integral equation in which the equilibrium radiance leaving a point is given as the sum of emitted plus reflected radiance under a geometric optics approximation. It was simultaneously introduced into computer graphics by David Immel et al. and James Kajiya in 1986. The various realistic rendering techniques in computer graphics attempt to solve this equation.

The physical basis for the rendering equation is the law of conservation of energy. Assuming that L denotes radiance, we have that at each particular position and direction, the outgoing light (L_o) is the sum of the emitted light (L_e) and the reflected light. The reflected light itself is the sum from all directions of the incoming light (L_i) multiplied by the surface reflection and cosine of the incident angle.

Equation Form

The rendering equation may be written in the form,

$$L_o(\mathrm{x},\omega_o,\lambda,t)=L_e(\mathrm{x},\omega_o,\lambda,t)+\int_\Omega f_r(\mathrm{x},\omega_i,\omega_o,\lambda,t)L_i(\mathrm{x},\omega_i,\lambda,t)(\omega_i\cdot\mathrm{n})\mathrm{d}\omega_i$$

where,

- $L_o(x,\omega_o,\lambda,t)$ is the total spectral radiance of wavelength λ directed outward along direction ω_o at time x, from a particular position X.

- x is the location in space.

- ω_o is the direction of the outgoing light.

- λ is a particular wavelength of light.

- t is time.

- $L_e(x,\omega_o,\lambda,t)$ is emitted spectral radiance.

- $\int_\Omega \ldots \, d\omega_i$ is an integral over Ω.

- Ω is the unit hemisphere centered around n containing all possible values for.

- $f_r(x,\omega_i,\omega_o,\lambda,t)$ is the bidirectional reflectance distribution function, the proportion of light reflected from ω_o to ω_o at position x, time t, and at wavelength.

- ω_i is the negative direction of the incoming light.

- $L_i(x,\omega_i,\lambda,t)$ is spectral radiance of wavelength λ coming inward toward x from direction t at time.

- n is the surface normal at x.

- $\omega_i \cdot n$ is the weakening factor of outward irradiance due to incident angle, as the light flux is smeared across a surface whose area is larger than the projected area perpendicular to the ray. This is often written as $\cos\theta_i$.

Two noteworthy features are: Its linearity—it is composed only of multiplications and additions, and its spatial homogeneity—it is the same in all positions and orientations. These mean a wide range of factorings and rearrangements of the equation are possible. It is a Fredholm integral equation of the second kind, similar to those that arise in quantum field theory.

Note this equation's spectral and time dependence — L_o may be sampled at or integrated over sections of the visible spectrum to obtain, for example, a trichromatic color sample. A pixel value for a single frame in an animation may be obtained by fixing t motion blur can be produced by averaging L_o over some given time interval (by integrating over the time interval and dividing by the length of the interval).

Note that a solution to the rendering equation is the function L_o. The function L_i is related to L_o via a ray-tracing operation: The incoming radiance from some direction at one point is the outgoing radiance at some other point in the opposite direction.

Applications

Solving the rendering equation for any given scene is the primary challenge in realistic rendering. One approach to solving the equation is based on finite element methods, leading to the radiosity algorithm. Another approach using Monte Carlo methods has led to many different algorithms including path tracing, photon mapping, and Metropolis light transport, among others.

Limitations

Although the equation is very general, it does not capture every aspect of light reflection. Some missing aspects include the following:

- Transmission, which occurs when light is transmitted through the surface, such as when it hits a glass object or a water surface,

- Subsurface scattering, where the spatial locations for incoming and departing light are different. Surfaces rendered without accounting for subsurface scattering may appear unnaturally opaque — however, it is not necessary to account for this if transmission is included in the equation, since that will effectively include also light scattered under the surface,

- Polarization, where different light polarizations will sometimes have different reflection distributions, for example when light bounces at a water surface,

- Phosphorescence, which occurs when light or other electromagnetic radiation is absorbed at one moment in time and emitted at a later moment in time, usually with a longer wavelength (unless the absorbed electromagnetic radiation is very intense),

- Interference, where the wave properties of light are exhibited,

- Fluorescence, where the absorbed and emitted light have different wavelengths,

- Non-linear effects, where very intense light can increase the energy level of an electron with more energy than that of a single photon (this can occur if the electron is hit by two photons at the same time), and emission of light with higher frequency than the frequency of the light that hit the surface suddenly becomes possible, and

- Relativistic Doppler effect, where light that bounces on an object that is moving in a very high speed will get its wavelength changed; if the light bounces at an object that is moving towards it, the impact will compress the photons, so the wavelength will become shorter and the light will be blueshifted and the photons will be packed more closely so the photon flux will be increased; if it bounces at an object that is moving away from it, it will be redshifted and the photons will be packed more sparsely so the photon flux will be decreased.

For scenes that are either not composed of simple surfaces in a vacuum or for which the travel time for light is an important factor, researchers have generalized the rendering equation to produce a volume rendering equation suitable for volume rendering and a transient rendering equation for use with data from a time-of-flight camera.

Pixels

In digital imaging, a pixel, pel, or picture element is a physical point in a raster image, or the smallest addressable element in an all points addressable display device; so it is the smallest controllable element of a picture represented on the screen.

Each pixel is a sample of an original image; more samples typically provide more accurate representations of the original. The intensity of each pixel is variable. In color imaging systems, a color is typically represented by three or four component intensities such as red, green, and blue, or cyan, magenta, yellow, and black.

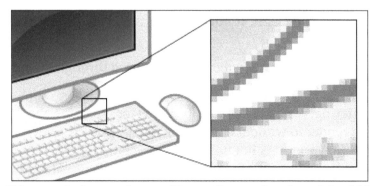

This example shows an image with a portion greatly enlarged, in which
the individual pixels are rendered as small squares and can easily be seen.

In some contexts (such as descriptions of camera sensors), pixel refers to a single scalar element of a multi-component representation (called a photosite in the camera sensor context, although sensel is sometimes used), while in yet other contexts it may refer to the set of component intensities for a spatial position.

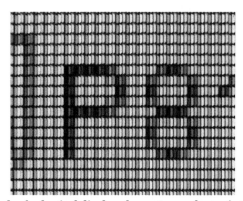

A photograph of sub-pixel display elements on a laptop's LCD screen.

Technical

A pixel is generally thought of as the smallest single component of a digital image. However, the definition is highly context-sensitive. For example, there can be "printed pixels" in a page, or pixels carried by electronic signals, or represented by digital values, or pixels on a display device, or pixels in a digital camera (photosensor elements). This list is not exhaustive and, depending on context, synonyms include pel, sample, byte, bit, dot, and spot. *Pixels* can be used as a unit of measure such as: 2400 pixels per inch, 640 pixels per line, or spaced 10 pixels apart.

The measures dots per inch (dpi) and pixels per inch (ppi) are sometimes used interchangeably, but have distinct meanings, especially for printer devices, where dpi is a measure of the printer's density of dot (e.g. ink droplet) placement. For example, a high-quality photographic image may be printed with 600 ppi on a 1200 dpi inkjet printer. Even higher dpi numbers, such as the 4800 dpi quoted by printer manufacturers since 2002, do not mean much in terms of achievable resolution.

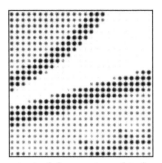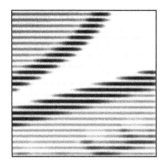

A pixel does not need to be rendered as a small square. This image shows alternative ways of reconstructing an image from a set of pixel values, using dots, lines, or smooth filtering.

The more pixels used to represent an image, the closer the result can resemble the original. The number of pixels in an image is sometimes called the resolution, though resolution has a more specific definition. Pixel counts can be expressed as a single number, as in a "three-megapixel" digital camera, which has a nominal three million pixels, or as a pair of numbers, as in a "640 by 480 display", which has 640 pixels from side to side and 480 from top to bottom (as in a VGA display) and therefore has a total number of $640 \times 480 = 307{,}200$ pixels, or 0.3 megapixels.

The pixels, or color samples, that form a digitized image (such as a JPEG file used on a web page) may or may not be in one-to-one correspondence with screen pixels, depending on how a computer displays an image. In computing, an image composed of pixels is known as a bitmapped image or a raster image. The word raster originates from television scanning patterns, and has been widely used to describe similar halftone printing and storage techniques.

Sampling Patterns

For convenience, pixels are normally arranged in a regular two-dimensional grid. By using this arrangement, many common operations can be implemented by uniformly applying the same operation to each pixel independently. Other arrangements of pixels are possible, with some sampling patterns even changing the shape (or kernel) of each pixel across the image. For this reason, care must be taken when acquiring an image on one device and displaying it on another, or when converting image data from one pixel format to another.

For example:

Text rendered using ClearType using subpixels.

- LCD screens typically use a staggered grid, where the red, green, and blue components are sampled at slightly different locations. Subpixel rendering is a technology which takes advantage of these differences to improve the rendering of text on LCD screens.

- The vast majority of color digital cameras use a Bayer filter, resulting in a regular grid of pixels where the *color* of each pixel depends on its position on the grid.

- A clipmap uses a hierarchical sampling pattern, where the size of the support of each pixel depends on its location within the hierarchy.

- Warped grids are used when the underlying geometry is non-planar, such as images of the earth from space.

- The use of non-uniform grids is an active research area, attempting to bypass the traditional Nyquist limit.

- Pixels on computer monitors are normally "square" (that is, have equal horizontal and vertical sampling pitch); pixels in other systems are often "rectangular" (that is, have unequal horizontal and vertical sampling pitch – oblong in shape), as are digital video formats with diverse aspect ratios, such as the anamorphic widescreen formats of the Rec. 601 digital video standard.

Resolution of Computer Monitors

Computers can use pixels to display an image, often an abstract image that represents a GUI. The resolution of this image is called the display resolution and is determined by the video card of the computer. LCD monitors also use pixels to display an image, and have a native resolution. Each pixel is made up of triads, with the number of these triads determining the native resolution. On some CRT monitors, the beam sweep rate may be fixed, resulting in a fixed native resolution. Most CRT monitors do not have a fixed beam sweep rate, meaning they do not have a native resolution at all - instead they have a set of resolutions that are equally well supported. To produce the sharpest images possible on an LCD, the user must ensure the display resolution of the computer matches the native resolution of the monitor.

Resolution of Telescopes

The pixel scale used in astronomy is the angular distance between two objects on the sky that fall one pixel apart on the detector (CCD or infrared chip). The scale s measured in radians is the ratio of the pixel spacing p and focal length f of the preceding optics, $s=p/f$. (The focal length is the product of the focal ratio by the diameter of the associated lens or mirror.) Because p is usually expressed in units of arcseconds per pixel, because 1 radian equals $180/\pi 3600 \approx 206,265$ arcseconds, and because diameters are often given in millimeters and pixel sizes in micrometers which yields another factor of 1,000, the formula is often quoted as $s=206p/f$.

Bits Per Pixel

The number of distinct colors that can be represented by a pixel depends on the number of bits per pixel (bpp). A 1 bpp image uses 1-bit for each pixel, so each pixel can be either on or off. Each additional bit doubles the number of colors available, so a 2 bpp image can have 4 colors, and a 3 bpp image can have 8 colors:

- 1 bpp, 2^1 = 2 colors (monochrome),

- 2 bpp, 2^2 = 4 colors,

- 3 bpp, 2^3 = 8 colors,

- ...,

- 8 bpp, 2^8 = 256 colors,

- 16 bpp, 2^{16} = 65,536 colors ("Highcolor"),

- 24 bpp, 2^{24} = 16,777,216 colors ("Truecolor").

For color depths of 15 or more bits per pixel, the depth is normally the sum of the bits allocated to each of the red, green, and blue components. Highcolor, usually meaning 16 bpp, normally has five bits for red and blue each, and six bits for green, as the human eye is more sensitive to errors in green than in the other two primary colors. For applications involving transparency, the 16 bits may be divided into five bits each of red, green, and blue, with one bit left for transparency. A 24-bit depth allows 8 bits per component. On some systems, 32-bit depth is available: this means that each 24-bit pixel has an extra 8 bits to describe its opacity (for purposes of combining with another image).

Subpixels

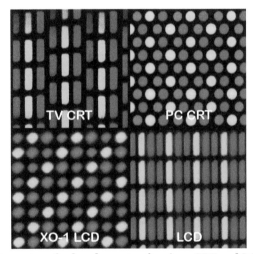

Geometry of color elements of various CRT and LCD
displays; phosphor dots in the color display of CRTs
(top row) bear no relation to pixels or subpixels.

Many display and image-acquisition systems are not capable of displaying or sensing the different color channels at the same site. Therefore, the pixel grid is divided into single-color regions that contribute to the displayed or sensed color when viewed at a distance. In some displays, such as LCD, LED, and plasma displays, these single-color regions are separately addressable elements, which have come to be known as subpixels. For example, LCDs typically divide each pixel vertically into three subpixels. When the square pixel is divided into three subpixels, each subpixel is nec- essarily rectangular. In display industry terminology, subpixels are often referred to as pixels, as they are the basic addressable elements in a viewpoint of hardware, and hence pixel circuits rather than subpixel circuits is used.

Most digital camera image sensors use single-color sensor regions, for example using the Bayer filter pattern, and in the camera industry these are known as pixels just like in the display industry, not subpixels.

For systems with subpixels, two different approaches can be taken:

- The subpixels can be ignored, with full-color pixels being treated as the smallest address-able imaging element; or

- The subpixels can be included in rendering calculations, which requires more analysis and processing time, but can produce apparently superior images in some cases.

This latter approach, referred to as subpixel rendering, uses knowledge of pixel geometry to ma-nipulate the three colored subpixels separately, producing an increase in the apparent resolution of color displays. While CRT displays use red-green-blue-masked phosphor areas, dictated by a mesh grid called the shadow mask, it would require a difficult calibration step to be aligned with the displayed pixel raster, and so CRTs do not currently use subpixel rendering.

The concept of subpixels is related to samples.

Megapixel

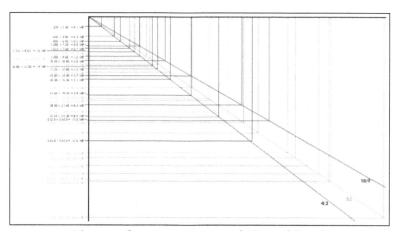

Diagram of common sensor resolutions of digital
cameras including megapixel values.

A megapixel (MP) is a million pixels; the term is used not only for the number of pixels in an im-age but also to express the number of image sensor elements of digital cameras or the number of display elements of digital displays. For example, a camera that makes a 2048 × 1536 pixel image (3,145,728 finished image pixels) typically uses a few extra rows and columns of sensor elements and is commonly said to have "3.2 megapixels" or "3.4 megapixels", depending on whether the number reported is the "effective" or the "total" pixel count.

Digital cameras use photosensitive electronics, either charge-coupled device (CCD) or comple-mentary metal–oxide–semiconductor (CMOS) image sensors, consisting of a large number of sin-gle sensor elements, each of which records a measured intensity level. In most digital cameras, the sensor array is covered with a patterned color filter mosaic having red, green, and blue regions in the Bayer filter arrangement so that each sensor element can record the intensity of a single pri-mary color of light. The camera interpolates the color information of neighboring sensor elements, through a process called demosaicing, to create the final image. These sensor elements are often called "pixels", even though they only record 1 channel (only red or green or blue) of the final color image. Thus, two of the three color channels for each sensor must be interpolated and a so-called

N-megapixel camera that produces an N-megapixel image provides only one-third of the information that an image of the same size could get from a scanner. Thus, certain color contrasts may look fuzzier than others, depending on the allocation of the primary colors (green has twice as many elements as red or blue in the Bayer arrangement).

DxO Labs invented the Perceptual MegaPixel (P-MPix) to measure the sharpness that a camera produces when paired to a particular lens – as opposed to the MP a manufacturer states for a camera product, which is based only on the camera's sensor. The new P-MPix claims to be a more accurate and relevant value for photographers to consider when weighing up camera sharpness. As of mid-2013, the Sigma 35 mm f/1.4 DG HSM lens mounted on a Nikon D800 has the highest measured P-MPix. However, with a value of 23 MP, it still wipes off more than one-third of the D800's 36.3 MP sensor.

One new method to add megapixels has been introduced in a Micro Four Thirds System camera, which only uses a 16 MP sensor but can produce a 64 MP RAW (40 MP JPEG) image by making two exposures, shifting the sensor by a half pixel between them. Using a tripod to take level multi-shots within an instance, the multiple 16 MP images are then generated into a unified 64 MP image.

Specular Highlight

A specular highlight is the bright spot of light that appears on shiny objects when illuminated. Specular highlights are important in 3D computer graphics, as they provide a strong visual cue for the shape of an object and its location with respect to light sources in the scene.

Microfacets

The term *specular* means that light is perfectly reflected in a mirror-like way from the light source to the viewer. Specular reflection is visible only where the surface normal is oriented precisely halfway between the direction of incoming light and the direction of the viewer; this is called the half-angle direction because it bisects (divides into halves) the angle between the incoming light and the viewer. Thus, a specularly reflecting surface would show a specular highlight as the perfectly sharp reflected image of a light source. However, many shiny objects show blurred specular highlights.

This can be explained by the existence of microfacets. We assume that surfaces that are not perfectly smooth are composed of many very tiny facets, each of which is a perfect specular reflector. These microfacets have normals that are distributed about the normal of the approximating smooth surface. The degree to which microfacet normals differ from the smooth surface normal is determined by the roughness of the surface.

The reason for blurred specular highlights is now clear. At points on the object where the smooth normal is close to the half-angle direction, many of the microfacets point in the half-angle direction and so the specular highlight is bright. As one moves away from the center of the highlight, the smooth normal and the half-angle direction get farther apart; the number of microfacets oriented in the half-angle direction falls, and so the intensity of the highlight falls off to zero.

The specular highlight often reflects the color of the light source, not the color of the reflecting object. This is because many materials have a thin layer of clear material above the surface of the pigmented material. For example plastic is made up of tiny beads of color suspended in a clear polymer and human skin often has a thin layer of oil or sweat above the pigmented cells. Such materials will show specular highlights in which all parts of the color spectrum are reflected equally. On metallic materials such as gold the color of the specular highlight will reflect the color of the material.

Models of Microfacets

A number of different models exist to predict the distribution of microfacets. Most assume that the microfacet normals are distributed evenly around the normal; these models are called isotropic. If microfacets are distributed with a preference for a certain direction along the surface, the distribution is anisotropic.

Phong Distribution

In Phong shading, the intensity of a specular highlight is usually calculated as $k_{spec} = \cos^n(N,H)$, where N is the smooth surface normal and H is the half-angle direction. (The notation $\cos(N,H)$ means the cosine of the angle between the directions N and H.) The number n is called the Phong exponent, and is a user-chosen value that controls the apparent smoothness of the surface. This equation implies that the distribution of microfacet normals is based on the cosine of the angle between the microfacet normal and the smooth surface normal, raised to a power. While this is a useful heuristic and produces believable results, it is not a physically based model.

Gaussian Distribution

A slightly better model of microfacet distribution can be created using a Gaussian distribution. The usual function calculates specular highlight intensity as:

$$k_{spec} = e^{-\left(\frac{\cos(N,H)}{m}\right)^2}$$

where m is a constant between 0 and 1 that controls the apparent smoothness of the surface.

Beckmann Distribution

A physically based model of microfacet distribution is the Beckmann distribution. This function gives very accurate results, but is also rather expensive to compute.

$$k_{spec} = \frac{1}{4m^2\cos^4(N,H)} e^{-\left(\frac{\tan(N,H)}{m}\right)^2}$$

where m is as before: a constant between 0 and 1 that controls the apparent smoothness of the surface.

Heidrich-Seidel Anisotropic Distribution

The Heidrich-Seidel distribution is a simple anisotropic distribution, based on the Phong model. It can be used to model surfaces that have small parallel grooves or fibers, such as brushed metal, satin, and hair. The specular highlight intensity for this distribution is:

$$k_{spec} = \left[\sin(L,T)\sin(V,T) - \cos(L,T)\cos(V,T)\right]^{n}$$

where n is the Phong exponent, V is the viewing direction, L is the direction of incoming light, and T is the direction parallel to the grooves or fibers at this point on the surface.

Using Multiple Distributions

If desired, different distributions (usually, using the same distribution function with different values of m or n) can be combined using a weighted average. This is useful for modelling, for example, surfaces that have small smooth and rough patches rather than uniform roughness.

References

- Foundation, Blender. "blender.org - Home of the Blender project - Free and Open 3D Creation Software". Blender.org. Retrieved 2019-04-24

- Webgl-graphics-pipeline, webgl: tutorialspoint.com, Retrieved 3 August, 2019

- Durand; Cutler. "Transformations" (powerpoint). Massachusetts Institute of Technology. Retrieved 12 September 2008.

- What-is-an-image-plane: wisegeek.com, Retrieved 19 May, 2019

- Michael Goesele (2004). New Acquisition Techniques for Real Objects and Light Sources in Computer Graphics. Books on Demand. ISBN 3-8334-1489-8. Archived from the original on 2018-01-22.

- "Image registration of blurred satellite images". Staff.utia.cas.cz. 28 February 2001. Archived from the original on 20 June 2008. Retrieved 2008-05-09.

- Specular-highlight: graphics.fandom.com, Retrieved 3 August, 2019

3
Computer Graphics: Hardware and Software

Graphics hardware are the different types of hardware components that are essential to quickly render 3D objects as pixels on the computer screen. The program which enables a person to manipulate images on a computer is known as graphics software. The topics elaborated in this chapter will help in gaining a better perspective about the diverse types of hardware and software used in computer graphics.

Graphics Hardware

Graphics pipelines consist of multiple shader stages, multiple fixed-function pipeline stages, and a pipeline layout Graphics hardware describes the hardware components necessary to quickly render 3D objects as pixels on your computer's screen using specialized rasterizationbased hardware architectures. The use of this term is meant to elicit a sense of the physical components necessary for performing these computations. In other words, we're talking about the chipsets, transistors, buses, and processors found on many current video cards.

One thing has been certain with graphics hardware: it changes very quickly with new extensions and features being added continually. One explanation for the fast pace is the video game industry and its economic momentum. Essentially what this means is that each new graphics card provides better performance and processing capabilities. As a result, graphics hardware is being used for tasks that support a much richer use of 3D graphics. For instance, researchers are performing computation on graphics hardware to perform ray-tracing and even solve the Navier-Stokes equations to simulate Real-Time Graphics: By fluid flow.

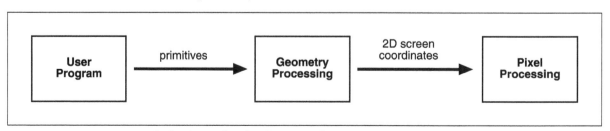

The basic graphics hardware pipeline consists of stages that
transform 3D data into 2D screen objects ready for rasterizing and
coloring by the pixel processing stages.

Most graphics hardware has been built to perform a set of fixed operations organized as a pipeline designed to push vertices and pixels through different stages. The fixed functionality of the pipeline ensures that basic coloring, lighting, and texturing can occur very quickly—often referred to as real-time graphics. Figure illustrates the real-time graphics pipeline. The important things to note about the pipeline follow:

- The user program, or application, supplies the data to the graphics hardware in the form of primitives, such as points, lines, or polygons describing the 3D geometry. Images or bitmaps are also supplied for use in texturing surfaces.

- Geometric primitives are processed on a per-vertex basis and are transformed from 3D coordinates to 2D screen triangles.

- Screen objects are passed to the pixel processors, rasterized, and then colored on a per-pixel basis before being output to the frame buffer, and eventually to the monitor.

Describing Geometry for the Hardware

As a graphics programmer, you need to be concerned with how the data associated with your 3D objects is transferred onto the memory cache of the graphics hardware. Unfortunately (or maybe fortunately), as a programmer you don't have complete control over this process. There are a variety of ways to place your data on the graphics hardware, and each has its own advantages. Any of the APIs you might use to program your video card will provide different methods to load data onto the graphics hardware memory. The examples that follow are presented in pseudo-code that is based loosely on the C function syntax of OpenGL, but semantically the examples should be applicable to other graphics APIs.

Most graphics hardware work with specific sets of geometric primitives. The primitive types leverage primitive complexity for processing speed on the graphics hardware. Simpler primitives can be processed very fast. The caveat is that the primitive types need to be general purpose so as to model a wide range of geometry from very simple to very complex. On typical graphics hardware, the primitive types are limited to one or more of the following:

- Points: Single vertices used to represent points or particle systems;

- Lines: Pairs of vertices used to represent lines, silhouettes, or edgehighlighting;

- Polygons: (e.g., triangles, triangle strips, indexed triangles, indexed triangle strips, quadrilaterals, general convex polygons, etc.), used for describing triangle meshes, geometric surfaces, and other solid objects, such as spheres, cones, cubes, or cylinders.

These three primitives form the basic building blocks for most geometry you will define. Using these primitives, you can build descriptions of your geometry using one of the graphics APIs and send the geometry to the graphics hardware for rendering. For instance, to transfer the description of a line to the graphics hardware, use the following:

```
beginLine();

  vertex( x1, y1, z1 );

  vertex( x2, y2, z2 );

endLine();
```

In above figure: How your geometry is organized will affect the performance of your application. This wireframe depiction of the Little Cottonwood Canyon terrain dataset shows tens of thousands of triangles organized in a triangle mesh running at real-time rates. (The image is rendered using the VTerrain Project terrain system courtesy of Ben Discoe.)

In this example, two things occur. First, one of the primitive types is declared and made active by the `beginLine()` function call. The line primitive is then made inactive by the `endLine()` function call. Second, all vertices declared between these two functions are copied directly to the graphics card for processing with the `vertex` function calls.

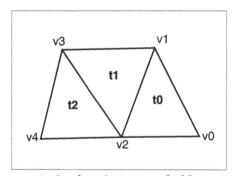

A triangle strip composed of five
vertices defining three triangles.

A second example creates a set of triangles grouped together in a strip; we could use the following code:

```
beginTriangleStrip();

    vertex( x0, y0, z0 );

    vertex( x1, y1, z1 );

    vertex( x2, y2, z2 );

    vertex( x3, y3, z3 );

    vertex( x4, y4, z4 );

endTriangleStrip();
```

In this example, the primitive type, `TriangleStrip`, is made active and the set of vertices that define the triangle strip are copied to the graphics card memory for processing. Note that ordering does matter when describing geometry. In the triangle strip example, connectivity between adjacent triangles is embedded within the ordering of the vertices. Triangle t0 is constructed from vertices (`v0, v1, v2`), triangle t1 from vertices (`v1, v3, v2`), and triangle t2 from vertices (`v2, v3, v4`).

The key point to learn from these simple examples is that geometry is defined for rendering on the graphics hardware using a primitive type along with a set of vertices. The previous examples are simple and push the vertices directly onto the graphics hardware. However, in practice, you will need to make conscious decisions about how you will push your data to the graphics hardware.

As geometry is passed to the graphics hardware, additional data can be specified for each vertex. This extra data is useful for defining state attributes, that might represent the `color` of the vertex, the `normal` direction at the vertex, texture coordinates at the vertex, or other per-vertex data. For instance, to set the `color` and normal state parameters at each vertex of a triangle strip, use the following code:

```
beginTriangleStrip();

   color( r0, g0, b0 ); normal( n0x, n0y, n0z );

   vertex( x0, y0, z0 );

   color( r1, g1, b1 ); normal( n1x, n1y, n1z );

   vertex( x1, y1, z1 );

   color( r2, g2, b2 ); normal( n2x, n2y, n2z );

   vertex( x2, y2, z2 );

   color( r3, g3, b3 ); normal( n3x, n3y, n3z );

   vertex( x3, y3, z3 );

   color( r4, g4, b4 ); normal( n4x, n4y, n4z );

   vertex( x4, y4, z4 );

endTriangleStrip();
```

Here, the color and normal direction at each vertex are specified just prior to the vertex being defined. Each vertex in this example has a unique `color` and `normal` direction. The color function sets the active `color` state using a RGB 3-tuple. The `normal` direction state at each vertex is set by the normal function. Both the color and normal function affect the current rendering state on the graphics hardware. Any vertices defined after these state attributes are set will be bound with those state attributes.

This is a good moment to mention that the graphics hardware maintains a fairly elaborate set of state parameters that determine how vertices and other components are rendered. Some state is bound to vertices, such as color, normal direction, and texture coordinates, while another state may affect pixel level rendering. The graphics state at any particular moment describes a large set of internal hardware parameters. This aspect of graphics hardware is important to consider when you write 3D applications. As you might suspect, making frequent changes to the graphics state affects performance at least to some extent. However, attempting to minimize graphics state changes is only one of many areas where thoughtful programming should be applied. You should attempt to minimize state changes when you can, but it is unlikely that you can group all of your geometry to completely reduce state context switches. One data structure that can help minimize state changes, especially on static scenes, is the scene graph data structure. Prior to rendering any geometry, the scene graph can re-organize the geometry and associated graphics state in an attempt to minimize state changes.

```
color( r, g, b );

normal( nx, ny, nz );

beginTriangleStrip();

    vertex( x0, y0, z0 );

    vertex( x1, y1, z1 );

    vertex( x2, y2, z2 );

    vertex( x3, y3, z3 );

    vertex( x4, y4, z4 );

endTriangleStrip();
```

All vertices in this TriangleStrip have the same color and normal direction, so these state parameters can be set prior to defining the vertices. This minimizes both function call overhead and changes to the internal graphics state.

Many things can affect the performance of a graphics program, but one of the potentially large contributors to performance (or lack thereof) is how your geometry is organized and whether it is stored in the memory cache of the graphics card. In the pseudo-code examples provided so far, geometry has been pushed onto the graphics hardware in what is often called immediate mode rendering. As vertices are defined, they are sent directly to the graphics hardware. The primary disadvantage of immediate mode rendering is that the geometry is sent to the graphics hardware each iteration of your application. If your geometry is static (i.e., it doesn't change), then there is no real need to resend the data each time you redraw a frame. In these and other circumstances, it is more desirable to store the geometry in the graphics card's memory.

The graphics hardware in your computer is connected to the rest of the system via a data bus, such as the PCI, AGP, or PCI-Express buses. When you send data to the graphics hardware, it is sent by the CPU on your machine across one of these buses, eventually being stored in the memory on your graphics hardware. If you have very large triangle meshes representing complex geometry, passing all this data across the bus can end up resulting in a large hit to performance. This is especially true if the geometry is being rendered in immediate mode, as the previous examples have illustrated.

There are various ways to organize geometry; some can help reduce the overall bandwidth needed for transmitting the geometry across the graphics bus. Some possible organization approaches include:

- Triangles: Triangles are specified with three vertices. A triangle mesh created in this manner requires that each triangle in the mesh be defined separately with many vertices potentially duplicated. For a triangle mesh containing m triangles, 3m vertices will be sent to the graphics hardware.

- Triangle strips: Triangles are organized in strips; the first three vertices specify the first triangle in the strip and each additional vertex adds a triangle. If you create a triangle mesh with m triangles organized as a single triangle strip, you send three vertices to the graphics hardware for the first triangle followed by a single vertex for each additional triangle in the strip for a total of m + 2 vertices.

- Indexed triangles: Triangle vertices are arranged as an array of vertices with a separate array defining the triangles using indices into the vertex array. Vertex arrays are sent to the graphics card with very few function calls.

- Indexed triangle strips: Similar to indexed triangles, triangle vertices are stored in a vertex array. However, triangles are organized in strips with the index array defining the strip layout. This is the most compact of the organizational structures for defining triangle meshes as it combines the benefits of triangles strips with the compactness of vertex arrays.

Of the different organizational structures, the use of vertex arrays, either through indexed triangles or indexed triangle strips, provides a good option for increasing the performance of your application. The tight encapsulation of the organization means that many fewer function calls need to be made as well. Once the vertices and indices are stored in an array, only a few function calls need to be made to transfer the data to the graphics hardware, whereas with the pseudo-code example, a function is called for each vertex.

At this point, you may be wondering how the graphics state such as colors, normals, or texture coordinates are defined when vertex arrays are used. In the immediate-mode rendering interleaving the graphics state with the associated vertices is obvious based on the order of the function calls. When vertex arrays are used, graphics state can either be interleaved in the vertex array or specified in separate arrays that are passed to the graphics hardware.

Even if the geometry is organized efficiently when it is sent to the graphics hardware, you can achieve higher performance gains if you can store your geometry in the graphics hardware's memory for the duration of your application. A somewhat unfortunate fact about current graphics hardware is that many of the specifications describing the layout of the graphics hardware memory and cache structure are often not widely publicized. Fortunately though, there are ways using graphics APIs that allow programmers to place geometry into the graphics hardware memory resulting in applications that run faster.

Two commonly used methods to store geometry and graphics state in the graphics hardware cache involve creating display lists or vertex buffer objects. Display lists compile a compact list representation of the geometry and the state associated with the geometry and store the list in the memory on the graphics hardware. The benefits of display lists are that they are general purpose and good at storing a static geometric representation plus associated graphics state on the hardware. They do not work well at all for continuously changing geometry and graphics state, since the display list must be recompiled and then stored again in the graphics hardware memory for every iteration in which the display list changes.

```
displayID = createDisplayList();

color( r, g, b );

normal( nx, ny, nz );

beginTriangleStrip();

  vertex( x0, y0, z0 );

  vertex( x1, y1, z1 );

  ...
```

```
  vertex( xN, yN, zN );

endTriangleStrip();

endDisplayList();
```

In the above example, a display list is created that contains the definition of a triangle strip with its associated color and normal information. The commands between the `createDisplayList` and `endDisplayList` function calls provide the elements that define the display list. Display lists are most often created during an initialization phase of an application. After the display list is created, it is stored in the memory of the graphics hardware and can be referenced for later use by the identifier assigned to the list.

```
// draw the display list created earlier

drawDisplayList(displayID);
```

When it is time to draw the contents of the display list, a single function call will instruct the graphics hardware to access the memory indexed through the display list identifier and display the contents.

A second method to store geometry on the graphics hardware for the duration of your application is through vertex buffer objects (VBOs). VBOs are specialized buffers that reside in high-performance memory on the graphics hardware and store vertex arrays and associated graphics state. They can also provide a mapping from your application to the memory on the graphics hardware to allow for fast access and updating to the contents of the VBO.

The chief advantage of VBOs is that they provide a mapping into the graphics hardware memory. With VBOs, geometry can be modified during an application with a minimal loss of performance as compared with using immediate mode rendering or display lists. This is extremely useful if portions of your geometry change during each iteration of your application or if the indices used to organize your geometry change.

VBOs are created in much the same way indexed triangles and indexed triangle strips are built. A buffer object is first created on the graphics card to make room for the vertex array containing the vertices of the triangle mesh. Next, the vertex array and index array are copied over to the graphics hardware. When it is time to render the geometry, the vertex buffer object identifier can be used to instruct the graphics hardware to draw your geometry. If you are already using vertex arrays in your application, modifying your code to use VBOs should likely require a minimal change.

Processing Geometry into Pixels

After the geometry has been placed in the graphics hardware memory, each vertex must be lit as well as transformed into screen coordinates during the geometry processing stage. In the fixed-function graphics pipeline illustrated in figure, vertices are transformed from a model coordinate system to a screen coordinate frame of reference. This process and the matrices involved .The model view and projection matrices needed for this transformation are defined using functions provided with the graphics API you decide to use.

Lighting is calculated on a per-vertex basis. Depending on the global shading parameters, the triangle face will either have a flat-shaded look or the face color will be diffusely shaded

(Gouraud shading) by linearly interpolating the color at each triangle vertex across the face of the triangle. The latter method produces a much smoother appearance. The color at each vertex is computed based on the assigned material properties, the lights in the scene, and various lighting parameters.

The lighting model in the fixed-function graphics pipeline is good for fast lighting of vertices; we make a tradeoff for increased speed over accurate illumination. As a result, Phong shaded surfaces are not supported with this fixed function framework.

In particular, the diffuse shading algorithm built into the graphics hardware often fails to compute the appropriate illumination since the lighting is only being calculated at each vertex. For example, when the distance to the light source is small, as compared with the size of the face being shaded, the illumination on the face will be incorrect. The center of the triangle will not be illuminated brightly despite being very close to the light source, since the lighting on the vertices, which are far from the light source, are used to interpolate the shading across the face.

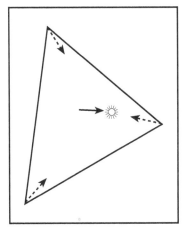

The distance to the light source is
small relative to the size of the triangle.

With the fixed-function pipeline, this issue can only be remedied by increasing the tessellation of the geometry. This solution works but is of limited use in real-time graphics as the added geometry required for more accurate illumination can result in slower rendering.

However, with current hardware, the problem of obtaining better approximations for illumination can be solved without necessarily increasing the geometric complexity of the objects. The solution involves replacing the fixed-function routines embedded within the graphics hardware with your own programs. These small programs run on the graphics hardware and perform a part of the geometry processing and pixel-processing stages of the graphics pipeline.

Programming the Pipeline

Fairly recent changes to the organization of consumer graphics hardware has generated a substantial buzz from game developers, graphics researchers, and many others. It is quite likely that you have heard about GPU programming, graphics hardware programming, or even shader programming. These terms and the changes in consumer hardware that have spawned them primarily have to do with how the graphics hardware rendering pipeline can now be programmed.

Specifically, the changes have opened up two specific aspects of the graphics hardware pipeline. Programmers now have the ability to modify how the hardware processes vertices and shades pixels by writing vertex shaders and fragment shaders (also sometimes referred to as vertex programs or fragment programs). Vertex shaders are programs that perform the vertex and normal transformations, texture coordinate generation, and per-vertex lighting computations normally computed in the geometry processing stage. Fragment shaders are programs that perform the computations in the pixel processing stage of the graphics pipeline and determine exactly how each pixel is shaded, how textures are applied, and if a pixel should be drawn or not. These small shader programs are sent to the graphics hardware from the user program, but they are executed on the graphics hardware.

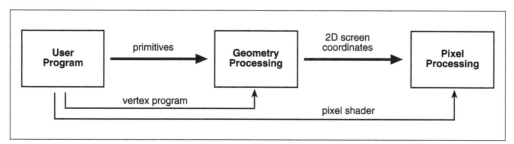

The programmable graphics hardware pipeline. The user program
supplies primitives, vertex programs, and fragment programs to the hardware.

What this programmability means for you is that you essentially have a multiprocessor machine. This turns out to be a good way to think about your graphics hardware, since it means that you may be able to use the graphics hardware processor to relieve the load on the CPU in some of your applications. The graphics hardware processors are often referred to as GPUs. GPU stands for Graphics Processing Unit and highlights the fact that graphics hardware components now contain a separate processor dedicated to graphics-related computations. Interestingly, modern GPUs contain more transistors than modern CPUs For the time being, GPUs are utilizing most of these transistors for computations and less for memory or cache management operations.

However, this will not always be the case as graphics hardware continues to advance. And just because the computations are geared towards 3D graphics, it does not mean that you cannot perform computations unrelated to computer graphics on the GPU. However, the manner in which the GPU is programmed is different from your general purpose CPU and will require a slightly modified way of thinking about how to solve problems and program the graphics hardware.

The GPU is a stream processor that excels at 3D vector operations such as vector multiplication, vector addition, dot products, and other operations necessary for basic lighting of surfaces and texture mapping. As stream processors, both the vertex and fragment processing components include the ability to process multiple primitives at the same time. In this regard, the GPU acts as a SIMD (Single Instruction, Multiple Data) processor, and in certain hardware implementations of the fragment processor, up to 16 pixels can be processed at a time. When you write programs for these processing components, it will be helpful, at least conceptually, to think of the computations being performed concurrently on your data. In other words, the vertex shader program will run for all vertices at the same time. The vertex computations will then be followed by a stage in which your fragment shader program will execute simultaneously on all fragments. It is important to note that while the computations on vertices or fragments occur concurrently, the staging of the pipeline components still occur in the same order.

The manner in which vertex and fragment shaders work is simple. You write a vertex shader program and a fragment shader program and send it to the graphics hardware. These programs can be used on specific geometry, and when your geometry is processed, the vertex shader is used to transform and light the vertices, while the fragment shader performs the final shading of the geometry on a per-pixel basis. Just as you can texture map different images onto different pieces of geometry, you can also write different shader programs to act upon different objects in your application. Shader programs are a part of the graphics state so you do need to be concerned with how your shader programs might get swapped in and out based on the geometry being rendered.

The details tend to be a bit more complicated, however. Vertex shaders usually perform two basic actions: set the color at the vertex and transform the vertex into screen coordinates by multiplying the vertex by the modelview and projection matrices. The perspective divide and clipping steps are not performed in a vertex program. Vertex shaders are also often used to set the stage for a fragment shader. In particular, you may have vertex attributes, such as texture coordinates or other application- dependent data, that the vertex shader calculates or modifies and then sends to the fragment processing stage for use in your fragment shader. It may seem strange at first, but vertex shaders can be used to manipulate the positions of the vertices. This is often useful for generating simulated ocean wave motion entirely on the GPU.

In a fragment shader, it is required that the program outputs the fragment color. This may involve looking up texture values and combining them in some manner with values obtained by performing a lighting calculation at each pixel; or, it may involve killing the fragment from being drawn entirely. Because operations in the fragment shader operate at the fragment level, the real power of the programmable graphics hardware is in the fragment shader. This added processing power represents one of the key differences between the fixed function pipeline and the programmable pipeline. In the fixed pipeline, fragment processing used illumination values interpolated between the vertices of the triangle to compute the fragment color. With the programmable pipeline, the color at each fragment can be computed independently. Gouraud shading of a triangle face fails to produce a reasonable solution because lighting only occurs at the vertices which are farther away from the light than the center of the triangle. In a fragment shader, the lighting equation can be evaluated at each fragment, rather than at each vertex, resulting in a more accurate rendering of the face.

Basic Execution Model

When writing vertex or fragment shaders, there are a few important things to understand in terms of how vertex and fragment programs execute and access data on the GPU. Because these programs run entirely on the GPU, the first details you will need to figure out are which data your shaders will use and how to get that data to them. There are several characteristics associated with the data types used in shader programs. The following terms, which come primarily from the OpenGL™ Shading Language framework, are used to describe the conceptual aspects of these data characteristics. The concepts are the same across different shading language frameworks. In the shaders you write, variables are characterized using one of the following terms:

- Attributes: Attribute variables represent data that changes frequently, often on a per-vertex basis. Attribute variables are often tied to the changing graphics state associated with each vertex. For instance, normal vectors or texture coordinates are considered to be attribute data since they are part of the graphics state associated with each vertex.

- Uniforms: Uniform variables represent data that cannot change during the execution of a shader program. However, uniform variables can be modified by your application between executions of a shader. This provides another way for your application to communicate data to a shader. Uniform data often represent the graphics state associated with an application. For instance, the modelview and projection matrices can be accessed through uniform variables. Information about light sources in your application can also be obtained through uniform variables. In these examples, the data does not change while the shader is executing, but could (e.g., the light could move) prior to the next iteration of the application.

- Varying: Varying data is used to pass data between a vertex shader and a fragment shader. The reason the data is considered varying is because it is written by vertex shaders on a per-vertex basis, but read by fragment shaders as value interpolated across the face of the primitive between neighboring vertices.

Variables defined using one of these three characteristics can either be built-in variables or user-defined variables. In addition to from accessing the built-in graphics state, attribute and uniform variables are one of the ways to communicate user-defined data to your vertex and fragment programs. Varying data is the only means to pass data from a vertex shader to a fragment shader. Figure illustrates the basic execution of the vertex and fragment processors in terms of the inputs and outputs used by the shaders.

Another way to pass data to vertex and fragment shaders is by using texture maps as sources and sinks of data. This may come as a surprise if you have been thinking of texture maps solely as images that are applied to the outside surface of geometry. The reason texture maps are important is because they give you access to the memory on the graphics hardware. When you write applications that run on the CPU, you control the memory your application requires and have direct access to it when necessary. On graphics hardware, memory is not accessed in the same manner. In fact, you are not directly able to allocate and deallocate general purpose memory chunks, and this particular aspect usually requires a slight change in thinking.

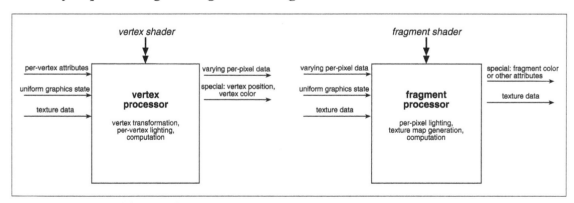

The execution model for shader programs. Input, such as per-vertex attributes, graphics state-related uniform variables, varying data, and texture maps are provided to vertex and fragment programs within the shader processor. Shaders output special variables used in later parts of the graphics pipeline.

Texture maps on graphics hardware, however, can be created, deleted, and controlled through the graphics API you use. In other words, for general data used by your shader, you will create texture maps that contain that data and then use texture access functions to look up the data in the texture map. Technically, textures can be accessed by both vertex and fragment shaders. However, in practice, texture lookups from the vertex shader are not currently supported on all graphics cards. An example that utilizes a texture map as a data source is bump mapping. Bump mapping uses a normal map which defines how the normal vectors change across a triangle face. A bump mapping fragment shader would look up the normal vector in the normal map "texture data" and use it in the shading calculations at that particular fragment.

You need to be concerned about the types of data you put into your texture maps. Not all numerical data types are well supported and only recently has graphics hardware included floating point textures with 16-bit components. Moreover, none of the computation being performed on your GPU is done with double-precision math! If numerical precision is important for your application, you will need to think through these issues very carefully to determine if using the graphics hardware for computation is useful.

So what do these shader programs look like? One way to write vertex and fragment shaders is through assembly language instructions. For instance, performing a matrix multiplication in shader assembly language looks something like this:

```
DP4  p[0].x,  M[0],  v[0];

DP4  p[0].y,  M[1],  v[0];

DP4  p[0].z,  M[2],  v[0];

DP4  p[0].w,  M[3],  v[0];
```

In this example, the DP4 instruction is a 4-component dot product function. It stores the result of the dot product in the first register and performs the dot product between the last two registers. In shader programming, registers hold 4-components corresponding to the x, y, z, and w components of a homogeneous coordinate, or the r, g, b, and a components of a RGBA tuple. So, in this example, a simple matrix multiplication, is computed by four DP4 instructions. Each instruction computes one element of the final result:

$$p = Mv$$

Fortunately though, you are not forced to program in assembly language. The good news is that higher-level languages are available to write vertex and fragment shaders. NVIDIA's Cg, the OpenGL™ Shading Language (GLSL), and Microsoft's High Level Shading Language (HLSL) all provide similar interfaces to the programmable aspects of graphics hardware. Using the notation of GLSL, the same matrix multiplication performed above looks like this:

$$p = M * v;$$

where p and v are vertex data types and M is a matrix data type. As evidenced here, one advantage of using a higher-level language over assembly language is that various data types are available to the programmer. In all of these languages, there are built-in data types for storing vectors and matrices, as well as arrays and constructs for creating structures. Many different functions are also built in to these languages to help compute trigonometric values (sin, cos, etc.), minimum and maximum values, exponential functions (log2, sqrt, pow, etc.), and other math or geometric-based functions.

Vertex Shader

Vertex shaders give you control over how your vertices are lit and transformed. They are also used to set the stage for fragment shaders. An interesting aspect to vertex shaders is that you still are able to use geometry-caching mechanisms, such as display lists or VBOs, and thus, benefit from their performance gains while using vertex shaders to do computation on the GPU. For instance, if the vertices represent particles and you can model the movement of the particles using a vertex shader, you have nearly eliminated the CPU from these computations. Any bottleneck in performance that may have occurred due to data being passed between the CPU and the GPU will be minimized. Prior to the introduction of vertex shaders, the computation of the particle movement would have been performed on the CPU and each vertex would have been re-sent to the graphics hardware on each iteration of your application. The ability to perform computations on the vertices already stored in the graphics hardware memory is a big performance win.

One of the simplest vertex shaders transforms a vertex into clip coordinates and assigns the front-facing color to the color attribute associated with the vertex.

```
void main(void)

{

    gl_Position = gl_ModelViewProjectionMatrix *

    gl_Vertex;

    gl_FrontColor = gl_Color;

}
```

In this example, gl_ModelViewProjectionMatrix is a built-in uniform variable supplied by the GLSL run-time environment. The variables gl_Vertex and gl_Color are built-in vertex attributes; the special output variables, gl_Position and gl_FrontColor are used by the vertex shader to set the transformed position and the vertex color.

A more interesting vertex shader that implements the surface- shading equations the effect of per-vertex shading using the Phong shading algorithm.

```
void main(void)

{

    vec4 v = gl_ModelViewMatrix * gl_Vertex;

    vec3 n = normalize(gl_NormalMatrix * gl_Normal);

    vec3 l = normalize(gl_LightSource.position - v);

    vec3 h = normalize(l - normalize(v));

    float p = 16;

    vec4 cr = gl_FrontMaterial.diffuse;

    vec4 cl = gl_LightSource.diffuse;

    vec4 ca = vec4(0.2, 0.2, 0.2, 1.0);
```

```
vec4 color;

if (dot(h,n) > 0)

color = cr * (ca + cl * max(0,dot(n,l))) +

cl * pow(dot(h,n), p);

else

color = cr * (ca + cl * max(0,dot(n,l)));

gl_FrontColor = color;

gl_Position = ftransform();

}
```

From the code presented in this shader, you should be able to gain a sense of shader programming and how it resembles C-style programming. Several things are happening with this shader. First, we create a set of variables to hold the vectors necessary for computing Phong shading: v, n, l, and h. Note that the computation in the vertex shader is performed in eye-space. This is done for a variety of reasons, but one reason is that the light-source positions accessible within a shader have already been transformed into the eye coordinate frame. When you create shaders, the coordinate system that you decide to use will likely depend on the types of computations being performed; this is an important factor to consider. Also, note the use of built-in functions and data structures in the example. In particular, there are several functions used in this shader: `normalize`, `dot`, `max`, `pow`, and `ftransform`. These functions are provided with the shader language. Additionally, the graphics state associated with materials and lighting can be accessed through built-in uniform variables: `gl FrontMaterial` and `gl LightSource`. The diffuse component of the material and light is accessed through the `diffuse` member of these variables. The color at the vertex is computed and then stored in the special output variable gl Front Color. The vertex position is transformed using the function `ftransform` which is a convenience function that performs the multiplication with the modelview and projection matrices. The results from running this vertex shader with differently tessellated spheres. Because the computations are performed on a per-vertex basis, a large amount of geometry is required to produce a Phong highlight on the sphere that appears correct.

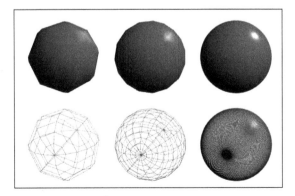

Figure: Each sphere is rendered using only a vertex shader that computes Phong shading. Because the computation is being performed on a per-vertex basis, the Phong highlight only begins to appear accurate after the amount of geometry used to model the sphere is increased drastically.

Fragment Shader

Fragment shaders are written in a manner very similar to vertex shaders. The vertex shader required for this example is fairly simple, but introduces the use of varying variables to communicate data to the fragment shader.

```
varying vec4 v;

varying vec3 n;

void main(void)

{

    v = gl_ModelViewMatrix * gl_Vertex;

    n = normalize(gl_NormalMatrix * gl_Normal);

    gl_Position = ftransform();

}
```

Recall that varying variables will be set on a per-vertex basis by a vertex shader, but when they are accessed in a fragment shader, the values will vary (i.e., be interpolated) across the triangle, or geometric primitive. In this case, the vertex position in eye-space v and the normal at the vertex n are calculated at each vertex. The final computation performed by the vertex shader is to transform the vertex into clip coordinates since the fragment shader will compute the lighting at each fragment. It is not necessary to set the front-facing color in this vertex shader.

The fragment shader program computes the lighting at each fragment using the Phong shading model.

```
varying vec4 v;

varying vec3 n;

void main(void)

{

vec3 l = normalize(gl_LightSource.position - v);

vec3 h = normalize(l - normalize(v));

float p = 16;

vec4 cr = gl_FrontMaterial.diffuse;

vec4 cl = gl_LightSource.diffuse;

vec4 ca = vec4(0.2, 0.2, 0.2, 1.0);

vec4 color;

if (dot(h,n) > 0)

    color = cr * (ca + cl * max(0,dot(n,l))) +

                cl * pow(dot(h,n),p);

else
```

```
    color = cr * (ca + cl * max(0,dot(n,l)));
gl_FragColor = color;

}
```

The first thing you should notice is the similarity between the fragment shader code in this example and the vertex shader code. The main difference is in the use of the varying variables, v and n. In the fragment shader, the view vectors and normal values are interpolated across the surface of the model between neighboring vertices. The results are shown in figure Immediately, you should notice the Phong highlight on the quadrilateral, which only contains four vertices. Because the shading is being calculated at the fragment level using the Phong equation with the interpolated (i.e., varying) data, more consistent and accurate Phong shading is produced with far less geometry.

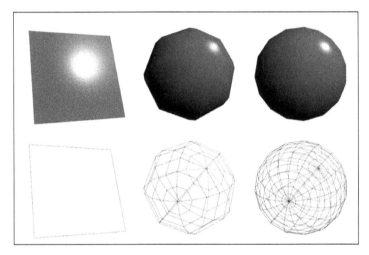

In figure the results of running the fragment shader from section. Note that the Phong highlight does appear on the left-most model which is represented by a single polygon. In fact, because lighting is calculated at the fragment, rather than at each vertex, the more coarsely tessellated sphere models also demonstrate appropriate Phong shading.

General Purpose Computing on the GPU

After studying the vertex and fragment shader examples, you may be wondering if you can write programs to perform other types of computations on the GPU. Obviously, the answer is yes, as many problems can be coded to run on the GPU given the various languages available for programming on the GPU. However, a few facts are important to remember. Foremost, floating point math processing on graphics hardware is not currently double-precision. Secondly, you will likely need to transform your problem into a form that fits within a graphics-related framework. In other words, you will need to use the graphics APIs to set up the problem, use texture maps as data rather than traditional memory, and write vertex and fragment shaders to frame and solve your problem.

Having stated that, the GPU may still be an attractive platform for computation, since the ratio of transistors that are dedicated to performing computation is much higher on the GPU than it is on the CPU. In many cases, algorithms running on GPUs run faster than on a CPU. Furthermore,

GPUs perform SIMD computation, which is especially true at the fragment-processing level. In fact, it can often help to think about the computation occurring on the fragment processor as a highly parallel version of a generic foreach construct, performing simultaneous operations on a set of elements.

There has been a large amount of investigation to perform General Purpose computation on GPUs, often referred to as GPGPU. Among other things, researchers are using the GPU as a means to simulate the dynamics of clouds, implement ray tracers, compute radiosity, perform 3D segmentation using level sets, or solve the Navier-Stokes equations.

General purpose computation is often performed on the GPU using multiple rendering "passes," and most computation is done using the fragment processor due to it's highly data-parallel setup. Each pass, called a kernel, completes a portion of the computation. Kernels work on streams of data with several kernels strung together to form the overall computation. The first kernel completes the first part of the computation, the second kernel works on the first kernel's data, and so on, until the calculation is complete. In this style of programming, working with data and data structures on the GPU is different than conventional programming and does require a bit of thought. Fortunately, recent efforts are providing abstractions and information for creating efficient data structures for GPU programming.

Using the GPU for general purpose programming does require that you understand how to program the graphics hardware. For instance, most applications that perform GPGPU will render a simple quadrilateral, or sets of quadrilaterals, with vertex and fragment shaders operating on that geometry. The geometry doesn't have to be visible, or drawn to the screen, but it is necessary to allow the vertex and fragment operations to occur.Fortunately, recent efforts are working to make the interface to the GPU more like traditional programming. The Brook for GPUs project is a system that provides a C-like interface to afford stream computations on the GPU, which should allow more people to take advantage of the computational power on modern graphics hardware.

Graphics Processing Unit

A GPU is a processor designed to handle graphics operations. This includes both 2D and 3D calculations, though GPUs primarily excel at rendering 3D graphics.

Early PCs did not include GPUs, which meant the CPU had to handle all standard calculations and graphics operations. As software demands increased and graphics became more important (especially in video games), a need arose for a separate processor to render graphics. On August 31, 1999, NVIDIA introduced the first commercially available GPU for a desktop computer, called the GeForce 256. It could process 10 million polygons per second, allowing it to offload a significant amount of graphics processing from the CPU.

The success of the first graphics processing unit caused both hardware and software developers alike to quickly adopt GPU support. Motherboards were manufactured with faster PCI slots and AGP slots, designed exclusively for graphics cards, became a common option as well. Software

APIs like OpenGL and Direct3D were created to help developers make use of GPUs in their programs. Today, dedicated graphics processing is standard – not just in desktop PCs – but also in laptops, smartphones, and video game consoles.

Function

The primary purpose of a GPU is to render 3D graphics, which are comprised of polygons. Since most polygonal transformations involve decimal numbers, GPUs are designed to perform floating point operations (as opposed to integer calculations). This specialized design enables GPUs to render graphics more efficiently than even the fastest CPUs. Offloading graphics processing to high-powered GPUs is what makes modern gaming possible.

While GPUs excel at rendering graphics, the raw power of a GPU can also be used for other purposes. Many operating systems and software programs now support GPGPU, or general-purpose computation on graphics processing units. Technologies like OpenCL and CUDA allow developers to utilize the GPU to assist the CPU in non-graphics computations. This can improve the overall performance of a computer or other electronic device.

General-purpose Computing on Graphics Processing Units

General-purpose computing on graphics processing units (GPGPU, rarely GPGP) is the use of a graphics processing unit (GPU), which typically handles computation only for computer graphics, to perform computation in applications traditionally handled by the central processing unit (CPU). The use of multiple video cards in one computer, or large numbers of graphics chips, further parallelizes the already parallel nature of graphics processing. In addition, even a single GPU-CPU framework provides advantages that multiple CPUs on their own do not offer due to the specialization in each chip.

Essentially, a GPGPU pipeline is a kind of parallel processing between one or more GPUs and CPUs that analyzes data as if it were in image or other graphic form. While GPUs operate at lower frequencies, they typically have many times the number of cores. Thus, GPUs can process far more pictures and graphical data per second than a traditional CPU. Migrating data into graphical form and then using the GPU to scan and analyze it can create a large speedup.

GPGPU pipelines were developed at the beginning of the 21st century for graphics processing (e.g., for better shaders). These pipelines were found to fit scientific computing needs well, and have since been developed in this direction.

In principle, any arbitrary boolean function, including those of addition, multiplication and other mathematical functions can be built-up from a functionally complete set of logic operators. In 1987, Conway's Game of Life became one of the first examples of general purpose computing using an early stream processor called a blitter to invoke a special sequence of logical operations on bit vectors.

General-purpose computing on GPUs became more practical and popular after about 2001, with the advent of both programmable shaders and floating point support on graphics processors. Notably, problems involving matrices and/or vectors – especially two-, three-, or four-dimensional vectors – were easy to translate to a GPU, which acts with native speed and support on those types.

The scientific computing community's experiments with the new hardware began with a matrix multiplication routine; one of the first common scientific programs to run faster on GPUs than CPUs was an implementation of LU factorization.

These early efforts to use GPUs as general-purpose processors required reformulating computational problems in terms of graphics primitives, as supported by the two major APIs for graphics processors, OpenGL and DirectX. This cumbersome translation was obviated by the advent of general-purpose programming languages and APIs such as Sh/RapidMind, Brook and Accelerator.

These were followed by Nvidia's CUDA, which allowed programmers to ignore the underlying graphical concepts in favor of more common high-performance computing concepts. Newer, hardware vendor-independent offerings include Microsoft's DirectCompute and Apple/Khronos Group's OpenCL. This means that modern GPGPU pipelines can leverage the speed of a GPU without requiring full and explicit conversion of the data to a graphical form.

Mobile Computers

Due to a trend of increasing power of mobile GPUs, general-purpose programming became available also on the mobile devices running major mobile operating systems.

Google Android 4.2 enabled running RenderScript code on the mobile device GPU. Apple introduced a proprietary Metal API for iOS applications, able to execute arbitrary code through Apple's GPU compute shaders.

Hardware Support

Computer video cards are produced by various vendors, such as Nvidia, and AMD and ATI. Cards from such vendors differ on implementing data-format support, such as integer and floating-point formats (32-bit and 64-bit). Microsoft introduced a *Shader Model* standard, to help rank the various features of graphic cards into a simple Shader Model version number (1.0, 2.0, 3.0, etc.).

Integer Numbers

Pre-DirectX 9 video cards only supported paletted or integer color types. Various formats are available, each containing a red element, a green element, and a blue element. Sometimes another alpha value is added, to be used for transparency. Common formats are:

- 8 bits per pixel – Sometimes palette mode, where each value is an index in a table with the real color value specified in one of the other formats. Sometimes three bits for red, three bits for green, and two bits for blue.

- 16 bits per pixel – Usually the bits are allocated as five bits for red, six bits for green, and five bits for blue.

- 24 bits per pixel – There are eight bits for each of red, green, and blue.

- 32 bits per pixel – There are eight bits for each of red, green, blue, and alpha.

Floating-point Numbers

For early fixed-function or limited programmability graphics (i.e., up to and including DirectX 8.1-compliant GPUs) this was sufficient because this is also the representation used in displays. It is important to note that this representation does have certain limitations. Given sufficient graphics processing power even graphics programmers would like to use better formats, such as floating point data formats, to obtain effects such as high dynamic range imaging. Many GPGPU applications require floating point accuracy, which came with video cards conforming to the DirectX 9 specification.

DirectX 9 Shader Model 2.x suggested the support of two precision types: full and partial precision. Full precision support could either be FP32 or FP24 (floating point 32- or 24-bit per component) or greater, while partial precision was FP16. ATI's Radeon R300 series of GPUs supported FP24 precision only in the programmable fragment pipeline (although FP32 was supported in the vertex processors) while Nvidia's NV30 series supported both FP16 and FP32; other vendors such as S3 Graphics and XGI supported a mixture of formats up to FP24.

The implementations of floating point on Nvidia GPUs are mostly IEEE compliant; however, this is not true across all vendors. This has implications for correctness which are considered important to some scientific applications. While 64-bit floating point values (double precision float) are commonly available on CPUs, these are not universally supported on GPUs. Some GPU architectures sacrifice IEEE compliance, while others lack double-precision. Efforts have occurred to emulate double-precision floating point values on GPUs; however, the speed tradeoff negates any benefit to offloading the computing onto the GPU in the first place.

Vectorization

Most operations on the GPU operate in a vectorized fashion: one operation can be performed on up to four values at once. For example, if one color <R1, G1, B1> is to be modulated by another color <R2, G2, B2>, the GPU can produce the resulting color <R1*R2, G1*G2, B1*B2> in one operation. This functionality is useful in graphics because almost every basic data type is a vector (either 2-, 3-, or 4-dimensional). Examples include vertices, colors, normal vectors, and texture coordinates. Many other applications can put this to good use, and because of their higher performance, vector instructions, termed single instruction, multiple data (SIMD), have long been available on CPUs.

GPU vs. CPU

Originally, data was simply passed one-way from a central processing unit (CPU) to a graphics processing unit (GPU), then to a display device. As time progressed, however, it became valuable for GPUs to store at first simple, then complex structures of data to be passed back to the CPU that analyzed an image, or a set of scientific-data represented as a 2D or 3D format that a video card can understand. Because the GPU has access to every draw operation, it can analyze data in these forms quickly, whereas a CPU must poll every pixel or data element much more slowly, as the speed of access between a CPU and its larger pool of random-access memory (or in an even worse case, a hard drive) is slower than GPUs and video cards, which typically contain smaller amounts of more expensive memory that is much faster to access. Transferring the portion of the data set to be actively analyzed to that GPU memory in the form of textures or other easily readable GPU forms results in speed increase. The distinguishing feature of a GPGPU design is the ability to transfer information bidirectionally back from the GPU to the CPU; generally the data throughput in both directions is ideally high, resulting in a multiplier effect on the speed of a specific high-use algorithm. GPGPU pipelines may improve efficiency on especially large data sets and/or data containing 2D or 3D imagery. It is used in complex graphics pipelines as well as scientific computing; more so in fields with large data sets like genome mapping, or where two- or three-dimensional analysis is useful – especially at present biomolecule analysis, protein study, and other complex organic chemistry. Such pipelines can also vastly improve efficiency in image processing and computer vision, among other fields; as well as parallel processing generally. Some very heavily optimized pipelines have yielded speed increases of several hundred times the original CPU-based pipeline on one high-use task.

A simple example would be a GPU program that collects data about average lighting values as it renders some view from either a camera or a computer graphics program back to the main program on the CPU, so that the CPU can then make adjustments to the overall screen view. A more advanced example might use edge detection to return both numerical information and a processed image representing outlines to a computer vision program controlling, say, a mobile robot. Because the GPU has fast and local hardware access to every pixel or other picture element in an image, it can analyze and average it (for the first example) or apply a Sobel edge filter or other convolution filter (for the second) with much greater speed than a CPU, which typically must access slower random-access memory copies of the graphic in question.

GPGPU is fundamentally a software concept, not a hardware concept; it is a type of algorithm, not a piece of equipment. Specialized equipment designs may, however, even further enhance the efficiency of GPGPU pipelines, which traditionally perform relatively few algorithms on very large amounts of data. Massively parallelized, gigantic-data-level tasks thus may be parallelized even further via specialized setups such as rack computing (many similar, highly tailored machines built into a *rack*), which adds a third layer – many computing units each using many CPUs to correspond to many GPUs. Some Bitcoin "miners" used such setups for high-quantity processing.

Caches

Historically, CPUs have used hardware-managed caches but the earlier GPUs only provided software-managed local memories. However, as GPUs are being increasingly used for general-purpose applications, state-of-the-art GPUs are being designed with hardware-managed multi-level caches which have helped the GPUs to move towards mainstream computing. For example, GeForce 200 series GT200 architecture GPUs did not feature an L2 cache, the Fermi GPU has 768 KiB last-level cache, the Kepler GPU has 1.5 MiB last-level cache, the Maxwell GPU has 2 MiB last-level cache and the Pascal GPU has 4 MiB last-level cache.

Register File

GPUs have very large register files, which allow them to reduce context-switching latency. Register file size is also increasing over different GPU generations, e.g., the total register file size on Maxwell (GM200) and Pascal GPUs are 6 MiB and 14 MiB, respectively. By comparison, the size of a register file on CPUs is small, typically tens or hundreds of kilobytes.

Energy Efficiency

Several research projects have compared the energy efficiency of GPUs with that of CPUs and FPGAs.

Stream Processing

GPUs are designed specifically for graphics and thus are very restrictive in operations and programming. Due to their design, GPUs are only effective for problems that can be solved using stream processing and the hardware can only be used in certain ways.

The following discussion referring to vertices, fragments and textures concerns mainly the legacy model of GPGPU programming, where graphics APIs (OpenGL or DirectX) were used to perform general-purpose computation. With the introduction of the CUDA and OpenCL general-purpose computing APIs, in new GPGPU codes it is no longer necessary to map the computation to graphics primitives. The stream processing nature of GPUs remains valid regardless of the APIs used.

GPUs can only process independent vertices and fragments, but can process many of them in parallel. This is especially effective when the programmer wants to process many vertices or fragments in the same way. In this sense, GPUs are stream processors – processors that can operate in parallel by running one kernel on many records in a stream at once.

A stream is simply a set of records that require similar computation. Streams provide data parallelism. Kernels are the functions that are applied to each element in the stream. In the GPUs, vertices and fragments are the elements in streams and vertex and fragment shaders are the kernels to be run on them. For each element we can only read from the input, perform operations on it, and write to the output. It is permissible to have multiple inputs and multiple outputs, but never a piece of memory that is both readable and writable.

Arithmetic intensity is defined as the number of operations performed per word of memory transferred. It is important for GPGPU applications to have high arithmetic intensity else the memory access latency will limit computational speedup. Ideal GPGPU applications have large data sets, high parallelism, and minimal dependency between data elements.

GPU Programming Concepts

Computational Resources

There are a variety of computational resources available on the GPU:

- Programmable processors – Vertex, primitive, fragment and mainly compute pipelines allow programmer to perform kernel on streams of data.

- Rasterizer – Creates fragments and interpolates per-vertex constants such as texture coordinates and color.

- Texture unit – Read-only memory interface.

- Framebuffer – Write-only memory interface.

In fact, a program can substitute a write only texture for output instead of the framebuffer. This is done either through Render to Texture (RTT), Render-To-Backbuffer-Copy-To-Texture (RTBCTT), or the more recent stream-out.

Textures as Stream

The most common form for a stream to take in GPGPU is a 2D grid because this fits naturally with the rendering model built into GPUs. Many computations naturally map into grids: matrix algebra, image processing, physically based simulation, and so on.

Since textures are used as memory, texture lookups are then used as memory reads. Certain operations can be done automatically by the GPU because of this.

Kernels

Compute kernels can be thought of as the body of loops. For example, a programmer operating on a grid on the CPU might have code that looks like this:

```
// Input and output grids have 10000 x 10000 or 100 million elements.

void transform_10k_by_10k_grid(float in, float out)

{

    for (int x = 0; x < 10000; x++) {

    for (int y = 0; y < 10000; y++) {

        // The next line is executed 100 million times

        out[x][y] = do_some_hard_work(in[x][y]);

    }

    }

}
```

On the GPU, the programmer only specifies the body of the loop as the kernel and what data to loop over by invoking geometry processing.

Flow control

In sequential code it is possible to control the flow of the program using if-then-else statements and various forms of loops. Such flow control structures have only recently been added to GPUs. Conditional writes could be performed using a properly crafted series of arithmetic/bit operations, but looping and conditional branching were not possible.

Recent GPUs allow branching, but usually with a performance penalty. Branching should generally be avoided in inner loops, whether in CPU or GPU code, and various methods, such as static branch resolution, pre-computation, predication, loop splitting, and Z-cull can be used to achieve branching when hardware support does not exist.

GPU Methods

Map

The map operation simply applies the given function (the kernel) to every element in the stream. A simple example is multiplying each value in the stream by a constant (increasing the brightness of an image). The map operation is simple to implement on the GPU. The programmer generates a fragment for each pixel on screen and applies a fragment program to each one. The result stream of the same size is stored in the output buffer.

Reduce

Some computations require calculating a smaller stream (possibly a stream of only 1 element) from a larger stream. This is called a reduction of the stream. Generally, a reduction can be performed in multiple steps. The results from the prior step are used as the input for the current step and the range over which the operation is applied is reduced until only one stream element remains.

Stream Filtering

Stream filtering is essentially a non-uniform reduction. Filtering involves removing items from the stream based on some criteria.

Scan

The scan operation, also termed *parallel prefix sum*, takes in a vector (stream) of data elements and an (arbitrary) associative binary function '+' with an identity element 'i'. If the input is [a0, a1, a2, a3, ...], an *exclusive scan* produces the output [i, a0, a0 + a1, a0 + a1 + a2, ...], while an *inclusive scan* produces the output [a0, a0 + a1, a0 + a1 + a2, a0 + a1 + a2 + a3, ...] and does not require an identity to exist. While at first glance the operation may seem inherently serial, efficient parallel scan algorithms are possible and have been implemented on graphics processing units. The scan operation has uses in e.g., quicksort and sparse matrix-vector multiplication.

Scatter

The scatter operation is most naturally defined on the vertex processor. The vertex processor is able to adjust the position of the vertex, which allows the programmer to control where information is deposited on the grid. Other extensions are also possible, such as controlling how large an area the vertex affects.

The fragment processor cannot perform a direct scatter operation because the location of each fragment on the grid is fixed at the time of the fragment's creation and cannot be altered by the programmer. However, a logical scatter operation may sometimes be recast or implemented with another gather step. A scatter implementation would first emit both an output value and an output address. An immediately following gather operation uses address comparisons to see whether the output value maps to the current output slot.

In dedicated compute kernels, scatter can be performed by indexed writes.

Gather

Gather is the reverse of scatter, after scatter reorders elements according to a map, gather can restore the order of the elements according to the map scatter used. In dedicated compute kernels, gather may be performed by indexed reads. In other shaders, it is performed with texture-lookups.

Sort

The sort operation transforms an unordered set of elements into an ordered set of elements. The most common implementation on GPUs is using radix sort for integer and floating point data and coarse-grained merge sort and fine-grained sorting networks for general comparable data.

Search

The search operation allows the programmer to find a given element within the stream, or possibly find neighbors of a specified element. The GPU is not used to speed up the search for an individual element, but instead is used to run multiple searches in parallel. Mostly the search method used is binary search on sorted elements.

Data Structures

A variety of data structures can be represented on the GPU:

- Dense arrays,

- Sparse matrixes (sparse array) – static or dynamic,

- Adaptive structures (union type).

Applications

The following are some of the areas where GPUs have been used for general purpose computing:

- Automatic parallelization.

- Computer clusters or a variant of a parallel computing (using GPU cluster technology) for highly calculation-intensive tasks:

    ○ High-performance computing (HPC) clusters, often termed supercomputers.

        ▪ Including cluster technologies like Message Passing Interface, and single-system image (SSI), distributed computing, and Beowulf.

    ○ Grid computing (a form of distributed computing) (networking many heterogeneous computers to create a virtual computer architecture).

    ○ Load-balancing clusters, sometimes termed a server farm.

- Physical based simulation and physics engines (usually based on Newtonian physics models).

    ○ Conway's Game of Life, cloth simulation, fluid incompressible flow by solution of Euler equations (fluid dynamics) or Navier–Stokes equations.

- Statistical physics.
  - Ising model.
- Lattice gauge theory.
- Segmentation – 2D and 3D.
- Level set methods.
- CT reconstruction.
- Fast Fourier transform.
- GPU learning – machine learning and data mining computations, e.g., with software BIDMach.
- k-nearest neighbor algorithm.
- Fuzzy logic.
- Tone mapping.
- Audio signal processing.
  - Audio and sound effects processing, to use a GPU for digital signal processing (DSP).
  - Analog signal processing.
  - Speech processing.
- Digital image processing.
- Video processing .
  - Hardware accelerated video decoding and post-processing.
    - Motion compensation (mo comp).
    - Inverse discrete cosine transform (iDCT).
    - Variable-length decoding (VLD), Huffman coding.
    - Inverse quantization (IQ (not to be confused by Intelligence Quotient)).
    - In-loop deblocking.
    - Bitstream processing (CAVLC/CABAC) using special purpose hardware for this task because this is a serial task not suitable for regular GPGPU computation.
    - Deinterlacing.
    - Spatial-temporal deinterlacing.
    - Noise reduction.
    - Edge enhancement.
    - Color correction.
  - Hardware accelerated video encoding and pre-processing.

- Global illumination – Ray tracing, photon mapping, radiosity among others, subsurface scattering.

- Geometric computing – Constructive solid geometry, distance fields, collision detection, transparency computation, shadow generation.

- Scientific computing.

  ◦ Monte Carlo simulation of light propagation.

  ◦ Weather forecasting.

  ◦ Climate research.

  ◦ Molecular modeling on GPU.

  ◦ Quantum mechanical physics.

  ◦ Astrophysics.

- Bioinformatics.

- Computational finance.

- Medical imaging.

- Clinical decision support system (CDSS).

- Computer vision.

- Digital signal processing / signal processing.

- Control engineering.

- Operations research.

  ◦ Implementations of: The GPU Tabu Search algorithm solving the Resource Constrained Project Scheduling problem is freely available on GitHub; the GPU algorithm solving the Nurse Rerostering problem is freely available on GitHub.

- Neural networks.

- Database operations.

- Computational Fluid Dynamics especially using Lattice Boltzmann methods.

- Cryptography and cryptanalysis.

- Performance modeling: computationally intensive tasks on GPU.

  ◦ Implementations of: MD6, Advanced Encryption Standard (AES), Data Encryption Standard (DES), RSA, elliptic curve cryptography (ECC).

  ◦ Password cracking.

  ◦ Cryptocurrency transactions processing ("mining") (Bitcoin mining).

- Electronic design automation.

- Antivirus software.

- Intrusion detection.

- Increase computing power for distributed computing projects like SETI@home, Einstein@home.

Texture Mapping Unit

A texture mapping unit (TMU) is a component in modern graphics processing units (GPUs). Historically it was a separate physical processor. A TMU is able to rotate, resize, and distort a bitmap image (performing texture sampling), to be placed onto an arbitrary plane of a given 3D model as a texture. This process is called texture mapping. In modern graphics cards it is implemented as a discrete stage in a graphics pipeline, whereas when first introduced it was implemented as a separate processor, e.g. as seen on the Voodoo2 graphics card.

The TMU came about due to the compute demands of sampling and transforming a flat image (as the texture map) to the correct angle and perspective it would need to be in 3D space. The compute operation is a large matrix multiply, which CPUs of the time (early Pentiums) could not cope with at acceptable performance.

Today, TMUs are part of the shader pipeline and decoupled from the Render Output Pipelines (ROPs). For example, in AMD's Cypress GPU, each shader pipeline (of which there are 20) has four TMUs, giving the GPU 80 TMUs. This is done by chip designers to closely couple shaders and the texture engines they will be working with.

Geometry

3D scenes are generally composed of two things: 3D geometry, and the textures that cover that geometry. Texture units in a video card take a texture and 'map' it to a piece of geometry. That is, they wrap the texture around the geometry and produce textured pixels which can then be written to the screen. Textures can be an actual image, a lightmap, or even normal maps for advanced surface lighting effects.

Texture Fill Rate

To render a 3D scene, textures are mapped over the top of polygon meshes. This is called texture mapping and is accomplished by texture mapping units (TMUs) on the videocard. Texture fill rate is a measure of the speed with which a particular card can perform texture mapping.

Though pixel shader processing is becoming more important, this number still holds some weight. Best example of this is the X1600 XT. This card has a 3 to 1 ratio of pixel shader processors/texture mapping units. As a result, the X1600 XT achieves lower performance when compared to other GPUs of the same era and class (such as nVidia's 7600GT). In the mid range, texture mapping can still very much be a bottleneck. However, at the high end, the X1900 XTX has this same 3 to 1 ratio, but does just fine because screen resolutions top out and it has more than enough texture mapping power to handle any display.

Texture Mapping Units (TMUs)

Textures need to be addressed and filtered. This job is done by TMUs that work in conjunction with pixel and vertex shader units. It is the TMU's job to apply texture operations to pixels. The number of texture units in a graphics processor is used when comparing two different cards for texturing performance. It is reasonable to assume that the card with more TMUs will be faster at processing texture information. In modern GPUs TMUs contain Texture Address Units(TA) and Texture Filtering Units(TF). Texture Address Units map texels to pixels and can perform texture addressing modes. Texture Filtering Units optionally perform hardware based texture filtering.

Pipelines

A pipeline is the graphics card's architecture, which provides a generally accurate idea of the computing power of a graphics processor.

A pipeline isn't formally accepted as a technical term. There are different pipelines within a graphics processor as there are separate functions being performed at any given time. Historically, it has been referred to as a pixel processor that is attached to a dedicated TMU. A Geforce 3 had four pixel pipelines, each of which had two TMUs. The rest of the pipeline handled things like depth and blending operations.

The ATI Radeon 9700 was first to break this mould, by placing a number of vertex shader engines independent of the pixel shaders. The R300 GPU used in the Radeon 9700 had four global vertex shaders, but split the rest of the rendering pipeline in half (it was, so to speak, dual core) each half, called a quad, had four pixel shaders, four TMUs and four ROPs.

Some units are used more than others, and in an effort to increase the processor's entire performance, they attempted to find a "sweet spot" in the number of units needed for optimum efficiency without the need for excess silicon. In this architecture the name pixel pipeline lost its meaning as pixel processors were no longer attached to single TMUs.

The vertex shader had long been decoupled, starting with the R300, but the pixel shader was not so easily done, as it required colour data (e.g. texture samples) to work with, and hence needed to be closely coupled to a TMU.

Said coupling remains to this day, where the shader engine, made of units able to run either vertex or pixel data, is tightly coupled to a TMU but has a crossbar dispatcher between its output and the bank of ROPs.

Render Output Pipelines (ROPs)

The Render Output Pipeline is an inherited term, and more often referred to as the render output unit. Its job is to control the sampling of pixels (each pixel is a dimensionless point), so it controls antialiasing, when more than one sample is merged into one pixel. All data rendered has to travel through the ROP in order to be written to the framebuffer, from there it can be transmitted to the display.

Therefore, the ROP is where the GPU's output is assembled into a bitmapped image ready for display.

Use in GPGPU

In GPGPU, texture maps in 1,2, or 3 dimensions may be used to store arbitrary data. By providing interpolation, the texture mapping unit provides a convenient means of approximating arbitrary functions with data tables.

Video Card

A video card (also called a display card, graphics card, display adapter, or graphics adapter) is an expansion card which generates a feed of output images to a display device (such as a computer monitor). Frequently, these are advertised as discrete or dedicated graphics cards, emphasizing the distinction between these and integrated graphics. At the core of both is the graphics processing unit (GPU), which is the main part that does the actual computations, but should not be confused with the video card as a whole, although "GPU" is often used to refer to video cards.

Most video cards are not limited to simple display output. Their integrated graphics processor can perform additional processing, removing this task from the central processor of the computer. For example, Nvidia and AMD (previously ATI) produced cards render the graphics pipeline OpenGL and DirectX on the hardware level. In the later 2010s, there has also been a tendency to use the computing capabilities of the graphics processor to solve non-graphic tasks.

Usually the graphics card is made in the form of a printed circuit board (expansion board) and inserted into an expansion slot, universal or specialized (AGP, PCI Express). Some have been made using dedicated enclosures, which are connected to the computer via a docking station or a cable.

Standards such as MDA, CGA, HGC, Tandy, PGC, EGA, VGA, MCGA, 8514 or XGA were introduced from 1982 to 1990 and supported by a variety of hardware manufacturers.

3dfx Interactive was one of the first companies to develop a GPU with 3D acceleration (with the Voodoo series) and the first to develop a graphical chipset dedicated to 3D, but without 2D support (which therefore required the presence of a 2D card to work). Now the majority of modern video cards are built with either AMD-sourced or Nvidia-sourced graphics chips. Until 2000, 3dfx Interactive was also an important, and often groundbreaking, manufacturer. Most video cards offer various functions such as accelerated rendering of 3D scenes and 2D graphics, MPEG-2/MPEG-4 decoding, TV output, or the ability to connect multiple monitors (multi-monitor). Video cards also have sound card capabilities to output sound – along with the video for connected TVs or monitors with integrated speakers.

Within the industry, video cards are sometimes called *graphics add-in-boards*, abbreviated as *AIB*s, with the word "graphics" usually omitted.

Dedicated vs. Integrated Graphics

As an alternative to the use of a video card, video hardware can be integrated into the motherboard, CPU, or a system-on-chip. Both approaches can be called integrated graphics. Motherboard-based implementations are sometimes called "on-board video". Almost all desktop computer mother-boards with integrated graphics allow the disabling of the integrated graphics chip in BIOS, and have a PCI, or PCI Express (PCI-E) slot for adding a higher-performance graphics card in place of the integrated graphics. The ability to disable the integrated graphics sometimes also allows the continued use of a motherboard on which the on-board video has failed. Sometimes both the integrated graphics and a dedicated graphics card can be used simultaneously to feed separate displays. The main advantages of integrated graphics include cost, compactness, simplicity and low energy consumption. The performance disadvantage of integrated graphics arises because the graphics processor shares system resources with the CPU. A dedicated graphics card has its own random access memory (RAM), its own cooling system, and dedicated power regulators, with all components designed specifically for processing video images. Upgrading to a dedicated graphics card offloads work from the CPU and system RAM, so not only will graphics processing be faster, but the computer's overall performance may also improve.

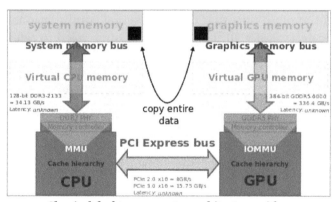

Classical desktop computer architecture with a
distinct graphics card over PCI Express.

Typical bandwidths for given memory technologies, missing are the memory latency. Zero-copy between GPU and CPU is not possible, since both have their distinct physical memories. Data must be copied from one to the other to be shared.

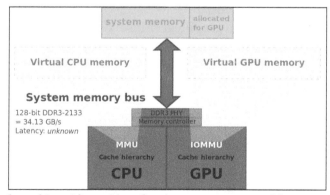

Integrated graphics with partitioned main memory: a part of the system memory
is allocated to the GPU exclusively. Zero-copy is not possible, data has to be copied,
over the system memory bus, from one partition to the other.

Both AMD and Intel have introduced CPUs and motherboard chipsets which support the integra-tion of a GPU into the same die as the CPU. AMD markets CPUs with integrated graphics under the trademark Accelerated Processing Unit (APU), while Intel markets similar technology under the "Intel HD Graphics and Iris" brands. With the 8th Generation Processors, Intel announced the Intel UHD series of Integrated Graphics for better support of 4K Displays. Although they are still not equivalent to the performance of discrete solutions, Intel's HD Graphics platform provides performance approaching discrete mid-range graphics, and AMD APU technology has been adopted by both the PlayStation 4 and Xbox One video game consoles.

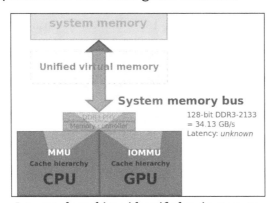

Integrated graphics with unified main memory,
to be found AMD "Kaveri" or PlayStation 4 (HSA).

Power Demand

As the processing power of video cards has increased, so has their demand for electrical power. Current high-performance video cards tend to consume a great deal of power. For example, the thermal design power (TDP) for the GeForce GTX TITAN is 250 watts. When tested while gaming, the GeForce GTX 1080 Ti Founder's Edition averaged 227 watts of power consumption. While CPU and power supply makers have recently moved toward higher efficiency, power demands of GPUs have continued to rise, so video cards may have the largest power consumption in a computer. Although power supplies are increasing their power too, the bottleneck is due to the PCI-Express connection, which is limited to supplying 75 watts. Modern video cards with a power consumption of over 75 watts usually include a combination of six-pin (75 W) or eight-pin (150 W) sockets that connect directly to the power supply. Providing adequate cooling becomes a challenge in such computers. Computers with multiple video cards may need power supplies in the 1000–1500 W range. Heat extraction becomes a major design consideration for computers with two or more high-end video cards.

Size

Video cards for desktop computers come in one of two size profiles, which can allow a graphics card to be added even to small-sized PCs. Some video cards are not of usual size, and are thus categorized as being low profile. Video card profiles are based on height only, with low-profile cards taking up less than the height of a PCIe slot, some can be as low as "half-height". Length and thickness can vary greatly, with high-end cards usually occupying two or three expansion slots, and with dual-GPU cards -such as the Nvidia GeForce GTX 690- generally exceeding 250 mm (10 in) in length. Generally, most users will prefer a lower profile card if the intention is to fit multiple cards or they run into clearance issues with other motherboard components like the DIMM or PCIE slots. This can be fixed with a larger case that comes in sizes like mid tower and full tower. Full towers can usually fit larger motherboards in sizes like ATX and micro ATX. The larger the case, the larger the motherboard, the larger the graphics card or multiple other components that will acquire case real-estate.

Multi-card Scaling

Some graphics cards can be linked together to allow scaling of the graphics processing across multiple cards. This is done using either the PCIe bus on the motherboard, or, more commonly, a data bridge. Generally, the cards must be of the same model to be linked, and most low power cards are not able to be linked in this way. AMD and Nvidia both have proprietary methods of scaling, CrossFireX for AMD, and SLI (since the Turing generation, renamed to NVLink) for Nvidia. Cards from different chipset manufacturers or architectures cannot be used together for multi card scaling. If a graphics card has different sizes of memory, the lowest value will be used, with the higher values being disregarded. Currently, scaling on consumer grade cards can be done using up to four cards. The use of four cards requires a large motherboard with a proper configuration. Nvidia's GeForce GTX 590 video card has the ability to be configured in this four card configuration. As stated above, users will want to stick to the same performance card for optimal use. Motherboards like ASUS Maximus 3 Extreme and Gigabyte GA EX58 Extreme are certified to work with this configuration. For proper performance of your 4 card configuration, it's recommend to use a core i7 CPU with turbo boost to avoid the bottleneck throughput. A certificated large power supply is necessary to run the cards in SLI or CrossFireX. Power demands must be known before a proper supply is installed. For the four card configuration, a 1000+ watt supply is needed. AcBel PC8055-000G and Corsair AX1200 supplies are examples. With any powerful video card like a GTX 1060+ or 1080, thermal management can be overlooked. Video cards require a well vented chassis and thermal solution. Water or air cooling are required for all video cards, with larger configurations needing water solutions to achieve proper performance without thermal throttling.

3D Graphic APIs

A graphics driver usually supports one or multiple cards by the same vendor, and has to be specifically written for an operating system. Additionally, the operating system or an extra software package may provide certain programming APIs for applications to perform 3D rendering.

3D rendering API availability across operating systems						
OS	Vulkan	Direct X	GNMX	Metal	OpenGL	OpenGL ES
Windows 10	Nvidia/AMD	Microsoft	No	No	Yes	Yes
macOS	MoltenVK	No	No	Apple	Apple	No
GNU/Linux	Yes	Via Wine	No	No	Yes	Yes
Android	Yes	No	No	No	Nvidia	Yes
iOS	MoltenVK	No	No	Apple	No	Apple
Tizen	In development	No	No	No	No	Yes
Sailfish OS	In development	No	No	No	No	Yes
Xbox One	No	Yes	No	No	No	No
Orbis OS (PS4)	No	No	Yes	No	No	No
Nintendo Switch	Yes	No	No	No	Yes	Yes

Usage Specific GPU

Some GPUs are designed with specific usage in mind:

- Gaming:
  - GeForce GTX
  - GeForce RTX
  - Nvidia Titan
  - Radeon HD
  - Radeon R5, R7, R9 and RX series
- Cloud gaming:
  - Nvidia Grid
  - Radeon Sky
- Workstation:
  - Nvidia Quadro
  - Nvidia Titan X
  - AMD FirePro
  - Radeon Pro
- Cloud Workstation:
  - Nvidia Tesla
  - AMD FireStream
- Artificial Intelligence Cloud:
  - Nvidia Tesla
  - Radeon Instinct
- Automated/Driverless car:
  - Nvidia Drive PX

Parts

A modern video card consists of a printed circuit board on which the components are mounted. These include:

Graphics Processing Unit

A graphics processing unit (GPU), also occasionally called visual processing unit (VPU), is a specialized electronic circuit designed to rapidly manipulate and alter memory to accelerate the building of images in a frame buffer intended for output to a display. Because of the large degree of programmable computational complexity for such a task, a modern video card is also a computer unto itself.

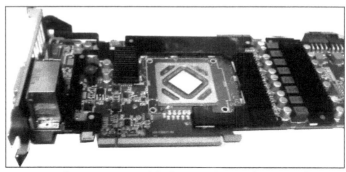

A Radeon HD 7970 with the main heatsink removed,
showing the major components of the card.

Heat Sink

A heat sink is mounted on most modern graphics cards. A heat sink spreads out the heat produced by the graphics processing unit evenly throughout the heat sink and unit itself. The heat sink commonly has a fan mounted as well to cool the heat sink and the graphics processing unit. Not all cards have heat sinks, for example, some cards are liquid cooled, and instead have a waterblock; additionally, cards from the 1980s and early 1990s did not produce much heat, and did not require heatsinks. Most modern graphics cards need a proper thermal solution. This can be the liquid solution or heatsinks with an additional connected heat pipe usually made of copper for the best thermal transfer. It should also be noted that the correct case; either Mid-tower or Full-tower or some other derivative, has to be properly configured for thermal management. This can be ample space with proper push pull or opposite configuration as well as liquid with a radiator either in lieu or with a fan setup.

Video BIOS

The video BIOS or firmware contains a minimal program for initial set up and control of the video card. It may contain information on the memory timing, operating speeds and voltages of the graphics processor, RAM, and other details which can sometimes be changed.

The modern Video BIOS does not support all the functions of the video card, being only sufficient to identify and initialize the card to display one of a few frame buffer or text display modes. It does not support YUV to RGB translation, video scaling, pixel copying, compositing or any of the multitude of other 2D and 3D features of the video card.

Video Memory

Type	Memory clock rate (MHz)	Bandwidth (GB/s)
DDR	200-400	1.6-3.2
DDR2	400-1066.67	3.2-8.533
DDR3	800-2133.33	6.4-17.066
DDR4	1600-4866	12.8-25.6

GDDR4	3000–4000	160–256
GDDR5	1000–2000	288–336.5
GDDR5X	1000–1750	160–673
GDDR6	1365-1770	336-672
HBM	250–1000	512–1024

The memory capacity of most modern video cards ranges from 1 GB to 12 GB. Since video memory needs to be accessed by the GPU and the display circuitry, it often uses special high-speed or multi-port memory, such as VRAM, WRAM, SGRAM, etc. Around 2003, the video memory was typically based on DDR technology. During and after that year, manufacturers moved towards DDR2, GDDR3, GDDR4, GDDR5 and GDDR5X. The effective memory clock rate in modern cards is generally between 1 GHz to 10 GHz.

Video memory may be used for storing other data as well as the screen image, such as the Z-buffer, which manages the depth coordinates in 3D graphics, textures, vertex buffers, and compiled shader programs.

RAMDAC

The RAMDAC, or random-access-memory digital-to-analog converter, converts digital signals to analog signals for use by a computer display that uses analog inputs such as cathode ray tube (CRT) displays. The RAMDAC is a kind of RAM chip that regulates the functioning of the graphics card. Depending on the number of bits used and the RAMDAC-data-transfer rate, the converter will be able to support different computer-display refresh rates. With CRT displays, it is best to work over 75 Hz and never under 60 Hz, in order to minimize flicker. (With LCD displays, flicker is not a problem.) Due to the growing popularity of digital computer displays and the integration of the RAMDAC onto the GPU die, it has mostly disappeared as a discrete component. All current LCD/plasma monitors and TVs and projectors with only digital connections, work in the digital domain and do not require a RAMDAC for those connections. There are displays that feature analog inputs (VGA, component, SCART, etc.) *only*. These require a RAMDAC, but they reconvert the analog signal back to digital before they can display it, with the unavoidable loss of quality stemming from this digital-to-analog-to-digital conversion. With VGA standard being phased out in favor of digital, RAMDACs are beginning to disappear from video cards.

Output Interfaces

Video In Video Out (VIVO) for S-Video (TV-out), Digital Visual Interface (DVI)
for High-definition television (HDTV), and DB-15 for Video Graphics Array (VGA).

The most common connection systems between the video card and the computer display are:

Video Graphics Array (VGA)

Also known as D-sub, VGA is an analog-based standard adopted in the late 1980s designed for

CRT displays, also called VGA connector. Some problems of this standard are electrical noise, image distortion and sampling error in evaluating pixels.

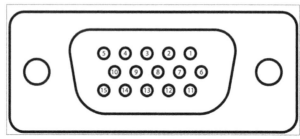

Video Graphics Array (VGA) (DE-15).

Today, the VGA analog interface is used for high definition video including 1080p and higher. While the VGA transmission bandwidth is high enough to support even higher resolution playback, there can be picture quality degradation depending on cable quality and length. How discernible this quality difference is depends on the individual's eyesight and the display; when using a DVI or HDMI connection, especially on larger sized LCD/LED monitors or TVs, quality degradation, if present, is prominently visible. Blu-ray playback at 1080p is possible via the VGA analog interface, if Image Constraint Token (ICT) is not enabled on the Blu-ray disc.

Digital Visual Interface (DVI)

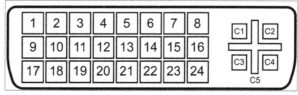

Digital Visual Interface (DVI-I).

Digital-based standard designed for displays such as flat-panel displays (LCDs, plasma screens, wide high-definition television displays) and video projectors. In some rare cases high-end CRT monitors also use DVI. It avoids image distortion and electrical noise, corresponding each pixel from the computer to a display pixel, using its native resolution. It is worth noting that most manufacturers include a DVI-I connector, allowing (via simple adapter) standard RGB signal output to an old CRT or LCD monitor with VGA input.

Video in Video out (VIVO) for S-video, Composite video and Component video

Included to allow connection with televisions, DVD players, video recorders and video game consoles. They often come in two 10-pin mini-DIN connector variations, and the VIVO splitter cable generally comes with either 4 connectors (S-Video in and out + composite video in and out), or 6 connectors (S-Video in and out + component P_B out + component P_R out + component Y out [also composite out] + composite in).

High-definition Multimedia Interface (HDMI)

HDMI is a compact audio/video interface for transferring uncompressed video data and compressed/uncompressed digital audio data from an HDMI-compliant device ("the source device") to a compatible digital audio device, computer monitor, video projector, or digital television. HDMI is a digital replacement for existing analog video standards. HDMI supports copy protection through HDCP.

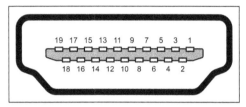

High-Definition Multimedia Interface (HDMI).

DisplayPort

DisplayPort is a digital display interface developed by the Video Electronics Standards Association (VESA). The interface is primarily used to connect a video source to a display device such as a computer monitor, though it can also be used to transmit audio, USB, and other forms of data. The VESA specification is royalty-free. VESA designed it to replace VGA, DVI, and LVDS. Backward compatibility to VGA and DVI by using adapter dongles enables consumers to use DisplayPort fitted video sources without replacing existing display devices. Although DisplayPort has a greater throughput of the same functionality as HDMI, it is expected to complement the interface, not replace it.

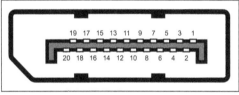

DisplayPort.

Other Types of Connection Systems

Composite video	
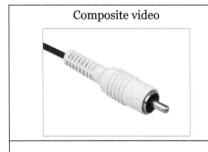	Analog systems with resolution lower than 480i use the RCA connector. The single pin connector carries all resolution, brightness and color information, making it the lowest quality dedicated video connection.
	It has three cables, each with RCA connector (YCBCR for digital component, or YPBPR for analog component); it is used in older projectors, video-game consoles, DVD players. It can carry SDTV 480i and EDTV 480p resolutions, and HDTV resolutions 720p and 1080i, but not 1080p due to industry concerns about copy protection. Contrary to popular belief it looks equal to HDMI for the resolutions it carries, but for best performance from Blu-ray, other 1080p sources like PPV, and 4K Ultra HD, a digital display connector is required.

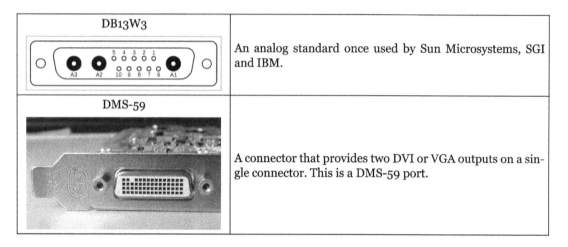

| DB13W3 | An analog standard once used by Sun Microsystems, SGI and IBM. |
| DMS-59 | A connector that provides two DVI or VGA outputs on a single connector. This is a DMS-59 port. |

Motherboard Interfaces

Chronologically, connection systems between video card and motherboard were, mainly:

- S-100 bus: Designed in 1974 as a part of the Altair 8800, it was the first industry-standard bus for the microcomputer industry.

- ISA: Introduced in 1981 by IBM, it became dominant in the marketplace in the 1980s. It was an 8- or 16-bit bus clocked at 8 MHz.

- NuBus: Used in Macintosh II, it was a 32-bit bus with an average bandwidth of 10 to 20 MB/s.

- MCA: Introduced in 1987 by IBM it was a 32-bit bus clocked at 10 MHz.

- EISA: Released in 1988 to compete with IBM's MCA, it was compatible with the earlier ISA bus. It was a 32-bit bus clocked at 8.33 MHz.

- VLB: An extension of ISA, it was a 32-bit bus clocked at 33 MHz. Also referred to as VESA.

- PCI: Replaced the EISA, ISA, MCA and VESA buses from 1993 onwards. PCI allowed dynamic connectivity between devices, avoiding the manual adjustments required with jumpers. It is a 32-bit bus clocked 33 MHz.

- UPA: An interconnect bus architecture introduced by Sun Microsystems in 1995. It had a 64-bit bus clocked at 67 or 83 MHz.

- USB: Although mostly used for miscellaneous devices, such as secondary storage devices and toys, USB displays and display adapters exist.

- AGP: First used in 1997, it is a dedicated-to-graphics bus. It is a 32-bit bus clocked at 66 MHz.

- PCI-X: An extension of the PCI bus, it was introduced in 1998. It improves upon PCI by extending the width of bus to 64 bits and the clock frequency to up to 133 MHz.

- PCI Express: Abbreviated PCIe, it is a point to point interface released in 2004. In 2006 provided double the data-transfer rate of AGP. It should not be confused with PCI-X, an enhanced version of the original PCI specification.

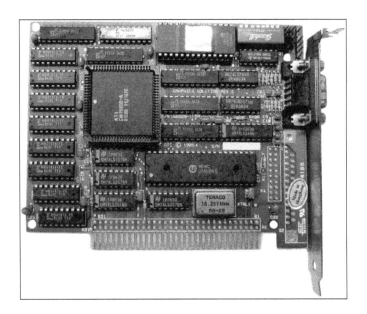

ATI Graphics Solution Rev 3 from 1985/1986, supporting Hercules graphics. As can be seen from the PCB the layout was done in 1985, whereas the marking on the central chip CW16800-A says "8639" meaning that chip was manufactured week 39, 1986. This card is using the ISA 8-bit (XT) interface.

Free and Open-source Graphics Device Driver

A free and open-source graphics device driver is a software stack which controls computer-graphics hardware and supports graphics-rendering application programming interfaces (APIs) and is released under a free and open-source software license. Graphics device drivers are written for specific hardware to work within a specific operating system kernel and to support a range of APIs used by applications to access the graphics hardware. They may also control output to the display if the display driver is part of the graphics hardware. Most free and open-source graphics device drivers are developed by the Mesa project. The driver is made up of a compiler, a rendering API, and software which manages access to the graphics hardware.

Drivers without freely (and legally) -available source code are commonly known as *binary drivers*. Binary drivers used in the context of operating systems that are prone to ongoing development and change (such as Linux) create problems for end users and package maintainers. These problems, which affect system stability, security and performance, are the main reason for the independent development of free and open-source drivers. When no technical documentation is available, an understanding of the underlying hardware is often gained by clean-room reverse engineering. Based on this understanding, device drivers may be written and legally published under any software license.

In rare cases, a manufacturer's driver source code is available on the Internet without a free license. This means that the code can be studied and altered for personal use, but the altered (and usually the original) source code cannot be freely distributed. Solutions to bugs in the driver cannot be easily shared in the form of modified versions of the driver. Therefore the utility of such drivers is significantly reduced comparison to free and open-source drivers.

Problems with Binary Drivers

Software Developer's View

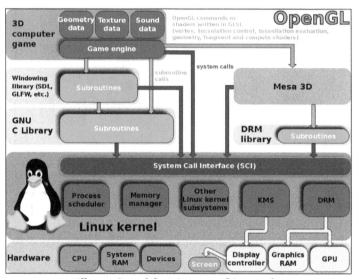

Illustration of the Linux graphics stack.

There are objections to binary-only drivers based on copyright, security, reliability and development concerns. As part of a wider campaign against binary blobs, OpenBSD lead developer Theo de Raadt said that with a binary driver there is "no way to fix it when it breaks (and it will break)"; when a product which relies on binary drivers is declared to be end-of-life by the manufacturer, it is effectively "broken forever." The project has also stated that binary drivers "hide bugs and workarounds for bugs", an observation which has been somewhat vindicated by flaws found in binary drivers (including an exploitable bug in Nvidia's 3D drivers discovered in October 2006 by Rapid7). It is speculated that the bug has existed since 2004; Nvidia have denied this, asserting that the issue was only communicated to them in July 2006 and the 2004 bug was a bug in X.Org (not in Nvidia's driver).

Binary drivers often do not work with current versions of open-source software, and almost never support development snapshots of open-source software; it is usually not directly possible for a developer to use Nvidia's or ATI's proprietary drivers with a development snapshot of an X server or a development snapshot of the Linux kernel. Features like kernel mode-setting cannot be added to binary drivers by anyone but the vendors, which prevents their inclusion if the vendor lacks capacity or interest.

In the Linux kernel development community, Linus Torvalds has made strong statements on the issue of binary-only modules:

> "I refuse to even consider tying my hands over some binary-only module. I want people to know that when they use binary-only modules, it's their problem". Another kernel developer, Greg Kroah-Hartman, has said that a binary-only kernel module does not comply with the kernel's license (the GNU General Public License); it "just violates the GPL due to

fun things like derivative works and linking and other stuff." Writer and computer scientist Peter Gutmann has expressed concern that the digital rights management scheme in Microsoft's Windows Vista operating system may limit the availability of the documentation required to write open drivers, since it "requires that the operational details of the device be kept confidential."

In the case of binary drivers, there are objections due to free software philosophy, software quality and security concerns. In 2006 Greg Kroah-Hartman concluded that:

> "Closed source Linux kernel modules are illegal. That's it, it is very simple. I've had the misfortune of talking to a lot of different IP lawyers over the years about this topic, and every one that I've talked to all agree that there is no way that anyone can create a Linux kernel module, today, that can be closed source. It just violates the GPL due to fun things like derivative works and linking."

The Linux kernel has never maintained a stable in-kernel application binary interface. There are also concerns that proprietary drivers may contain backdoors, like the one found in Samsung Galaxy-series modem drivers.

Hardware Developer's View

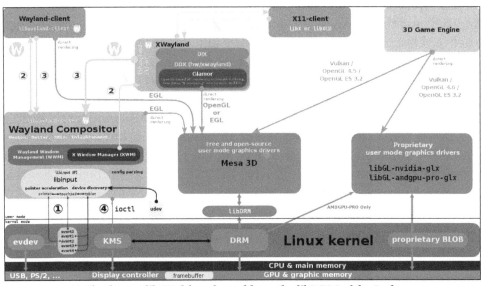

In the future, libGL-fglrx-glx could use the libDRM of the Radeon open-source driver instead of the proprietary binary blob; most of the investment is in the userspace driver.

When applications such as a 3D game engine or a 3D computer graphics software shunt calculations from the CPU to the GPU, they usually use a special-purpose API like OpenGL or Direct3D and do not address the hardware directly. Because all translation (from API calls to GPU opcodes) is done by the device driver, it contains specialized knowledge and is an object of optimization. Due to the history of the rigidity of proprietary driver development there has been a recent surge in the number of community-backed device drivers for desktop and mobile GPUs. Free and Open Hardware organizations like FOSSi, LowRISC, and others, would also benefit from the development of an open graphical hardware standard. This would then provide computer manufacturers, hobbyists, and the like with a complete, royalty-free platform with which to develop computing hardware and related devices.

The desktop computer market was long dominated by PC hardware using the x86/x86-64 instruction set and GPUs available for the PC. With three major competitors (Nvidia, AMD and Intel). The main competing factor was the price of hardware and raw performance in 3D computer games, which is greatly affected by the efficient translation of API calls into GPU opcodes. The display driver and the video decoder are inherent parts of the graphics card: hardware designed to assist in the calculations necessary for the decoding of video streams. As the market for PC hardware has dwindled, it seems unlikely that new competitors will enter this market and it is unclear how much more knowledge one company could gain by seeing the source code of other companies' drivers.

The mobile sector presents a different situation. The functional blocks (the application-specific integrated circuit display driver, 2- and 3D acceleration and video decoding and encoding) are separate semiconductor intellectual property (SIP) blocks on the chip, since hardware devices vary substantially; some portable media players require a display driver that accelerates video decoding, but do not require 3D acceleration. The development goal is not only raw 3D performance, but system integration, power consumption and 2D capabilities. There is also an approach which abandons the traditional method (Vsync) of updating the display and makes better use of sample and hold technology to lower power consumption.

During the second quarter of 2013 79.3 percent of smartphones sold worldwide were running a version of Android, and the Linux kernel dominates smartphones. Hardware developers have an incentive to deliver Linux drivers for their hardware but, due to competition, no incentive to make these drivers free and open-source. Additional problems are the Android-specific augmentations to the Linux kernel which have not been accepted in mainline, such as the Atomic Display Framework (ADF). ADF is a feature of 3.10 AOSP kernels which provides a dma-buf-centric framework between Android's hwcomposer HAL and the kernel driver. ADF significantly overlaps with the DRM-KMS framework. ADF has not been accepted into mainline, but a different set of solutions addressing the same problems (known as atomic mode setting) is under development. Projects such as libhybris harness Android device drivers to run on Linux platforms other than Android.

Software Architecture

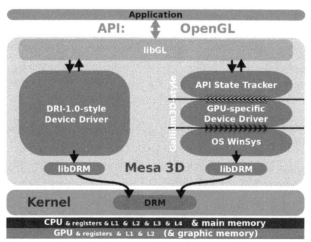

Although Mesa (DRI) and Gallium3D have different driver
models, they share free and open-source code.

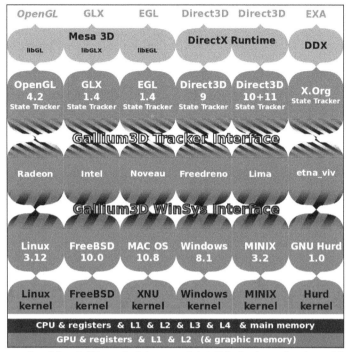

An example matrix of the Gallium3D driver model. With the introduction of the Gallium3D
tracker and WinSys interfaces, 18 modules are required instead of 36. Each WinSys module
can work with each Gallium3D device driver module and each State Tracker module.

Free and open-source drivers are primarily developed on and for Linux by Linux kernel developers, third-party programming enthusiasts and employees of companies such as Advanced Micro Devices. Each driver has five parts:

1. A Linux kernel component DRM.

2. A Linux kernel component KMS driver (the display controller driver).

3. A libDRM user-space component (a wrapper library for DRM system calls, which should only be used by Mesa 3D).

4. A Mesa 3D user-space component. This component is hardware-specific; it is executed on the CPU and translates OpenGL commands, for example, into machine code for the GPU. Because the device driver is split, marshalling is possible. Mesa 3D is the only free and open-source implementation of OpenGL, OpenGL ES, OpenVG, GLX, EGL and OpenCL. In July 2014, most of the components conformed to Gallium3D specifications. A fully functional State Tracker for Direct3D version 9 is written in C, and an unmaintained tracker for Direct3D versions 10 and 11 is written in C++. Wine has Direct3D version 9. Another Wine component translates Direct3D calls into OpenGL calls, working with OpenGL.

5. Device Dependent X (DDX), another 2D graphics device driver for X.Org Server.

The DRM is kernel-specific. A VESA driver is generally available for any operating system. The VESA driver supports most graphics cards without acceleration and at display resolutions limited to a set programmed in the video BIOS by the manufacturer.

The Linux graphics stack has evolved, detoured by the X Window System core protocol.

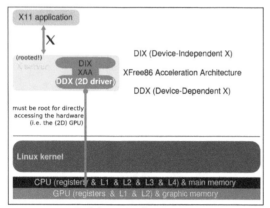
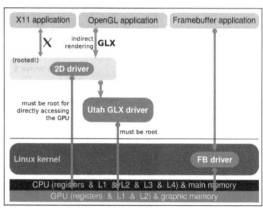

2D drivers in the X server.   Indirect rendering over GLX using Utah GLX.

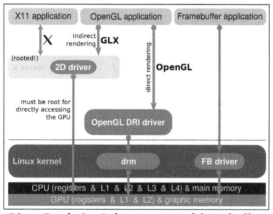
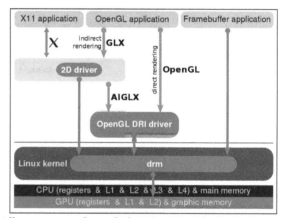

Direct Rendering Infrastructure and framebuffer.   All access goes through the Direct Rendering Manager.

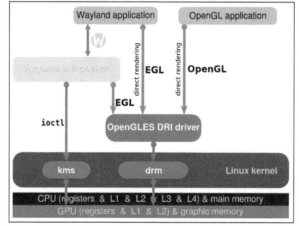

In Linux kernel 3.12, render nodes are merged and mode setting
split off. Wayland implements direct rendering over EGL.

Free and Open-source Drivers

Radeon

AMD's proprietary driver, AMD Catalyst for their Radeon, is available for Microsoft Windows and

Linux (formerly fglrx). A current version can be downloaded from AMD's site, and some Linux distributions contain it in their repositories. It is in the process of being replaced with an AMDGPU-PRO hybrid driver combining the open-source kernel, X and Mesa multimedia drivers with closed-source OpenGL, OpenCL and Vulkan drivers derived from Catalyst.

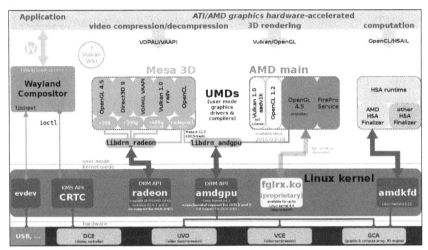

Linux device drivers for AMD hardware in August 2016.

The FOSS drivers for ATI-AMD GPUs are being developed under the name Radeon (xf86-video-ati or xserver-xorg-video-radeon). They still must load proprietary microcode into the GPU to enable hardware acceleration.

Radeon 3D code is split into six drivers, according to GPU technology: the radeon, r200 and r300 classic drivers and r300g, r600g and radeonsi Gallium3D drivers:

- Radeon supports the R100 series.

- R200 supports the R200 series.

- R300g supports pre-unified shader model microarchitectures: R300, R400 and R500.

- R600g supports all TeraScale (VLIW5/4)-based GPUs: R600, R700, HD 5000 (Evergreen) and HD 6000 (Northern Islands).

- Radeonsi supports all Graphics Core Next-based GPUs: HD 7000, HD 8000 and Rx 200 (Southern Islands, Sea Islands and Vulcanic Islands).

An up-to-date feature matrix is available, and there is support for Video Coding Engine and Unified Video Decoder. The free and open-source Radeon graphics device drivers are not reverse-engineered, but are based on documentation released by AMD without the requirement to sign a non-disclosure agreement (NDA). Documentation began to be gradually released in 2007. This is in contrast to AMD's main competitor in the graphics field, Nvidia, which has a proprietary driver similar to AMD Catalyst but provides no support to free-graphics initiatives.

In addition to providing the necessary documentation, AMD employees contribute code to support their hardware and features. At the 2014 Game Developers Conference, the company announced that they were exploring a strategy change to re-base the user-space part of Catalyst on a free and open-source DRM kernel module instead of their proprietary kernel blob.

All components of the Radeon graphics device driver are developed by core contributors and interested parties worldwide. In 2011, the r300g outperformed Catalyst in some cases.

AMDGPU

The release of the AMDGPU stack was announced on the dri-devel mailing list in April 2015. Although AMDGPU only officially supports *GCN* 1.2 and later graphics cards, experimental support for GCN 1.0 and 1.1 graphics cards (which are only officially supported by the Radeon driver) may be enabled via a kernel parameter. A separate libdrm, libdrm-amdgpu, has been included since libdrm 2.4.63.

Nvidia

Screenshot of REnouveau, a program which collects data for most of Nouveau's reverse-engineering work.

Nvidia's proprietary driver, Nvidia GeForce driver for GeForce, is available for Windows XP x86-x86-64 and later, Linux x86-x86-64-ARMv7-A, OS X 10.5 and later, Solaris x86-x86-64 and FreeBSD x86/x86-64. A current version can be downloaded from the Internet, and some Linux distributions contain it in their repositories. In 2013 beta Nvidia GeForce driver 331.13 supports the EGL interface, enabling support for Wayland in conjunction with this driver.

Nvidia's free and open-source driver is named nv. It is limited (supporting only 2D acceleration), and Matthew Garrett, Dirk Hohndel and others have called its source code confusing. Nvidia decided to deprecate nv, not adding support for Fermi or later GPUs and DisplayPort, in March 2010.

In 2009, Nvidia announced they would not support free graphics initiatives. In 2013, the company announced that they would release some documentation of their GPUs.

Nouveau is based almost entirely on information gained through reverse engineering. This project aims to produce 3D acceleration for X.Org/Wayland using Gallium3D. In 2012, Nouveau's DRM component was marked stable and promoted from the staging area of the Linux kernel. Nouveau supports Tesla- (and earlier), Fermi-, Kepler- and Maxwell-based GPUs. On 31 January 2014, Nvidia employee Alexandre Courbot committed an extensive patch set which adds initial support for the GK20A (Tegra K1) to Nouveau. In 2014, Codethink reportedly ran a Wayland-based Weston compositor with Linux kernel 3.15, using EGL and a "100% open-source graphics driver stack" on a Tegra K1. A feature matrix is available. In 2014, Nouveau was unable to outperform the Nvidia GeForce driver due to missing re-clocking support. Tegra-re is a project which is working to reverse-engineer nVidia's VLIW-based Tegra series of GPUs that predate Tegra K1.

Nvidia distributes proprietary device drivers for Tegra through OEMs and as part of its Linux for Tegra (formerly L4T) development kit. Nvidia and a partner, Avionic Design, were working on submitting Grate (free and open-source drivers for Tegra) upstream of the mainline Linux kernel in April 2012. The company's co-founder and CEO laid out the Tegra processor roadmap with Ubuntu Unity at the 2013 GPU Technology Conference.

Nvidia's Unified Memory driver (nvidia-uvm.ko), which implements memory management for Pascal and Volta GPUs on Linux, is MIT licensed. The source code is available in the Nvidia Linux driver downloads on systems that support nvidia-uvm.ko.

Intel

Intel has a history of producing (or commissioning) open-source drivers for its graphics chips, with the exception of their PowerVR-based chips. Their 2D X.Org driver is called xf86-video-intel. The kernel mode-setting driver in the Linux kernel does not use the video BIOS for switching video modes; since some BIOSes have a limited range of modes, this provides more reliable access to those supported by Intel video cards.

The company worked on optimizing their free Linux drivers for performance approaching their Windows counterparts, especially on Sandy Bridge and newer hardware where performance optimizations have allowed the Intel driver to outperform their proprietary Windows drivers in certain tasks, in 2011. Some of the performance enhancements may also benefit users of older hardware.

Support for Intel's LLC (Last Level Cache, L4-Cache, Crystalwell and Iris Pro) was added in Linux kernel 3.12, and the company has 20 to 30 full-time Linux graphics developers.

Matrox

Matrox develops and manufactures the Matrox Mystique, Parhelia, G200, G400 and G550. Although the company provides free and open-source drivers for their chipsets which are older than the G550; chipsets newer than the G550 are supported by a closed-source driver.

S3 Graphics

S3 Graphics develops the S3 Trio, ViRGE, Savage and Chrome, supported by OpenChrome.

Arm Holdings

Arm Holdings is a fabless semiconductor company which licenses semiconductor intellectual property cores. Although they are known for the licensing the ARM instruction set and CPUs based on it, they also develop and license the Mali series of GPUs. On January 21, 2012, Phoronix reported that Luc Verhaegen was driving a reverse-engineering attempt aimed at the Arm Holdings Mali series of GPUs (specifically, the Mali-200 and Mali-400 versions). The reverse-engineering project, known as Lima, was presented at FOSDEM on February 4, 2012. On February 2, 2013, Verhaegen demonstrated Quake III Arena in timedemo mode, running on top of the Lima driver. In May 2018, a Lima developer posted the driver for inclusion in the Linux kernel.

ARM has indicated no intention of providing support for their graphics acceleration hardware licensed under a free and open-source license. However, ARM employees sent patches for the Linux kernel to support their ARM HDLCD display controller and Mali DP500, DP550 and DP650 SIP blocks in December 2015 and April 2016.

Imagination Technologies

Imagination Technologies is a fabless semiconductor company which develops and licenses semiconductor intellectual property cores, among which are the PowerVR GPUs. Intel has manufactured a number of PowerVR-based GPUs. PowerVR GPUs are widely used in mobile SoCs. The company does not provide a FOSS driver or public documentation for the PowerVR. Due to its wide use in embedded devices, the Free Software Foundation has put reverse-engineering of the PowerVR driver on its high-priority project list.

Vivante

Vivante Corporation is a fabless semiconductor company which licenses semiconductor intellectual property cores and develops the GCxxxx series of GPUs. A Vivante proprietary, closed-source Linux driver consists of kernel- and user-space parts. Although the kernel component is open-source (GPL), the user-space components—consisting of the GLES(2) implementations and a HAL library—are not; these contain the bulk of the driver logic.

Wladimir J. van der Laan found and documented the state bits, command stream and shader ISA by studying how the blobs work, examining and manipulating command-stream dumps. The Etnaviv Gallium3D driver is being written based on this documentation. Van der Laan's work was inspired by the Lima driver, and the project has produced a functional-but-unoptimized Gallium3D LLVM driver. The Etnaviv driver has performed better than Vivante's proprietary code in some benchmarks, and it supports Vivante's GC400, GC800, GC1000, GC2000, and GC3000 series. In January 2017, Etnaviv was added to Mesa with both OpenGL ES 2.0 and Desktop OpenGL 2.0 support.

Qualcomm

Qualcomm develops the Adreno (formerly ATI Imageon) GPU series, and includes it as part of their Snapdragon system. Phoronix and Slashdot reported in 2012 that Rob Clark, inspired by the Lima driver, was working on reverse-engineering drivers for the Adreno GPU series. In a referenced blog post, Clark wrote that he was doing the project in his spare time and that the Qualcomm platform was his only viable target for working on open 3D graphics. His employers (Texas Instruments and Linaro) were affiliated with the Imagination PowerVR and ARM Mali cores, which would have been his primary targets; he had working command streams for 2D support, and 3D commands seemed to have the same characteristics. The driver code was published on Gitorious "freedreno", and has been moved to Mesa. In 2012, a working shader assembler was completed; demonstration versions were developed for texture mapping and phong shading, using the reverse-engineered shader compiler. Clark demonstrated Freedreno running desktop compositing, the XBMC media player and Quake III Arena at FOSDEM in 2013.

In August 2013, the kernel component of freedreno (MSM driver) was accepted into mainline and is available in Linux kernel 3.12 and later. The DDX driver gained support for server-managed file descriptors requiring X.Org Server version 1.16 and above in July 2014. In January 2016, the Mesa Gallium3D-style driver gained support for Adreno 430; in November of that year, the driver added support for the Adreno 500 series. Freedreno can be used on devices such as 96Boards Dragonboard 410c and Nexus 7 (2013) in traditional Linux distributions (like Debian and Fedora) and on Android.

Broadcom

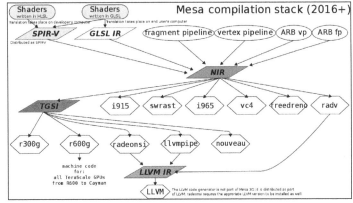

The Mesa driver for VideoCore4, VC4, was written
from scratch by Broadcom's Eric Anholt.

Broadcom develops and designs the VideoCore GPU series as part of their SoCs. Since it is used by the Raspberry Pi, there has been considerable interest in a FOSS driver for VideoCore. The Raspberry Pi Foundation, in co-operation with Broadcom, announced on October 24, 2012 that they open-sourced "all the ARM (CPU) code that drives the GPU". However, the announcement was misleading; according to the author of the reverse-engineered Lima driver, the newly open-sourced components only allowed message-passing between the ARM CPU and VideoCore but offered little insight into Videocore and little additional programability. The Videocore GPU runs an RTOS which handles the processing; video acceleration is done with RTOS firmware coded for its proprietary GPU, and the firmware was not open-sourced on that date. Since there was neither a toolchain targeting the proprietary GPU nor a documented instruction set, no advantage could be taken if the firmware source code became available. The Videocoreiv project attempted to document the VideoCore GPUs.

On February 28, 2014 (the Raspberry Pi's second anniversary), Broadcom and the Raspberry Pi Foundation announced the release of full documentation for the VideoCore IV graphics core and a complete source release of the graphics stack under a 3-clause BSD license. The free-license 3D graphics code was committed to Mesa on 29 August 2014, and first appeared on Mesa's 10.3 release.

Other Vendors

Although Silicon Integrated Systems and VIA Technologies have expressed limited interest in open-source drivers, both have released source code which has been integrated into X.Org by FOSS developers. In July 2008, VIA opened documentation of their products to improve its image in the Linux and open-source communities. The company has failed to work with the open-source community to provide documentation and a working DRM driver, leaving expectations of Linux support unfulfilled. In 2011, it was announced that VIA was no longer interested in supporting free graphics initiatives.

DisplayLink announced an open-source project, Libdlo, with the goal of bringing support for their USB graphics technology to Linux and other platforms. Its code is available under the LGPL license, but it has not been integrated into an X.Org driver. DisplayLink graphics support is available through the kernel udlfb driver (with fbdev) in mainline and udl/drm driver, which in 2012 was only available in the drm-next tree.

Non-hardware-related vendors may also assist free graphics initiatives. Red Hat has two full-time employees working on Radeon software, and the Fedora Project sponsors a Fedora Graphics Test Week event before the launch of their new Linux distribution versions to test free graphics drivers. Other companies which have provided development or support include Novell and VMware.

Graphic Art Software

Graphic art software is a subclass of application software used for graphic design, multimedia development, stylized image development, technical illustration, general image editing, or simply to access graphic files. Art software uses either raster or vector graphic reading and editing methods to create, edit, and view art.

Many artists and other creative professionals today use personal computers rather than traditional media. Using graphic art software may be more efficient than rendering using traditional media by requiring less hand–eye coordination, requiring less mental imaging skill, and utilizing the computer's quicker (sometimes more accurate) automated rendering functions to create images. However, advanced level computer styles, effects and editing methods may require a steeper learning curve of computer technical skills than what was required to learn traditional hand rendering and mental imaging skills. The potential of the software to enhance or hinder creativity may depend on the intuitiveness of the interface.

Software

Most art software includes common functions, creation tools, editing tools, filters, and automated rendering modes. Many, however, are designed to enhance a specialized skill or technique. Specialized software packages may be discontinued for various reasons such as lack of appreciation for the result, lack of expertise and training for the product, or simply not worth the time and money investment, but most likely due to obsolescence compared to newer methods or integration as a feature of newer more complete software packages.

Graphic Design Software

Graphic design professionals favor general image editing software and page layout software commonly referred to as desktop publishing software. Graphic designers that are also image developers or multimedia developers may use a combination of page layout software with the following:

Multimedia Development Software

Multimedia development professionals favor software with audio, motion and interactivity such as software for creating and editing hypermedia, electronic presentations, computer simulations and games.

Stylized Image Development Software

Image development professionals may use general graphic editors or may prefer more specialized software for rending or capturing images with style. Although images can be created from scratch with most art software, specialized software applications or advanced features of generalized applications are used for more accurate visual effects. These visual effects include:

Traditional Medium Effects

Watercolor painted in Auryn Ink.

Vector editors are ideal for solid crisp lines seen in line art, poster, woodcut ink effects, and mosaic effects.

Some generalized image editors, such as Adobe Photoshop are used for digital painting (representing real brush and canvas textures such as watercolor or burlap canvas) or handicraft textures such as mosaic or stained glass. However, unlike Adobe Photoshop, which was originally designed for photo editing, software such as Corel Painter and Photo-Paint were originally designed for rendering with digital painting effects and continue to evolve with more emphasis on hand-rendering styles that don't appear computer generated.

Photorealistic Effects

Unlike traditional medium effects, photorealistic effects create the illusion of a photographed image. Specialized software may contain 3D modeling and ray tracing features to make images appear photographed. Some 3D software is for general 3D object modeling, whereas other 3D software is more specialized, such as Poser for characters or Bryce for scenery. Software such as Adobe Photoshop may be used to create 3D effects from 2D (flat) images instead of 3D models. AddDepth is a discontinued software for extruding 2D shapes into 3D images with the option of beveled effects. MetaCreations Detailer and Painter 3D are discontinued software applications specifically for painting texture maps on 3D Models.

Hyperrealistic Effects

Specialized software may be used to combine traditional medium effects and photorealistic effects. 3-D modeling software may be exclusively for, include features for, or include the option of 3rd party plugins for rendering 3-D models with 2-D effects (e.g. cartoons, illustrations) for hyperrealistic effects. Other 2-D image editing software may be used to trace photographs or rotoscope animations from film. This allows artists to rapidly apply unique styles to what would be purely photorealistic images from computer generated imagery from 3-D models or photographs. Some styles of hyperrealism may require motion visual effects (e.g. geometrically accurate rotation, accurate kinetics, simulated organic growth, lifelike motion constraints) to notice the realism of the imagery. Software may be used to bridge the gap between the imagination and the laws of physics.

Technical Graphic Software

Technical professionals and technical illustrators may use technical graphic software that might allow for stylized effects with more emphasis on clarity and accuracy and little or no emphasis on creative expression and aesthetics. For this reason, the results are seldom referred to as "art." For designing or technical illustration of synthetic physical objects, the software is usually referred to as CAD or CADD, Computer-Aided Design and Drafting. This software allows for more precise handling of measurements and mathematical calculations, some of which simulate physics to conduct virtual testing of the models. Aside from physical objects, technical graphic software may include software for visualizing concepts, manually representing scientific data, visualizing algorithms, visual instructions, and navigational aids in the form of information graphics. Specialized software for concept maps may be used for both technical purposes and non-technical conceptualizing, which may or may not be considered technical illustration.

Specialized Graphic Format Handling

This may include software for handling specialized graphic file formats such as Fontographer software, which is dedicated to creating and editing computer fonts. Some general image editing software has unique image file handling features as well. Vector graphic editors handle vector graphic files and are able to load PostScript files natively. Some tools enable professional photographers to use nondestructive image processing for editing digital photography without permanently changing or duplicating the original, using the Raw image format. Other special handling software includes software for capturing images such as 2D scanning software, 3D scanning software and screen-capturing, or software for specialized graphic format processing such as raster image processing and file format conversion. Some tools may reduce the file size of graphics for web performance optimization while maintaining the image quality as best as possible.

Amira

Amira is a software platform for 3D and 4D data visualization, processing, and analysis.

Amira is an extendable software system for scientific visualization, data analysis, and presentation of 3D and 4D data. It is used by thousands of researchers and engineers in academia and industry around the world. Its flexible user interface and modular architecture make it a universal tool for processing and analysis of data from various modalities; e.g. micro-CT, PET, Ultrasound. Its ever-expanding functionality has made it a versatile data analysis and visualization solution, applicable to and being used in many fields, such as microscopy in biology and materials science, molecular biology, quantum physics, astrophysics, computational fluid dynamics (CFD), finite element modeling (FEM), non-destructive testing (NDT), and many more. One of the key features, besides data visualization, is Amira's set of tools for image segmentation and geometry reconstruction. This allows the user to mark (or segment) structures and regions of interest in 3D image volumes using automatic, semi-automatic, and manual tools. The segmentation can then be used for a variety of subsequent tasks, such as volumetric analysis, density analysis, shape analysis, or the generation of 3D computer models for visualization, numerical simulations, or rapid prototyping or 3D printing, to name a few. Other key Amira features are multi-planar and volume visualization, image registration, filament tracing, cell separation and analysis, tetrahedral mesh generation, fiber-tracking from diffusion tensor imaging (DTI) data, skeletonization, spatial graph analysis, and stereoscopic rendering of 3D data over multiple displays and immersive virtual reality environments, including CAVEs. As a commercial product Amira requires the purchase of a license or an academic subscription. A time-limited, but full-featured evaluation version is available for download free of charge.

Amira's roots go back to 1993 and the Department for Scientific Visualization, headed by Hans-Christian Hege at the Zuse Institute Berlin (ZIB). The ZIB is a research institute for mathematics and informatics. The Scientific Visualization department's mission is to help solve computationally and scientifically challenging tasks in medicine, biology, engineering and materials science. For this purpose, it develops algorithms and software for 2D, 3D, and 4D data visualization and visually supported exploration and analysis. At that time, the young visualization group at the ZIB had experience with the extendable, data flow-oriented visualization environments apE, IRIS Explorer, and Advanced Visualization Studio (AVS), but was not satisfied with these products' interactivity, flexibility, and ease-of-use for non-computer scientists.

Therefore, the development of a new software system was started in a research project within a medically oriented, multi-disciplinary collaborative research center. Based on experiences that Tobias Höllerer had gained in late 1993 with the new graphics library IRIS Inventor, it was decided to utilize that library. The development of the medical planning system was performed by Detlev Stalling, who later became the chief software architect of Amira. The new software was called "HyperPlan", highlighting its initial target application – a planning system for hyperthermia cancer treatment. The system was being developed on Silicon Graphics (SGI) computers, which at the time were the standard workstations used for high-end graphics computing. The software was based on libraries such as OpenGL (originally IRIS GL), Open Inventor (originally IRIS Inventor), and the graphical user interface libraries X11, Motif (software), and ViewKit. In 1998, X11/Motif/Viewkit were replaced by the Qt toolkit.

The HyperPlan framework served as the base for more and more projects at the ZIB and was used by a growing number of researchers in collaborating institutions. The projects included applications in medical image computing, medical visualization, neurobiology, confocal microscopy, flow visualization, molecular analytics and computational astrophysics.

Commercially Supported Product

The growing number of users of the system started to exceed the capacities that ZIB could spare for software distribution and support, as ZIB's primary mission was algorithmic research. Therefore, the spin-off company Indeed – Visual Concepts GmbH was founded by Hans-Christian Hege, Detlev Stalling, and Malte Westerhoff with the vision of making the extensive capabilities of the software available to researchers in industry and academia worldwide and to provide the product support and robustness needed in today's fast-paced and competitive world.

In 1998 the HyperPlan software was given the new, application-neutral name "Amira". This name is not an acronym, but was chosen for being pronounceable in different languages and providing a suitable connotation, namely "to look at" or "to wonder at", from the Latin verb "admirare" (to admire), which reflects a basic situation in data visualization.

A major re-design of the software was undertaken by Detlev Stalling and Malte Westerhoff in order to make it a commercially supportable product and to make it available on non-SGI computers as well. In 1999, the first version of the commercial Amira was exhibited at the CeBIT tradeshow in Hannover, Germany on SGI IRIX and Hewlett-Packard UniX (HP-UX) booths. Versions for Linux and Microsoft Windows followed within the following twelve months. Later Mac OS X support was added. Indeed – Visual Concepts GmbH selected the Bordeaux, France and San Diego, United States based company TGS, Inc. as the worldwide distributor for Amira and completed five major releases (up to version 3.1) in the subsequent four years.

In 2003 both Indeed – Visual Concepts GmbH, as well as TGS, Inc. were acquired by Massachusetts-based Mercury Computer Systems, Inc. (NASDAQ:MRCY) and became part of Mercury's newly formed life sciences business unit, later branded Visage Imaging. In 2009, Mercury Computer Systems, Inc. spun off Visage Imaging again and sold it to Melbourne, Australia based Promedicus Ltd (ASX:PME), a leading provider of radiology information systems and medical IT solutions. During this time, Amira continued to be developed in Berlin, Germany and in close collaboration with the ZIB, still headed by the original creators of Amira. TGS, located in Bordeaux, France was sold by Mercury Computer systems to a French investor and renamed to Visualization Sciences Group (VSG). VSG continued the work on a complementary product named Avizo, based on the same source code but customized for material sciences.

In 2012, FEI, to that date the largest OEM reseller of Amira, purchased VSG and the Amira business from Promedicus. This brought the two software sisters Amira and Avizo back into one hand. In 2013, Visualization Sciences Group (VSG) became a business unit of FEI. In 2016 FEI has been bought by Thermo Fisher Scientific and became part of its Materials & Structural Analysis division in early 2017.

Amira and Avizo are still being marketed as two different products; Amira for life sciences and Avizo for materials science, but the development efforts are now joined once again. In the meantime, the number of scientific articles using the Amira / Avizo software, is in the order of 10 thousands. As in the beginning, the Amira roadmap continues to be driven by the challenging scientific questions that Amira users around the world are trying to answer, often at the leading edge in their fields.

Amira Options

Microscopy Option

- Specific readers for microscopy data.

- Image deconvolution.

- Exploration of 3D imagery obtained from virtually any microscope.

- Extraction and editing of filament networks from microscopy images.

DICOM Reader

- Import of clinical and preclinical data in DICOM format.

Mesh Option

- Generation of 3D finite element (FE) meshes from segmented image data.

- Support for many state-of-the-art FE solver formats.

- High-quality visualization of simulation mesh-based results, using scalar, vector, and tensor field display modules.

Skeletonization Option

- Reconstruction and analysis of neural and vascular networks.

- Visualization of skeletonized networks.

- Length and diameter quantification of network segments.

- Ordering of segments in a tree graph.

- Skeletonization of very large image stacks.

Molecular Option

- Advanced tools for the visualization of molecule models.

- Hardware-accelerated volume rendering.

- Powerful molecule editor.

- Specific tools for complex molecular visualization.

Developer Option

- Creation of new custom components for visualizing or data processing.

- Implementation of new file readers or writers.

- C++ programming language.

- Development wizard for getting started quickly.

Neuro Option

- Medical image analysis for DTI and brain perfusion.

- Fiber tracking supporting several stream-line based algorithms.

- Fiber separation into fiber bundles based on user defined source and destination regions.

- Computation of tensor fields, diffusion weighted maps.

- Eigenvalue decomposition of tensor fields.

- Computation of mean transit time, cerebral blood flow, and cerebral blood volume.

VR Option

- Visualization of data on large tiled displays or in immersive Virtual Reality (VR) environments.

- Support of 3D navigation devices.

- Fast multi-threaded and distributed rendering.

Very Large Data Option

- Support for visualization of image data exceeding the available main memory, using efficient out-of-core data management.

- Extensions of many standard modules, such as orthogonal and oblique slicing, volume rendering, and isosurface rendering, to work on out-of-core data.

Scenery Generator

A scenery generator refers to software used to create landscape images, 3D models, and animations. These programs often use procedural generation to generate the landscapes. If not using procedural generation to create the landscapes, then normally a 3D artist would render and create the landscapes. These programs are often used in video games or movies. Basic elements of landscapes created by scenery generators include terrain, water, foliage, and clouds. The process for basic random generation uses a diamond square algorithm.

A landscape created in Terragen.

Most scenery generators can create basic heightmaps to simulate the variation of elevation in basic terrain. Common techniques include Simplex noise, fractals, or the Diamond-Square Algorithm, which can generate 2-dimensional heightmaps. A version of scenery generator can be very simplistic. Using a Diamond-Square Algorithm with some extra steps involving fractals an algorithm for random generation of terrain can be made with only 120 lines of code. The program in example takes a grid and then divides the grid repeatedly. Each smaller grid is then split into squares and diamonds and the algorithm then makes the randomized terrain for each square and diamond. Most programs for creating the landscape can also allow for adjustment and editing of the landscape. For example World Creator allows for terrain sculpting which uses a similar "brush" system as Photoshop and allows to enhance it additionally with its procedural techniques such as erosion, sediments, and more. Other tools the World Creator program can use are terrain stamping which you can import height-maps and uses them as a base. The programs tend to also allow for additional placement of rocks, trees, Etc. These can be done procedurally or by hand depending on the program. Typically the models used for the placement objects are the same as to lessen the amount of work that would be done if the user was to create a multitude of different trees.

The terrain generated the compute does a generation of multifractals then integrates them until finally rendering them onto the screen. These techniques are typically done "on-the-fly" which typically for a 128x128 resolution terrain would mean 1.5 seconds on a CPU from the early 90's.

Applications

Scenery generators are commonly used in movies, animations and video games. For example, Industrial Light & Magic used E-on Vue to create the fictional environments for Pirates of the Caribbean: Dead Man's Chest. In such live-action cases, a 3D model of the generated environment is rendered and blended with live-action footage. Scenery generated by the software may also be used to create completely computer-generated scenes. In the case of animated movies such as Kung-Fu Panda, the raw generation is assisted by hand-painting to accentuate subtle details.

Environment elements not commonly associated with landscapes, such as or ocean waves have also been handled by the software.

Scenery Generation is used in most 3D based video-games. These typically use either custom or purchased engines that contain their own scenery generators. For some games they tend to use a procedurally generated terrain. These typically use a form of height mapping and use of Perlin noise. This will create a grid that with one point in a 2D coordinate will create the same heightmap as it is pseudo-random, meaning it will result in the same output with the same input. This can then easily be translated into the product 3D image. These can then be changed from the editor tools in most engines if the terrain will be custom built. With recent developments neural networks can be built to create or texture the terrain based off previously suggested artwork or heightmap data. These would be generated using algorithms that have been able to identify images and similarities between them. With the info the machine can take other heightmaps and render a very similar looking image to the style image. This can be used to create similar images in example a Studio Ghibli or Van Gogh art-style.

Blender

Blender is a free and open source 3D computer graphics suite built with the combined efforts of artists, scientists, students, visual effects experts, animators, game artists, artists, and other professionals around the world. Feature-rich and intuitive, the software is used for creating animated films, visual effects, arts, 3D printed models, 3D applications, and video games.

Blender has a built-in path-tracer engine that allows users to achieve ultra-realistic rendering. It is equipped with comprehensive modeling tools; enabling them to create, edit, and transform their models quickly. Also, with its camera and object tracking features, they will be able to import raw footage, track the footage, and view camera movements in 3D scenes.

Additionally, Blender offers rigging and animation tools which are ideal for creating short films, advertisements, and TV series. Users can also combine 2D with 3D in the viewport. Last but not the least, the 3D creation suite provides a Python API that is helpful in customizing the layout, colors, fonts, and size of its interface.

Benefits of Blender

Path-tracer Engine for Realistic Rendering

Among the interesting features in Blender is its ray-trace based production render engine called Cycles. Basically, a render engine is a set of codes that controls the usage of materials and lighting, and the appearance of the rendered image in 3D scenes. Cycles is a path-tracer render engine that provides users with the ability to add more realistic lighting to their scenes by tracing the path of light as pixels in an image and simulating the effects of its interaction with objects.

Speed up Rendering Processes

Cycles provides the capability to perform rendering using a graphics card rather than the CPU, a feature known as GPU rendering. As a result, it speeds up the rendering process allowing modern GPUs to perform plenty of number crunching. Number crunching is the process of performing 3D calculations which are required especially for developing video games and 3D-heavy applications.

Create 3D Games

Speaking of video game development, Blender offers a game engine which allows users to create 3D games. This includes the ability to code their own game logic and port models to third-party game engines. They can create interactive visualizations and prototypes for their games.

Film Animation

Blender also has animation tools and features that are very useful for creating short and feature-length films. It has a character pose animator editor, as well as features for independent movements and inverse kinematics. Users will be able to do automatic skinning as they create posable characters, and work on bone layers and colored groups through the aid of its fast rigging tools.

Visual Effects Features

Meanwhile, the VFX features of the software include a built-in compositor that enables users to access a library of nodes as they create camera effects, vignettes, and color grading. They will also be able to render to multilayer OpenEXR files. OpenEXR is a high dynamic-range (HDR) image file format used in movies such as Harry Potter and the Sorcerer's Stone, Men In Black II, and Signs.

Scripting

As part of its scripting capabilities, Blender offers extensions users can activate to obtain more functionalities. An option for them will also be to add such functionalities via Python scripts (an object-oriented programming language). These functionalities include animation, rendering, import and export, and object creation.

Features of Blender

- Rendering,
- High-End Production Path Tracer,
- GPU Rendering,
- Game Creation,
- Animation Toolset,
- Fast Rigging,
- Visual Effects,
- Camera and Object Motion Tracking,

- Masking,

- Compositing,

- Phyton Scripts,

- Video Editing,

- Simulation,

- Modeling,

- Customizable UI,

- Integrate with Pipeline Tools.

References

- David Airlie (2007-09-13). "AMD hand me specs on a CD". Archived from the original on 2012-10-22. Retrieved 2014-07-15

- Mittal, S.; Vetter, J. (2015). "A Survey of CPU-GPU Heterogeneous Computing Techniques". ACM Computing Surveys. 47 (4): 1–35. Doi:10.1145/2788396

- "Use F# for GPU Programming". F# Software Foundation. Archived from the original on 18 December 2016. Retrieved 15 December 2016

- Awasthi, V.; Holter, J.; Thorp, K.; Anderson, S.; Epstein, R. (2010). "F-18-fluorothymidine-PET evaluation of bone marrow transplant in a rat model". Nuclear Medicine Communications. 31 (2): 152–158. Doi:10.1097/mnm.ob013e3283339f92. PMID 19966596

- Obenaus, A.; Hayes, P. (2011). Drill hole defects: induction, imaging, and analysis in the rodent. Methods in Molecular Biology. 690. Pp. 301–314. Doi:10.1007/978-1-60761-962-8_20. ISBN 978-1-60761-961-1. PMID 21043001

4

Techniques and Methods in Computer Graphics

Various types of techniques and methods used in computer graphics include ray tracing, texture filtering, visualization, fluid animation, multiview projection, shaders, 3D modeling, reflection mapping, normal mapping, bump mapping, texture mapping and displacement mapping. The diverse applications of these techniques and methods in computer graphics have been thoroughly discussed in this chapter.

A-Buffer Method

A-Buffer method in computer graphics is a general hidden face detection mechanism suited to medium scale virtual memory computers. This method is also known as anti-aliased or area-averaged or accumulation buffer. This method extends the algorithm of depth-buffer (or Z Buffer) method. As the depth buffer method can only be used for opaque object but not for transparent object, the A-buffer method provides advantage in this scenario. Although the A buffer method requires more memory, but different surface colors can be correctly composed using it. Being a descendent of the Z-buffer algorithm, each position in the buffer can reference a linked list of surfaces. The key data structure in the A buffer is the accumulation buffer.

Each position in the A buffer has 2 fields:

1. Depth field,

2. Surface data field or Intensity field.

A depth field stores a positive or negative real number. A surface data field can stores surface intensity information or a pointer to a linked list of surfaces that contribute to that pixel position.

depth >= 0	RGB and other info
(a) When a pixel overlap by only one surface	

As shown in the above figure, if the value of depth is >= 0, the number stored at that position is the depth of single surface overlapping the corresponding pixel area. The 2nd field, i.e, the intensity field then stores the RGB components of the surface color at that point and the percent of pixel coverage.

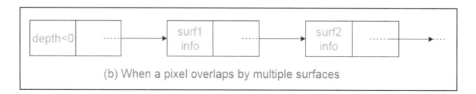

(b) When a pixel overlaps by multiple surfaces

As shown in the above figure, multiple-surface contributions to the pixel intensity is indicated by depth < 0. The 2nd field, i.e, the intensity field then stores a pointer to a linked list of surface data.

A buffer method is slightly costly than Z-buffer method because it requires more memory in comparison to the Z-buffer method. It proceeds just like the depth buffer algorithm. Here, the depth and opacity are used to determine the final color of the pixel. As shown in the figure below, the A buffer method can be used to show the transparent objects.

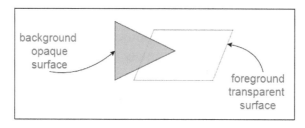

The surface buffer in the A buffer method includes:

1. Depth,

2. Surface Identifier,

3. Opacity Parameter,

4. Percent of area coverage,

5. RGB intensity components,

6. Pointer to the next surface.

The other advantage of A buffer method is that it provides anti-aliasing in addition to what Z-buffer does. The usage of A-buffer algorithm for the transparent surfaces is as shown below :

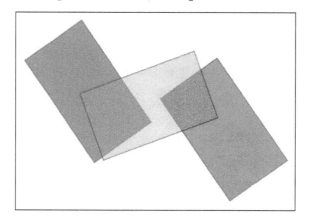

On applying the A-buffer method on all the six surfaces indicated below, the corresponding colors are as:

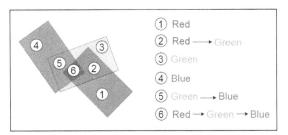

In A-buffer method, each pixel is made up of a group of sub-pixels. The final color of a pixel is computed by summing up all of its sub-pixels. Due to this accumulation taking place at sub-pixel level, A-buffer method gets the name accumulation buffer.

Rendering

A variety of rendering techniques applied to a single 3D scene.

Rendering or image synthesis is the automatic process of generating a photorealistic or non-photorealistic image from a 2D or 3D model (or models in what collectively could be called a *scene* file) by means of computer programs. Also, the results of displaying such a model can be called a render. A scene file contains objects in a strictly defined language or data structure; it would contain geometry, viewpoint, texture, lighting, and shading information as a description of the virtual scene. The data contained in the scene file is then passed to a rendering program to be processed and output to a digital image or raster graphics image file. The term "rendering" may be by analogy with an "artist's rendering" of a scene.

Though the technical details of rendering methods vary, the general challenges to overcome in producing a 2D image from a 3D representation stored in a scene file are outlined as the graphics pipeline along a rendering device, such as a GPU. A GPU is a purpose-built device able to assist a CPU in performing complex rendering calculations. If a scene is to look relatively realistic and predictable under virtual lighting, the rendering software should solve the rendering equation. The rendering equation doesn't account for all lighting phenomena, but is a general lighting model for computer-generated imagery. 'Rendering' is also used to describe the process of calculating effects in a video editing program to produce final video output.

An image created by using POV-Ray 3.6.

Rendering is one of the major sub-topics of 3D computer graphics, and in practice is always connected to the others. In the graphics pipeline, it is the last major step, giving the final appearance to the models and animation. With the increasing sophistication of computer graphics since the 1970s, it has become a more distinct subject.

Rendering has uses in architecture, video games, simulators, movie or TV visual effects, and design visualization, each employing a different balance of features and techniques. As a product, a wide variety of renderers are available. Some are integrated into larger modeling and animation packages, some are stand-alone, some are free open-source projects. On the inside, a renderer is a carefully engineered program, based on a selective mixture of disciplines related to: light physics, visual perception, mathematics, and software development.

In the case of 3D graphics, rendering may be done slowly, as in pre-rendering, or in realtime. Pre-rendering is a computationally intensive process that is typically used for movie creation, while real-time rendering is often done for 3D video games which rely on the use of graphics cards with 3D hardware accelerators.

Usage

When the pre-image (a wireframe sketch usually) is complete, rendering is used, which adds in bitmap textures or procedural textures, lights, bump mapping and relative position to other objects. The result is a completed image the consumer or intended viewer sees.

For movie animations, several images (frames) must be rendered, and stitched together in a program capable of making an animation of this sort. Most 3D image editing programs can do this.

Features

A rendered image can be understood in terms of a number of visible features. Rendering research and development has been largely motivated by finding ways to simulate these efficiently. Some relate directly to particular algorithms and techniques, while others are produced together.

- Shading – How the color and brightness of a surface varies with lighting.

- Texture-mapping – A method of applying detail to surfaces.

- Bump-mapping – A method of simulating small-scale bumpiness on surfaces.

- Fogging/participating medium – How light dims when passing through non-clear atmosphere or air.

- Shadows – The effect of obstructing light.

- Soft shadows – Varying darkness caused by partially obscured light sources.

- Reflection – Mirror-like or highly glossy reflection.

- Transparency (optics), transparency (graphic) or opacity – Sharp transmission of light through solid objects.

- Translucency – Highly scattered transmission of light through solid objects.

- Refraction – Bending of light associated with transparency.

- Diffraction – Bending, spreading, and interference of light passing by an object or aperture that disrupts the ray.

- Indirect illumination – Surfaces illuminated by light reflected off other surfaces, rather than directly from a light source (also known as global illumination).

- Caustics (a form of indirect illumination) – Reflection of light off a shiny object, or focusing of light through a transparent object, to produce bright highlights on another object.

- Depth of field – Objects appear blurry or out of focus when too far in front of or behind the object in focus.

- Motion blur – Objects appear blurry due to high-speed motion, or the motion of the camera.

- Non-photorealistic rendering – Rendering of scenes in an artistic style, intended to look like a painting or drawing.

Techniques

Many rendering algorithms have been researched, and software used for rendering may employ a number of different techniques to obtain a final image.

Tracing every particle of light in a scene is nearly always completely impractical and would take a stupendous amount of time. Even tracing a portion large enough to produce an image takes an inordinate amount of time if the sampling is not intelligently restricted.

Therefore, a few loose families of more-efficient light transport modelling techniques have emerged:

- Rasterization, including scanline rendering, geometrically projects objects in the scene to an image plane, without advanced optical effects;

- Ray casting considers the scene as observed from a specific point of view, calculating the observed image based only on geometry and very basic optical laws of reflection intensity, and perhaps using Monte Carlo techniques to reduce artifacts;

- Ray tracing is similar to ray casting, but employs more advanced optical simulation, and usually uses Monte Carlo techniques to obtain more realistic results at a speed that is often orders of magnitude faster.

The fourth type of light transport technique, radiosity is not usually implemented as a rendering technique, but instead calculates the passage of light as it leaves the light source and illuminates surfaces. These surfaces are usually rendered to the display using one of the other three techniques.

Most advanced software combines two or more of the techniques to obtain good-enough results at reasonable cost.

Another distinction is between image order algorithms, which iterate over pixels of the image plane, and object order algorithms, which iterate over objects in the scene. Generally object order is more efficient, as there are usually fewer objects in a scene than pixels.

Scanline Rendering and Rasterisation

Rendering of the European Extremely Large Telescope.

A high-level representation of an image necessarily contains elements in a different domain from pixels. These elements are referred to as primitives. In a schematic drawing, for instance, line segments and curves might be primitives. In a graphical user interface, windows and buttons might be the primitives. In rendering of 3D models, triangles and polygons in space might be primitives.

If a pixel-by-pixel (image order) approach to rendering is impractical or too slow for some task, then a primitive-by-primitive (object order) approach to rendering may prove useful. Here, one loops through each of the primitives, determines which pixels in the image it affects, and modifies those pixels accordingly. This is called rasterization, and is the rendering method used by all current graphics cards.

Rasterization is frequently faster than pixel-by-pixel rendering. First, large areas of the image may be empty of primitives; rasterization will ignore these areas, but pixel-by-pixel rendering must pass through them. Second, rasterization can improve cache coherency and reduce redundant work by taking advantage of the fact that the pixels occupied by a single primitive tend to be contiguous in the image. For these reasons, rasterization is usually the approach of choice when interactive rendering is required; however, the pixel-by-pixel approach can often produce higher-quality images and is more versatile because it does not depend on as many assumptions about the image as rasterization.

The older form of rasterization is characterized by rendering an entire face (primitive) as a single color. Alternatively, rasterization can be done in a more complicated manner by first rendering the vertices of a face and then rendering the pixels of that face as a blending of the vertex colors. This version of rasterization has overtaken the old method as it allows the graphics to flow without complicated textures (a rasterized image when used face by face tends to have a very block-like effect if not covered in complex textures; the faces are not smooth because there is no gradual color change from one primitive to the next). This newer method of rasterization utilizes the graphics card's more taxing shading functions and still achieves better performance because the simpler textures stored in memory use less space. Sometimes designers will use one rasterization method on some faces and the other method on others based on the angle at which that face meets other joined faces, thus increasing speed and not hurting the overall effect.

Ray Casting

In ray casting the geometry which has been modeled is parsed pixel by pixel, line by line, from the point of view outward, as if casting rays out from the point of view. Where an object is intersected, the color value at the point may be evaluated using several methods. In the simplest, the color value of the object at the point of intersection becomes the value of that pixel. The color may be determined from a texture-map. A more sophisticated method is to modify the colour value by an illumination factor, but without calculating the relationship to a simulated light source. To reduce artifacts, a number of rays in slightly different directions may be averaged.

Ray casting involves calculating the "view direction" (from camera position), and incrementally following along that "ray cast" through "solid 3d objects" in the scene, while accumulating the resulting value from each point in 3D space. This is related and similar to "ray tracing" except that the raycast is usually not "bounced" off surfaces (where the "ray tracing" indicates that it is tracing out the lights path including bounces). "Ray casting" implies that the light ray is following a straight path (which may include travelling through semi-transparent objects). The ray cast is a vector that can originate from the camera or from the scene endpoint ("back to front", or "front to back"). Sometimes the final light value is a derived from a "transfer function" and sometimes it's used directly.

Rough simulations of optical properties may be additionally employed: a simple calculation of the ray from the object to the point of view is made. Another calculation is made of the angle of incidence of light rays from the light source(s), and from these as well as the specified intensities of the light sources, the value of the pixel is calculated. Another simulation uses illumination plotted from a radiosity algorithm, or a combination of these two.

Ray Tracing

Ray tracing aims to simulate the natural flow of light, interpreted as particles. Often, ray tracing methods are utilized to approximate the solution to the rendering equation by applying Monte Carlo methods to it. Some of the most used methods are path tracing, bidirectional path tracing, or Metropolis light transport, but also semi realistic methods are in use, like Whitted Style Ray Tracing, or hybrids. While most implementations let light propagate on straight lines, applications exist to simulate relativistic spacetime effects.

Spiral Sphere and Julia, Detail, a computer-generated image
created by visual artist Robert W. McGregor using only POV-Ray
3.6 and its built-in scene description language.

In a final, production quality rendering of a ray traced work, multiple rays are generally shot for each pixel, and traced not just to the first object of intersection, but rather, through a number of sequential 'bounces', using the known laws of optics such as "angle of incidence equals angle of reflection" and more advanced laws that deal with refraction and surface roughness.

Once the ray either encounters a light source, or more probably once a set limiting number of bounces has been evaluated, then the surface illumination at that final point is evaluated using techniques and the changes along the way through the various bounces evaluated to estimate a value observed at the point of view. This is all repeated for each sample, for each pixel.

In distribution ray tracing, at each point of intersection, multiple rays may be spawned. In path tracing, however, only a single ray or none is fired at each intersection, utilizing the statistical nature of Monte Carlo experiments.

As a brute-force method, ray tracing has been too slow to consider for real-time, and until recently too slow even to consider for short films of any degree of quality, although it has been used for special effects sequences, and in advertising, where a short portion of high quality (perhaps even photorealistic) footage is required.

However, efforts at optimizing to reduce the number of calculations needed in portions of a work where detail is not high or does not depend on ray tracing features have led to a realistic possibility of wider use of ray tracing. There is now some hardware accelerated ray tracing equipment, at least in prototype phase, and some game demos which show use of real-time software or hardware ray tracing.

Radiosity

Radiosity is a method which attempts to simulate the way in which directly illuminated surfaces act as indirect light sources that illuminate other surfaces. This produces more realistic shading and seems to better capture the 'ambience' of an indoor scene. A classic example is the way that shadows 'hug' the corners of rooms.

The optical basis of the simulation is that some diffused light from a given point on a given surface is reflected in a large spectrum of directions and illuminates the area around it.

The simulation technique may vary in complexity. Many renderings have a very rough estimate of radiosity, simply illuminating an entire scene very slightly with a factor known as ambiance. However, when advanced radiosity estimation is coupled with a high quality ray tracing algorithm, images may exhibit convincing realism, particularly for indoor scenes.

In advanced radiosity simulation, recursive, finite-element algorithms 'bounce' light back and forth between surfaces in the model, until some recursion limit is reached. The colouring of one surface in this way influences the colouring of a neighbouring surface, and vice versa. The resulting values of illumination throughout the model (sometimes including for empty spaces) are stored and used as additional inputs when performing calculations in a ray-casting or ray-tracing model.

Due to the iterative/recursive nature of the technique, complex objects are particularly slow to emulate. Prior to the standardization of rapid radiosity calculation, some digital artists used a technique referred to loosely as false radiosity by darkening areas of texture maps corresponding to corners, joints and recesses, and applying them via self-illumination or diffuse mapping for scanline rendering. Even now, advanced radiosity calculations may be reserved for calculating the ambiance of the room, from the light reflecting off walls, floor and ceiling, without examining the contribution that complex objects make to the radiosity—or complex objects may be replaced in the radiosity calculation with simpler objects of similar size and texture.

Radiosity calculations are viewpoint independent which increases the computations involved, but makes them useful for all viewpoints. If there is little rearrangement of radiosity objects in the scene, the same radiosity data may be reused for a number of frames, making radiosity an effective way to improve on the flatness of ray casting, without seriously impacting the overall rendering time-per-frame.

Because of this, radiosity is a prime component of leading real-time rendering methods, and has been used from beginning-to-end to create a large number of well-known recent feature-length animated 3D-cartoon films.

Sampling and Filtering

One problem that any rendering system must deal with, no matter which approach it takes, is the sampling problem. Essentially, the rendering process tries to depict a continuous function from image space to colors by using a finite number of pixels. As a consequence of the Nyquist–Shannon sampling theorem (or Kotelnikov theorem), any spatial waveform that can be displayed must consist of at least two pixels, which is proportional to image resolution. In simpler terms, this expresses the idea that an image cannot display details, peaks or troughs in color or intensity, that are smaller than one pixel.

If a naive rendering algorithm is used without any filtering, high frequencies in the image function will cause ugly aliasing to be present in the final image. Aliasing typically manifests itself as jaggies, or jagged edges on objects where the pixel grid is visible. In order to remove aliasing, all rendering algorithms (if they are to produce good-looking images) must use some kind of low-pass filter on the image function to remove high frequencies, a process called antialiasing.

Optimization

Due to the large number of calculations, a work in progress is usually only rendered in detail appropriate to the portion of the work being developed at a given time, so in the initial stages of modeling, wireframe and ray casting may be used, even where the target output is ray tracing with radiosity. It is also common to render only parts of the scene at high detail, and to remove objects that are not important to what is currently being developed.

For real-time, it is appropriate to simplify one or more common approximations, and tune to the exact parameters of the scenery in question, which is also tuned to the agreed parameters to get the most 'bang for the buck'.

Academic Core

The implementation of a realistic renderer always has some basic element of physical simulation or emulation — some computation which resembles or abstracts a real physical process.

The term "physically based" indicates the use of physical models and approximations that are more general and widely accepted outside rendering. A particular set of related techniques have gradually become established in the rendering community.

The basic concepts are moderately straightforward, but intractable to calculate; and a single elegant algorithm or approach has been elusive for more general purpose renderers. In order to meet demands of robustness, accuracy and practicality, an implementation will be a complex combination of different techniques.

Rendering research is concerned with both the adaptation of scientific models and their efficient application.

Rendering Equation

This is the key academic/theoretical concept in rendering. It serves as the most abstract formal expression of the non-perceptual aspect of rendering. All more complete algorithms can be seen as solutions to particular formulations of this equation.

$$L_o(x, \vec{w}) = L_e(x, \vec{w}) + \int_\Omega f_r(x, \vec{w}', \vec{w}) L_i(x, \vec{w}')(\vec{w}' \cdot \vec{n}) \mathrm{d}\vec{w}'$$

Meaning: at a particular position and direction, the outgoing light (L_o) is the sum of the emitted light (L_e) and the reflected light. The reflected light being the sum of the incoming light (L_i) from all directions, multiplied by the surface reflection and incoming angle. By connecting outward light to inward light, via an interaction point, this equation stands for the whole 'light transport' — all the movement of light — in a scene.

Bidirectional Reflectance Distribution Function

The bidirectional reflectance distribution function (BRDF) expresses a simple model of light interaction with a surface as follows:

$$f_r(x, \vec{w}', \vec{w}) = \frac{\mathrm{d}L_r(x, \vec{w})}{L_i(x, \vec{w}')(\vec{w}' \cdot \vec{n}) \mathrm{d}\vec{w}'}$$

Light interaction is often approximated by the even simpler models: diffuse reflection and specular reflection, although both can ALSO be BRDFs.

Geometric Optics

Rendering is practically exclusively concerned with the particle aspect of light physics — known as geometrical optics. Treating light, at its basic level, as particles bouncing around is a simplification, but appropriate: the wave aspects of light are negligible in most scenes, and are significantly more difficult to simulate. Notable wave aspect phenomena include diffraction (as seen in the colours of CDs and DVDs) and polarisation (as seen in LCDs). Both types of effect, if needed, are made by appearance-oriented adjustment of the reflection model.

Visual Perception

Though it receives less attention, an understanding of human visual perception is valuable to rendering. This is mainly because image displays and human perception have restricted ranges. A renderer can simulate an almost infinite range of light brightness and color, but current displays — movie screen, computer monitor, etc. — cannot handle so much, and something must be discarded or compressed. Human perception also has limits, and so does not need to be given large-range images to create realism. This can help solve the problem of fitting images into displays, and, furthermore, suggest what short-cuts could be used in the rendering simulation, since certain subtleties won't be noticeable. This related subject is tone mapping.

Mathematics used in rendering includes: linear algebra, calculus, numerical mathematics, signal processing, and Monte Carlo methods.

Rendering for movies often takes place on a network of tightly connected computers known as a render farm.

The current state of the art in 3-D image description for movie creation is the mental ray scene description language designed at mental images and RenderMan Shading Language designed at Pixar. (compare with simpler 3D fileformats such as VRML or APIs such as OpenGL and DirectX tailored for 3D hardware accelerators).

Other renderers (including proprietary ones) can and are sometimes used, but most other renderers tend to miss one or more of the often needed features like good texture filtering, texture caching, programmable shaders, highend geometry types like hair, subdivision or nurbs surfaces with tesselation on demand, geometry caching, raytracing with geometry caching, high quality shadow mapping, speed or patent-free implementations. Other highly sought features these days may include interactive photorealistic rendering (IPR) and hardware rendering/shading.

Some renderers execute on the GPU instead of the CPU (e.g. FurryBall, Redshift, Octane). The parallelized nature of GPUs can be used for shorter render times. However, GPU renderers are constrained by the amount of video memory available.

Non-photorealistic Rendering

Non-photorealistic rendering (NPR) is an area of computer graphics that focuses on enabling a wide variety of expressive styles for digital art. In contrast to traditional computer graphics, which has focused on photorealism, NPR is inspired by artistic styles such as painting, drawing, technical illustration, and animated cartoons. NPR has appeared in movies and video games in the form of "toon shading", as well as in scientific visualization, architectural illustration and experimental animation. An example of a modern use of this method is that of cel-shaded animation.

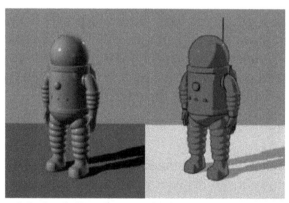

A normal shader (left) and a NPR shader using cel-shading (right).

The term "non-photorealistic rendering" is believed to have been coined by the SIGGRAPH 1990 papers committee, who held a session entitled "Non Photo Realistic Rendering" The term, however, has received criticism; some criticisms include:

- The term "photorealism" has different meanings for graphics researchers and artists. For artists, who are the target consumers of NPR techniques, it refers to a school of painting that focuses on reproducing the effect of a camera lens, with all the distortion and hyper-reflections that it involves. For graphics researchers, it refers to an image that is visually indistinguishable from reality. In fact, graphics researchers lump the kinds of visual distortions that are used by photorealist painters into non-photorealism.

- Describing something by what it is not is problematic. Equivalent comparisons might be "non-elephant biology", or "non-geometric mathematics". NPR researchers have stated that they expect the term will disappear eventually, and be replaced by the more general term "computer graphics", with "photorealistic graphics" being used to describe traditional computer graphics.

- Many techniques that are used to create 'non-photorealistic' images are not rendering techniques. They are modelling techniques, or post-processing techniques. While the latter are coming to be known as 'image-based rendering', sketch-based modelling techniques, cannot technically be included under this heading, which is very inconvenient for conference organisers.

The first conference on Non-Photorealistic Animation and Rendering included a discussion of possible alternative names. Among those suggested were "expressive graphics", "artistic rendering", "non-realistic graphics", "art-based rendering", and "psychographics". All of these terms have been used in various research papers on the topic, but the term NPR seems to have nonetheless taken hold.

The first technical meeting dedicated to NPR was the ACM sponsored Symposium on Non-Photorealistic Rendering and Animation (NPAR) in 2000. NPAR is traditionally co-located with the

Annecy Animated Film Festival, running on even numbered years. From 2007 NPAR began to also run on odd-numbered years, co-located with ACM SIGGRAPH.

3D

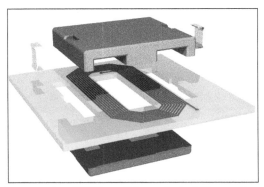

An example of NPR used for technical illustrations.

Three-dimensional NPR is the style that is most commonly seen in video games and movies. The output from this technique is almost always a 3D model that has been modified from the original input model to portray a new artistic style. In many cases, the geometry of the model is identical to the original geometry, and only the material applied to the surface is modified. With increased availability of programmable GPU's, shaders have allowed NPR effects to be applied to the rasterised image that is to be displayed to the screen. The majority of NPR techniques applied to 3D geometry are intended to make the scene appear two-dimensional.

NPR techniques for 3D images include cel shading and Gooch shading.

For enhanced legibility, the most useful technical illustrations for technical communication are not necessarily photorealistic. Non-photorealistic renderings, such as exploded view diagrams, greatly assist in showing placement of parts in a complex system.

2D

The input to a two dimensional NPR system is typically an image or video. The output is a typically an artistic rendering of that input imagery (for example in a watercolor, painterly or sketched style) although some 2D NPR serves non-artistic purposes e.g. data visualization.

The artistic rendering of images and video (often referred to as Image Stylization) traditionally focused upon heuristic algorithms that seek to simulate the placement of brush strokes on a digital canvas.

Arguably, the earliest example of 2D NPR is Paul Haeberli's 'Paint by Numbers' at SIGGRAPH 1990. This (and similar interactive techniques) provide the user with a canvas that they can "paint" on using the cursor — as the user paints, a stylized version of the image is revealed on the canvas. This is especially useful for people who want to simulate different sizes of brush strokes according to different areas of the image.

Subsequently basic image processing operations using gradient operators or statistical moments were used to automate this process and minimize user interaction in the late nineties (although artistic control remains with the user via setting parameters of the algorithms). This automation enabled practical application of 2D NPR to video, for the first time in the living paintings of the movie What Dreams May Come.

An example of a non-photoreal rendering
of an existing 2D image.

More sophisticated image abstractions techniques were developed in the early 2000s harnessing Computer Vision operators e.g. image salience, or segmentation operators to drive stroke placement. Around this time, machine learning began to influence image stylization algorithms notably image analogy that could learn to mimic the style of an existing artwork.

The advent of deep learning has re-kindled activity in image stylization, notably with Neural Style Transfer (NST) algorithms that can mimic a wide gamut of artistic styles from single visual examples. These algorithms underpin mobile apps capable of the same e.g. Prisma.

In addition to the above stylization methods, a related class of techniques in 2D NPR address the simulation of artistic media. These methods include simulating the diffusion of ink through different kinds of paper, and also of pigments through water for simulation of watercolor.

Artistic Rendering

Artistic rendering is the application of visual art styles to rendering. For photorealistic rendering styles, the emphasis is on accurate reproduction of light-and-shadow and the surface properties of the depicted objects, composition, or other more generic qualities. When the emphasis is on unique interpretive rendering styles, visual information is interpreted by the artist and displayed accordingly using the chosen art medium and level of abstraction in abstract art. In computer graphics, interpretive rendering styles are known as non-photorealistic rendering styles, but may be used to simplify technical illustrations. Rendering styles that combine photorealism with non-photorealism are known as hyperrealistic rendering styles.

Volume Rendering

Rapid advances in hardware have been transforming revolutionary approaches in computer graphics into reality. One typical example is the raster graphics that took place in the seventies, when hardware innovations enabled the transition from vector graphics to raster graphics. Another example which has a similar potential is currently shaping up in the field of volume graphics.

This trend is rooted in the extensive research and development effort in scientific visualization in general and in volume visualization in particular.

Visualization is the usage of computer-supported, interactive, visual representations of data to amplify cognition. Scientific visualization is the visualization of physically based data.

Volume visualization is a method of extracting meaningful information from volumetric datasets through the use of interactive graphics and imaging, and is concerned with the representation, manipulation, and rendering of volumetric datasets. Its objective is to provide mechanisms for peering inside volumetric datasets and to enhance the visual understanding.

Traditional 3D graphics is based on surface representation. Most common form is polygon-based surfaces for which affordable special-purpose rendering hardware have been developed in the recent years. Volume graphics has the potential to greatly advance the field of 3D graphics by offering a comprehensive alternative to conventional surface representation methods.

The object of this thesis is to examine the existing methods for volume visualization and to find a way of efficiently rendering scientific data with commercially available hardware, like PC's, without requiring dedicated systems.

Volume Rendering

Our display screens are composed of a two-dimensional array of pixels each representing a unit area. A volume is a three-dimensional array of cubic elements, each representing a unit of space. Individual elements of a three-dimensional space are called volume elements or voxels. A number associated with each point in a volume is called the value at that point. The collection of all these values is called a scalar field on the volume. The set of all points in the volumewith a given scalar value is called a level surface. Volume rendering is the process of displaying scalar fields. It is a method for visualizing a three dimensional data set. The interior information about a data set is projected to a display screen using the volume rendering methods. Along the ray path from each screen pixel, interior data values are examined and encoded for display. How the data are encoded for display depends on the application. Seismic data, for example, is often examined to find the maximum and minimum values along each ray. The values can then be color coded to give information about the width of the interval and the minimum value. In medical applications, the data values are opacity factors in the range from 0 to 1 for the tissue and bone layers. Bone layers are completely opaque, while tissue is somewhat transparent. Voxels represent various physical characteristics, such as density, temperature, velocity, and pressure. Other measurements, such as area, and volume, can be extracted from the volume datasets. Applications of volume visualization are medical imaging (e.g., computed tomography, magnetic resonance imaging, ultrasonography), biology (e.g., confocal microscopy), geophysics (e.g., seismic measurements from oil and gas exploration), industry (e.g., finite element models), molecular systems (e.g., electron density maps), meteorology (e.g., stormy (prediction), computational fluid dynamics (e.g., water flow), computational chemistry (e.g., new materials), digital signal and image processing (e.g., CSG) . Numerical simulations and sampling devices such as magnetic resonance imaging (MRI), computed tomography (CT), positron emission tomography (PET), ultrasonic imaging, confocal microscopy, supercomputer simulations, geometric models, laser scanners, depth images estimated by stereo disparity, satellite imaging, and sonar are sources of large 3D datasets.

3D scientific data can be generated in a variety of disciplines by using sampling methods. Volumetric data obtained from biomedical scanners typically come in the form of 2D slices of a regular, Cartesian grid, sometimes varying in one or more major directions. The typical output of super-computer and Finite Element Method (FEM) simulations is irregular grids. The raw output of an ultrasound scan is a sequence of arbitrarily oriented, fan-shaped slices, which constitute partially structured point samples. A sequence of 2D slices obtained from these scanners is reconstructed into a 3D volume model. Imaging machines have a resolution of millimeters scale so that many details important for scientific purposes can be recorded.

It is often necessary to view the dataset from continuously changing positions to better understand the data being visualized. The real-time interaction is the most essential requirement and preferred even if it is rendered in a somewhat less realistic way. A real-time rendering system is important for the following reasons:

- To visualize rapidly changing datasets,

- For real-time exploration of 3D datasets, (e.g. virtual reality)

- >for interactive manipulation of visualization parameters, (e.g. classification)

- For interactive volume graphics.

Rendering and processing does not depend on the object's complexity or type, it depends only on volume resolution. The dataset resolutions are generally anywhere from 128^3 to 1024^3 and may be non-symmetric (i.e. 1024 x 1024 x 512).

Volumetric Data

Volumetric data is typically a set of samples $S(x, y, z, v)$, representing the value v of some property of the data, at a 3D location (x, y, z). If the value is simply a 0 or a 1, with a value of 0 indicating background and a value of 1 indicating the object, then the data is referred to as binary data. The data may instead be multi-valued, with the value representing some measurable property of the data, including, for example, color, density, heat or pressure. The value v may even be a vector, representing, for example, velocity at each location. In general, the samples may be taken at purely random locations in space, but in most cases the set S is isotropic containing samples taken at regularly spaced intervals along three orthogonal axes. When the spacing between samples along each axis is a constant, then S is called isotropic, but there may be three different spacing constants for the three axes. In that case the set S is anisotropic. Since the set of samples is defined on a regular grid, a 3D array (called also volume buffer, cubic frame buffer, 3D raster) is typically used to store the values, with the element location indicating position of the sample on the grid. For this reason, the set S will be referred to as the array of values $S(x, y, z)$, which is defined only at grid locations. Alternatively, either rectilinear, curvilinear (structured), or unstructured grids, are employed.

In a rectilinear grid the cells are axis-aligned, but grid spacing along the axes are arbitrary. When such a grid has been non-linearly transformed while preserving the grid topology, the grid becomes curvilinear. Usually, the rectilinear grid defining the logical organization is called computational space, and the curvilinear grid is called physical space. Otherwise the grid is called unstructured or irregular. An unstructured or irregular volume data is a collection of cells whose connectivity has to be specified explicitly. These cells can be of an arbitrary shape such as tetrahedra, hexahedra, or prisms.

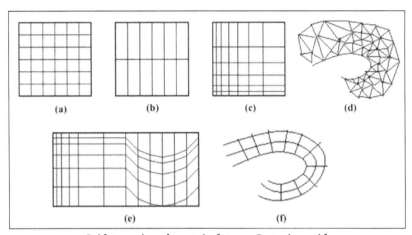

Grid types in volumetric data. a. Cartesian grid,
b. Regular grid, c. Rectilinear grid, d. Curvilinear grid,
e. Block structured grid, and f. Unstructured grid.

The array S only defines the value of some measured property of the data at discrete locations in space. A function f(x, y, z) may be defined over the volume in order to describe the value at any continuous location. The function f(x, y, z) = S(x, y, z) if (x, y, z) is a grid location, otherwise f(x, y, z) approximates the sample value at a location (x, y, z) by applying some interpolation function to S. There are many possible interpolation functions. The simplest interpolation function is known as zero-order interpolation, which is actually just a nearest-neighbor function. The value at any location in the volume is simply the value of the closest sample to that location. With this interpolation method there is a region of a constant value around each sample in S. Since the samples in S are regularly spaced, each region is of a uniform size and shape. The region of the constant value that surrounds each sample is known as a voxel with each voxel being a rectangular cuboid having six faces, twelve edges, and eight corners.

Higher-order interpolation functions can also be used to define f(x, y, z) between sample points. One common interpolation function is a piecewise function known as first-order interpolation, or trilinear interpolation. With this interpolation function, the value is assumed to vary linearly along directions parallel to one of the major axes.

Voxels and Cells

Volumes of data are usually treated as either an array of voxels or an array of cells. These two approaches stem from the need to resample the volume between grid points during the rendering process. Resampling, requiring interpolation, occurs in almost every volume visualization algorithm. Since the underlying function is not usually known, and it is not known whether the function was sampled above the Nyquist frequency, it is impossible to check the reliability of the interpolation used to find data values between discrete grid points. It must be assumed that common interpolation techniques are valid for an image to be considered valid.

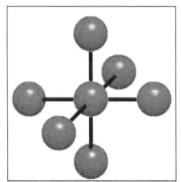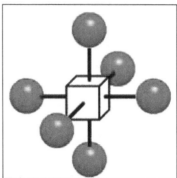

Voxels: Each grid point has a sample value.
Data values do not vary within voxels.

The voxel approach dictates that the area around a grid point has the same value as the grid point. A voxel is, therefore, an area of non-varying value surrounding a central grid point. The voxel approach has the advantage that no assumptions are made about the behavior of data between grid points, only known data values are used for generating an image.

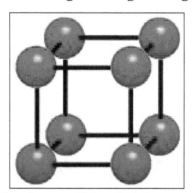

Cells: Data values do vary within cells. It is assumed that values
between grid points can be estimated.

The cell approach views a volume as a collection of hexahedra whose corners are grid points and whose value varies between the grid points. This technique attempts to estimate values inside the cell by interpolating between the values at the corners of the cell. Trilinear and tricubic are the most commonly used interpolation functions. Images generated using the cell approach, appear smoother than those images created with the voxel approach. However, the validity of the cell-based images cannot be verified.

Classification of Volume Rendering Algorithms

The classification of the algorithms given below is therefore not binding. All of the names of the algorithms are carefully taken into consideration and emphasized.

Volume visualization has been the most active sub-area of researches during last 20 years in scientific visualization. To be useful, volume visualization techniques must offer understandable data representations, quick data manipulation, and reasonably fast rendering. Scientific users should be able to change parameters and see the resultant image instantly. Few present day systems are capable of this type of performance; therefore researchers are still studying many new ways to use volume visualization effectively.

The rendering approaches differ in several aspects which can be used for their detailed classification in various ways. Coarsely, volume visualization is done using two different approaches based on the portion of the volume raster set which they render:

1. Surface rendering (or indirect volume rendering),

2. Volume rendering (or direct volume rendering).

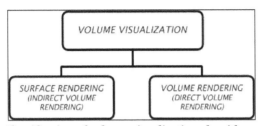

Classification of volume visualization algorithms.

Surface rendering (indirect rendering or surface oriented) algorithms are standard for nearly all 3D visualization problems. Surface oriented algorithms first fit geometric primitives to values in the data, and then render these primitives. The data values are usually chosen from an iso-surface, which is the set of locations in the data where the scalar field equals some value. In typical datasets from medical or scientific applications, the iso-surface forms a connected surface, such as the air/skin or brain/bone boundary in a CT dataset. With dedicated vector hardware, these models can be calculated very efficiently. Examples of surface oriented hardware are Reality Engine, HP, SUN, IBM, and PIXAR. Typical visualization problems to be solved in the medical context are e.g. tissues that have no defined surface or blood vessels whose size is close to the limit of imaging resolution. However surface oriented methods leave these problems unsolved.

An indirect volume rendering system transforms the data into a different domain (e.g., compression, boundary representation, etc.). Typically, the data is transformed into a set of polygons representing a level surface (or iso-surface); then conventional polygon rendering methods are used to project the polygons into an image. Many methods exist for indirect volume rendering (surface rendering), which are defined as visualizing a volumetric dataset by first transferring the data into a different domain and rendering directly from the new domain. Indirect volume rendering can be classified as *surface tracking*, *iso-surfacing*, and *domain-based rendering*. Indirect methods are often chosen because of a particular form of hardware acceleration or because of a speed advantage.

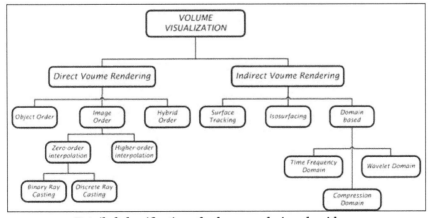

Detailed classification of volume rendering algorithms.

Volume rendering (oriented) algorithmsrender every voxel in the volume raster directly, without conversion to geometric primitives or first converting to a different domain and then rendering from that domain. They usually include an illumination model which supports semi-transparent voxels; this allows rendering where every voxel in the volume is (potentially) visible. Each voxel contributes to the final 2D projection.

Surface Tracking

Surface tracking is a surface reconstruction process that constructs a geometric surface from a volumetric dataset by following the faces of the voxels residing on the surface boundary. The boundary is defined by a *thresholding, classification,* or *surface detection* process. Given a threshold value, a closed contour is traced for each data slice and then the contours in adjacent slices are connected and a tessellation, usually of triangles, is performed.

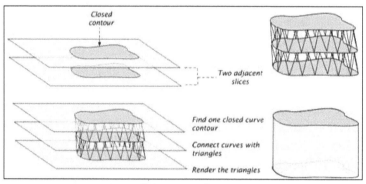

Contour tracing.

Thres holdingis a segmentation operation that assigns a value 1 to a cell in Scene B if the corresponding cell in Scene A has an intensity that falls within a specified intensity interval and that assigns a value 0 to the cell otherwise. A less general thresholding operation is one in which a single intensity value is specified. If a cell's intensity in Scene A is above this value, it is assigned a value 1 in Scene B, and a value 0, otherwise. Classification is a process of converting a given set of scenes into a scene, all with identical domains, or into a non-binary shell. If the output is a scene, its cell intensity represents fuzziness or a membership value of the cell in the object of interest. In the case of a non-binary shell, the fuzziness or the membership value is retained as one of the property values associated with the shell elements.

Examples of a contoured data that are tessellated.

Surface tracking methods are well-known and effectively used for smooth surfaces. These algorithms are known as surface extraction, feature extraction, surface tiling, polygonization, tessellation, triangulation, tracing or meshing.

Iso-surfacing

Surface Detection (iso-surface) is an operation that given a scene outputs a connected surface as a binary shell. Connectedness means that within the output shell it is possible to reach to any shell element from any shell element without leaving the shell. If the input is a binary scene, the shell constitutes a connected interface between 1-cells and 0-cells. If the input is a (grey) scene, the interface between the interior and exterior of the structure is usually difficult to determine. Thresholding can be used to determine this interface, in which the shell constitutes essentially a connected interface between cells that satisfy the threshold criterion and cells that do not. In a particular thresholding operation specified by a single intensity value, the resulting surface is called an *iso-surface*. The common iso-surfacing algorithms are Opaque Cubes (Cuberille), Marching Cubes, Marching Tetrahedra, and Dividing Cubes.

Cuberille (Opaque Cubes)

This algorithm was one of the first widely used methods for visualizing volume data. It was first proposed in, and involves deciding whether a particular volume element is a part of the surface or not. It simply visualizes the cells that are a part of the iso-surface. The first step in the cuberilles algorithm is to ensure that the volume is made up of cubic voxels. A large number of volume datasets consist of a stack of 2 dimensional slices. If the distance between the slices is larger than the size of the pixels in the slice then the data must be resampled so that the gap between the slices is in the same size as the pixels. The second stage of the algorithm involves using a binary segmentation to decide which voxels belong to the object and which do not. This should, hopefully, produce a continuous surface of voxels through which the surface in the data passes. These voxels are joined together and the surface of the object is then approximated by the surfaces of the individual voxels which make up the surface.

The algorithm visualizes the cells that are intersected by the iso-surface in the following way. In the first stage, for each cell in the dataset intersected by the iso-surface, 6 polygons are generated representing the faces of the cell. In the second stage, for each polygon, polygon is rendered in an appropriate color.

The algorithm is easy and straightforward to implement. Finding and rendering the surface is fast. The first stage of the algorithm is parallelizable at the cell level. On the other hand, the final image might look jaggy, due to too less cells in the dataset, and the algorithm is fundamentally bad at showing small features. The blocky look of the final image can be reduced by using gradient shading during rendering.

Marching Cubes

A variation on the Opaque Cubes (Cuberille) algorithm is provided by marching cubes. The basic notion is that we can define a voxel by the pixel values at the eight corners of the cube. If one or more pixels of a cube have values less than a user-specified isovalue (threshold), and one or more have values greater than this value, we conclude that the voxel must contribute some component of the iso-surface. By determining which edges of the cube are intersected by the iso-surface, we can create triangular patches which divide the cube between regions within the iso-surface and regions outside. By connecting the patches from all cubes on the iso-surface boundary, we get a surface representation.

The basic idea of the algorithm is for each cell through which an iso-surface passes to create small polygons approximating the surface within the cell. For the threshold value, some voxels will be entirely inside or outside the corresponding iso-surface and some voxels will be intersected by the iso-surface. In the first pass of the algorithm the voxels that are intersected by the threshold value are identified. In the second pass these voxels are examined and a set of one or more polygons is produced, which are then output for rendering. Each of the 8 vertices of a voxel can be either inside or outside the iso-surface value. The exact edge intersection points are determined and using 15 predefined polygon sets the polygons are created.

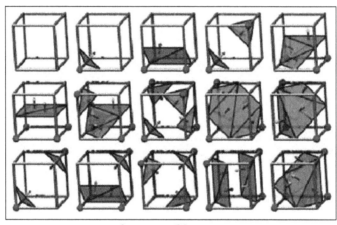

The 15 possible cases.

The original algorithm proposed has several ambiguous cases which can lead to holes in the final image. These ambiguities occur either when a wrong decision is made about whether a vertex is inside or outside a surface, or if the triangles chosen do not fit together properly. A number of extensions have been proposed to the marching cubes algorithm to avoid the ambiguous cases. These include marching tetrahedra and dividing cubes. Both the marching cubes and opaque cubes (cuberille) algorithms involve an intermediate approximation of the surfaces in the data set using geometric primitives. This technique has a number of disadvantages:

1. There is a loss of accuracy when visualizing small or fuzzy details.

2. The assumptions which are made about the data may not necessarily be valid. This particularly applies to the assumption that the surfaces exist within the data to map the geometric primitives onto.

3. Unless the original information is stored along with the geometric representation, the information on the interior of the surfaces is lost.

The first two disadvantages listed here are directly linked to the requirement to map geometric primitives onto the data. While this method works well for some data sets, it breaks down when there are small details on a similar scale to the grid size in the data, and when well defined surfaces do not exist. These issues, along with the worry of losing the original data, led to the development of another class of algorithm, volume rendering.

One obvious problem with marching cubes is the amount of memory needed to store the resulting surface. Another problem arises when a filled space of voxels is not available. Depending on how the volume data was acquired there may be voids which need to be assigned values or circumnavigated in the surface generation algorithm. Any interpolated value used may reduce the validity of the resulting surface.

Dividing Cubes

The Dividing cubes algorithm is an extension to or optimization of the Marching Cubes. It was designed to overcome the problem of the superfluous number of triangles with that algorithm. Instead of, as in the marching cube algorithm, calculating the approximate iso-surface through a cell, the Dividing cubes algorithm first projects all cells that are intersected by the iso-surface to the image/screen space. If a cell projects to a larger area than a pixel it is divided into sub-cells and rendered as a surface point. Otherwise the whole cell is rendered as a surface point. After the surface points are determined, the gradients can be calculated, using interpolation between the original cells. With the given gradient, the shading can be calculated and finally the image can be rendered. Surface points can be rendered into the image buffer directly, because there are no intermediate surface primitives used. This is done by using standard computer graphics hidden-surface removal algorithms. This algorithm works far more faster than the marching cubes even when there is no any rendering hardware available. The algorithm is also parallelizable.

Marching Tetrahedra

To perform the marching cubes algorithm, one way is to split a cube into some number of tetrahedra, and perform a marching tetrahedra algorithm. The general idea here is so simple that the number of cases to consider in marching tetrahedra is far less than the number of cases in marching cubes. Cells can be divided into 5, 6, or 24 tetrahedra.

The Marching Tetrahedra Algorithm is the same as the Marching Cubes Algorithm up to the point that, the cube is divided into 5 tetrahedron instead of 15 as depicted in figure.

As we step across the cubic space, we must alternate the decomposition of the cubes into tetrahedra. For a given tetrahedron, each of it's vertices are classified as either lying inside or outside the tetrahedron. There are originally 16 possible configurations. If we remove the two cases where all four vertex are either inside or outside the iso-value, we are left with 14 configurations. Due to symmetry there are only three real cases.

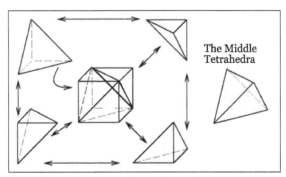

The Tetrahedra orientation within a cube.

Based on these cases, triangles are generated to approximate the iso-surface intersection with the tetrahedron. Like the Marching Cubes Algorithm, when all of the triangles generated by marching these tetrahedrons are rendered across the cubic region, an iso-surface approximation is obtained.

The 5 Tetrahedra case requires flipping adjacent cells; otherwise anomalous, unconnected surfaces are encountered. The Marching Tetrahedra Algorithm has great advantages over the Marching Cubes Algorithm because the three cases are easier to deal with than 15, and the code is more manageable. Another advantage of using the Marching Tetrahedra Algorithm to approximate an iso-surface is that a higher resolution is achieved. Basically the cubes of the Marching Cubes Algorithm are subdivided into smaller geometries (tetrahedrons). More triangles are generated per cube, and these triangles are able to approximate the iso-surface better.

The disadvantages of the Marching Tetrahedra Algorithm is basically that because it sub-divides the cubes into 5 more sub-regions, the number of triangles generated by the Marching Tetrahedra Algorithm is greater than the number of triangles generated by the Marching Cubes Algorithm. While the Marching Tetrahedra Algorithm generates better iso-surfaces, the time to render the iso-surfaces is higher than that of the Marching Cubes Algorithm.

Factors that affect the performance of the marching tetrahedra algorithm are 3D grid size, grid resolution, number of objects, threshold, radius of influence for an individual object, and strength of an individual object.

Frequency Domain Rendering

The frequency domain rendering applies the Fourier slice projection theorem, which states that a projection of a 3D data volume from a certain view direction can be obtained by extracting a 2D slice perpendicular to that view direction out of the 3D Fourier spectrum and then inverse Fourier transforming it.

It is well-known that the integral of a 1D signal is equal to the value of its spectrum at the origin. The Fourier projection slice theorem extends this notion to higher dimensions. For a 3D volume, the theorem states that the following two are a Fourier transform pair:

1. The 2D image obtained by taking line integrals of the volume along rays perpendicular to the image plane,

2. The 2D spectrum obtained by extracting a slice from the Fourier transform of the volume along a plane that includes the origin and is parallel to the image plane.

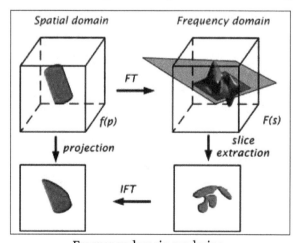

Frequency domain rendering.

Using this theorem, once a volume data is Fourier transformed an (orthographic) image for any viewing direction can be obtained by extracting a 2D slice of the 3D spectrum at the appropriate orientation and than inverse Fourier transforming it. This approach obtains the 3D volume projection directly from the 3D spectrum of the data, and therefore reduces the computational complexity for volume rendering. The complexity is dominated by the 2D inverse Fourier transform that is $O(N^2 logN)$. Since $logN$ grows slowly, the advantage of this approach over spatial domain algorithms is greater at large data sizes.

Despite their theoretical speed advantage, frequency domain volume rendering algorithms suffer from several well-known problems such as a high interpolation cost, high memory usage, and the lack of depth information. The first two problems are technical in nature and several solutions are proposed. The lack of occlusion is fundamental and so far no projection-slice-theorem is known that reproduces the integro-differential equation approximated by volume rendering algorithms.

Compression Domain Rendering

As volume data sets grow bigger and larger, data compression algorithms are required to reduce the disk storage size, and potentially the memory size during rendering as well. Data compression is an essential technology to achieve efficient volume visualization. Not only can it reduce the disk storage space with some effort, sometimes it can also be used to reduce the run-time memory requirement during the rendering process. There are basically two types of compression: lossless, and lossy compression. While lossless compression targets mainly at text documents, it can also be used to compress regular grids if data fidelity is crucial. Lossy compression, however, provides much higher compression efficiency, of course if data fidelity is not so crucial.

There are several possibilities to integrate volume data compression and volume rendering. The most naive way is to decompress the entire volume data set before rendering. This is simple and most flexible: different compression methods can be easily paired with different visualization methods. However there are three problems with this scheme. The extra decompression time introduces a long start-up latency for the renderer. The data loading time, from the renderer's point of view does not decrease despite the fact that the data sets are stored on disk in compressed form. The memory usage required for the renderer does not decrease, either. One might modify the renderer's interface to eliminate the second problem by storing the uncompressed data set in memory without incurring additional disk I/O, but the first and third problems still remain.

To address the first issue, one can perform "on-the-fly" rendering during compression. This means the renderer can start working almost immediately as soon as the first "indivisible" unit of the data set is decompressed. This essentially reduces the start-up delay to the data loading time of the minimal data unit that the renderer can work on. In fact, the second issue is also solved, because the renderer does not need to hold the entire uncompressed data set but only the compressed form of it, by decompressing it on-the-fly. Furthermore, sometimes with the help of a "garbage collection" scheme, the memory requirement for rendering could also be reduced, thus solving the third problem as well. However, this scheme may require significant modification to the rendering algorithm and some coordination effort between the decompressor and the renderer.

Another scheme to address the start-up latency and memory requirement problems is to perform on-the-fly decompression during rendering. This usually means the data set was initially partitioned into units of the same or different sizes and during rendering only these units that the renderer need will be decompressed. As the final goal here is to produce a rendered image, the on-the-fly decompression scheme is favorable since unnecessary decompression work may be avoided. Although the on-the-fly decompression scheme requires only a minor modification effort to the renderer, it suffers from the following problem: In order for each data unit to be compressed/decompressed independently of each other, some kind of partitioning must be done. If all these partitions are mutually disjointed, then rendered images may exhibit a "blocky" effect. On the other hand, overlapping these partitions to remove these blocky artifacts leads to substantial severe storage overhead.

Another elegant way to integrate volume data compression and rendering is to perform rendering directly in the compression/transformed domain, thus avoiding decompression completely. Several methods have been proposed but each of them has its drawbacks: loss of quality, undesired artifacts, large storage overhead or exceedingly high implementation complexity.

Many compression algorithms applied to volume data sets are borrowed from the image compression world, simply because most of the time it can be directly generalized to deal with regular volume data. Among them are Discrete Fourier Transform, Discrete Cosine Transform, Vector Quantization, Fractal Compression, Laplacian Decomposition/Compression, and Wavelet Decomposition /Compression.

Wavelet Domain Rendering

A wavelet is a fast decaying function with zero averaging. The nice features of wavelets are that they have a local property in both spatial and frequency domain, and can be used to fully represent the volumes with a small number of wavelet coefficients. Muraki first applied wavelet transform to volumetric data sets, Gross et al. found an approximate solution for the volume rendering equation using orthonormal wavelet functions, and Westermann combined volume rendering with wavelet-based compression. However, all of these algorithms have not focused on the acceleration of volume rendering using wavelets. The greater potential of wavelet domain, based on the elegant multi-resolution hierarchy provided by the wavelet transform, is still far from being fully utilized for volume rendering. A possible research and development is to exploit the local frequency variance provided by wavelet transform and accelerate the volume rendering in homogeneous area.

Object Order Rendering

Direct volume rendering algorithms can be classified according to the order that the algorithm traverses the volume data. Object-order rendering is also called forward rendering, or object-space rendering or voxel space projection. The simplest way to implement viewing is to traverse all the volume regarding each voxel as a 3D point that is transformed by the viewing matrix and then projected onto a Z-buffer and drawn onto the screen. The data samples are considered with a uniform spacing in all three directions. If an image is produced by projecting all occupied voxels to the image plane in an arbitrary order, a correct image is not guaranteed. If two voxels project to the same pixel on the image plane, the one that was projected later will prevail, even if it is farther from the image plane than the earlier projected voxel. This problem can be solved by traversing the data samples in a back-to-front or front-to-back order. This visibility ordering is used for the detailed classification of object order rendering.

Back-to Front (BTF) Algorithm

Earliest rendering algorithms sorted the geometric primitives according to their distance to the viewing plane. These algorithms solve the hidden surface problem by visiting the primitives in depth order, from farthest to nearest, and scan-converting each primitive into the screen buffer. Because of the order in which the primitives are visited, closer objects overwrite farther objects, which solve the hidden surface problem (at least as long as the primitives do not form a visibility cycle). Such methods are referred to as *painter's algorithms* and as *list-priority algorithms*. By definition, any painter's algorithm requires sorting the primitives. However, because of their structure, volume grids often afford a trivial sort, which simply involves indexing the volume elements in the proper order.

This algorithm is essentially the same as the Z-buffer method with one exception that is based on the observation that the voxel array is presorted in a fashion that allows scanning of its components in an order of decreasing distance from the observer. This avoids the need for a Z-buffer for hidden voxel removal considerations by applying the painter's algorithm by simply drawing the current voxel on top of previously drawn voxels or by compositing the current voxel with the screen value.

It is based on the simple observation that, given a volume grid and a view plane, for each grid axis there is a traversal direction that visits the voxels in the order of decreasing distances to the view plane. A 2D example of this is given in figure.

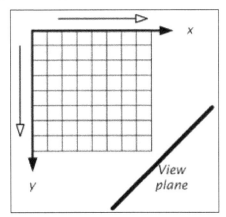

A 2D example of the BTF visibility ordering.

Here the origin is the farthest point from the view plane, and traversing the grid in the order of increasing values of x and y always visits voxels in the order of decreasing distances. This extends naturally to 3D. The choice of which index changes fastest can be arbitrary – although.

A cube rendered with the BTF visibility ordering.
Note the visibility error along the top of the cube.

BTF method can support efficient methods of accessing the volume data by taking into account how the data is stored on disk. It also allows rendering when only some slices but not the entire volume will fit into memory. While the BTF ordering correctly renders orthographic projections, it does not to work for perspective projections.

Westover gives the Westover back-to-front (WBTF) visibility ordering. The WBTF ordering is similar to the BTF ordering in that each grid axis is traversed in the direction that visits voxels in the order of decreasing distances to the view plane. The algorithm goes farther than the BTF technique in that it also chooses a permutation of the grid axes, such that the slowest changing axis is the axis that is most perpendicular to the view plane, while the quickest changing axis is the one that is most parallel to the view plane.

The V-BUFFER traversal ordering is similar to the WBTF traversal in that it processes the volume data in slices which are as parallel as possible to the view plane hence the orderings are the same. It differs in that it uses a more complicated "concentric sweep" to order the voxels in each slice. The sweep strictly orders the voxels according to increasing distances from the view plane. An example of the ordering for one slice is shown in figure. When the viewing plane is beyond one corner of the slice, the voxels are visited in the diagonal pattern shown. This differs from the WBTF ordering, which accesses each slice in a scanline fashion, and hence does not visit the voxels in a strict distance ordering.

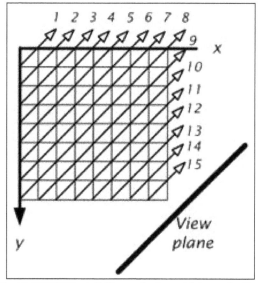

The V-BUFFER visibility ordering within each slice.

Front-to Back (FTB) Algorithm

This algorithm is essentially the same as BTF only that now the voxels are traversed in an increasing distance order. It should be observed that while in the basic Z-buffer method it is impossible to support the rendition of semitransparent materials since the voxels are mapped to the screen in an arbitrary order. Compositing is based on a computation that simulates the passage of light through several materials. In this computation the order of materials is crucial. Therefore, translucency can easily be realized in both BTF and FTB in which objects are mapped to the screen in the order in which the light traverses the scene.

Splatting

The most important algorithm of the object order family is the splatting algorithm. One way of achieving volume rendering is to try to reconstruct the image from the object space to the image space, by computing the contribution of every element in the dataset to the image. Each voxel's contribution to the image is computed and added to the other contributions. The algorithm works by virtually "throwing" the voxels onto the image plane. In this process every voxel in the object space leaves a *footprint* in the image space that will represent the object. The computation is processed by virtually slice by slice, and by accumulating the result in the image plane.

The first step is to determine in what order to traverse the volume. The closest face (and corner) to the image plane is determined. Then the closest voxels are splatted first. Each voxel is given a color and opacity according to the look up tables set by the user. These values are modified according to the gradient.

Next, the voxel is projected into the image space. To compute the contribution for a particular voxel, a reconstruction kernel is used. For an orthographic projection a common kernel is a round Gaussian . The projection of this kernel into the image space (called its footprint) is computed. The size is adjusted according to the relative sizes of the volume and the image plane so that the volume can fill the image. Then the center of the kernel is placed at the center of the voxel's projection in the image plane (note that this does not necessarily correspond to a pixel center). Then the resultant shade and opacity of a pixel is determined by the sum of all the voxel contributions for that pixel, weighted by the kernel.

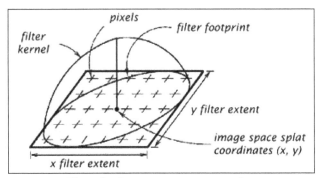

The splatting process reconstruction
and resampling with the 2D filter kernel.

Image Order Rendering

Image-order rendering (also called backward mapping, ray casting, pixel space projection, or image-space rendering) techniques are fundamentally different from object-order rendering techniques. Instead of determining how a data sample affects the pixels on the image plane, we determine the data samples for each pixel on the image plane, which contribute to it.

In ray casting, rays are cast into the dataset. Each ray originates from the viewing (eye) point, and penetrates a pixel in the image plane (screen), and passes through the dataset. At evenly spaced intervals along the ray, sample values are computed using interpolation. The sample values are mapped to display properties such as opacity and color. A local gradient is combined with a local illumination model at each sample point to provide a realistic shading of the object. Final pixel values are found by compositing the color and opacity values along the ray. The composition models the physical reflection and absorption of light.

In ray casting, because of high computational requirements of volume rendering, the data needs to be processed in a pipelined and parallel manner. They offer a flexibility for algorithmic optimizations, but accessing the volume memory in a non-predictable manner significantly slows down the memory performance. The data flow diagram of a ray casting system is shown in figure.

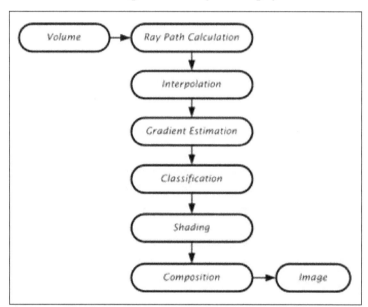

The data flow diagram of a ray casting system.

Any ray casting implementation requires a memory system, ray path calculation, interpolation, gradient estimation, classification, shading, and composition. The *memory system* provides the necessary voxel values at a rate which ultimately dictates the performance of the architecture. The *ray-path calculation* determines the voxels that are penetrated by a given ray: it is tightly coupled with the organization of the memory system. The *interpolation* estimates the value at a re-sample location using a small neighborhood of voxel values. The *gradient estimation* estimates a surface normal using a neighborhood of voxels surrounding the re-sample location. The *classification* maps interpolated sample values and the estimated surface normal to a color and opacity. The *shading* uses the gradient and classification information to compute a color that takes the interaction of light into account on the estimated surfaces in the dataset. The *composition* uses shaded color values and the opacity to compute a final pixel color to display. Ray casting can be classified into two sub-classes according to the level of interpolation used:

1. Algorithms that use a zero order interpolation,

2. Algorithms that use a higher order interpolation.

Algorithms that use a zero order interpolation are Binary Ray Casting, and Discrete Ray Casting. Binary Ray Casting was developed to generate images of surfaces contained within binary volumetric data without the need to explicitly perform boundary detection and hidden-surface removal. For each pixel on the image plane, a ray is cast from that pixel to determine if it intersects the surface contained within the data. In order to determine the first intersection along the ray a stepping technique is used where the value is determined at regular intervals along the ray until the object is intersected. Data samples with a value of 0 are considered to be the background while those with a value of 1 are considered to be a part of the object. In Discrete Ray Casting, instead of traversing a continuous ray and determining the closest data sample for each step, a discrete representation of the ray is traversed. This discrete ray is generated using a 3D Bresenham-like algorithm or a 3D line scan-conversion (voxelization) algorithm. As in the previous algorithms, for each pixel in the image plane, the data samples which contribute to it need to be determined. This could be done by casting a ray from each pixel in the direction of the viewing ray. This ray would be discretized (voxelized), and the contribution from each voxel along the path is considered when producing the final pixel value.

Algorithms that use a higher order interpolation are the image order volume rendering algorithm of Levoy, V-Buffer image order ray casting, and V-Buffer cell-by-cell processing. The image-order volume rendering algorithm developed by Levoy states that given an array of data samples, two new arrays which define the color and opacity at each grid location can be generated using preprocessing techniques. The interpolation functions which specify the sample value, color, and opacity at any location in volume, are then defined by using transfer functions proposed by him. Generating the array of color values involves performing a shading operation. In V-Buffer image order ray casting method, rays are cast from each pixel on the image plane into the volume. For each cell in the volume along the path of this ray, a scalar value is determined at the point where the ray first intersects the cell. The ray is then stepped along until it traverses the entire cell, with calculations for scalar values, shading, opacity, texture mapping, and depth cuing performed at each stepping point. This process is repeated for each cell along the ray, accumulating color and opacity, until the ray exits the volume, or the accumulated opacity reaches to unity. At this point, the accumulated color and opacity for that pixel are stored, and the next ray is cast. The goal of this method is not to produce a realistic image, but instead to provide a representation of the volumetric data which can be interpreted by a scientist or an engineer. In V-Buffer cell-by-cell processing method each cell in the volume is processed in a front-to-back order. Processing begins on the plane closest to the viewpoint, and progresses in a plane-by-plane manner. Within each plane, processing begins with the cell closest to the viewpoint, and then continues in the order of increasing distance from the viewpoint. Each cell is processed by first determining for each scan line in the image plane which pixels are affected by the cell. Then, for each pixel an integration volume is determined. This process continues in a front-to-back order, until all cells have been processed, with an intensity accumulated into pixel values.

Hybrid Order Rendering

This approach to volume rendering adopts the advantages of both object-order and image-order algorithms, and is known as *hybrid projection*. They may be a combination of both image order approach and object order approach or do not fall into either one of them. V-Buffer algorithm divides data set into cells, and render it cell-by-cell, which makes it an object order method. But within each cell ray-casting is used, therefore it is a hybrid approach. In the volume data set is rendered by first shearing the volume slice to make ray traversal trivial, and then warps the intermediate image to the final image. EM-Cube is a parallel ray casting engine that implements a hybrid order algorithm. The most popular hybrid algorithm is the shear-warp factorization.

The Shear-warp Factorization

Image-order algorithms have the disadvantage that the spatial data structure must be traversed once for every ray, resulting in redundant computations. Object-order algorithms operate through the volume data in the storage order making it difficult to implement an early ray termination, an effective optimization in ray-casting algorithms. The shear-warp algorithm combines the advantages of image-order and object-order algorithms. The method is based on a factorization of the viewing matrix into a 3D shear parallel to the slices of the volume data, a projection to form a distorted intermediate image, and a 2D warp to produce the final image. The advantage of shear-warp factorizations is that scanlines of the volume data and scanlines of the intermediate image are always aligned.

The arbitrary nature of the transformation from object space to image space complicates efficient, high-quality filtering and projection in object-order volume rendering algorithms. This problem is solved by transforming the volume to an intermediate coordinate system for which there is a very simple mapping from the object coordinate system and which allows an efficient projection. The intermediate coordinate system is called *sheared object space* and by construction, in sheared object space all viewing rays are parallel to the third coordinate axis.

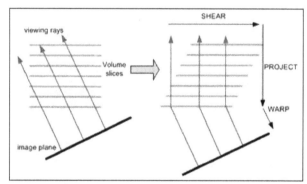

A volume is transformed to sheared object space for a parallel projection by translating each slice. The projection in sheared object space is simple and efficient.

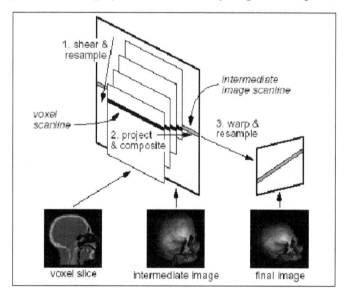

The shear-warp algorithm includes three conceptual steps: shear and resample the volume slices, project resampled voxel scanlines onto intermediate image scanlines, and warp the intermediate image into the final image.

Figure illustrates the transformation from object space to sheared object space for a parallel projection. The volume is assumed to be sampled on a rectilinear grid. After the transformation the volume data is sheared parallel to the set of slices that is most perpendicular to the viewing direction and the viewing rays are perpendicular to the slices.

There are three variations of shear warp algorithm. Parallel projection rendering algorithm is optimized for parallel projections and assumes that the opacity transfer function does not change between renderings, but the viewing and shading parameters can be modified. Perspective projection rendering algorithm supports perspective projections. Fast classification algorithm allows the opacity transfer function to be modified as well as the viewing and shading parameters, with a moderate performance penalty.

Optimization in Volume Rendering

Volume rendering can produce informative images that can be useful in data analysis, but a major drawback of the techniques is the time required to generate a high-quality image. Several volume rendering optimizations are developed which decrease rendering times, and therefore increase interactivity and productivity It is obvious that one can not hope to have a real time volume rending in the near future without investing time, effort, and ingenuity in accelerating the process through software optimizations and hardware implementations. There are five main approaches to overcoming this seemingly insurmountable performance barrier:

1. Data reduction by means of model extraction or data simplification,

2. Software-based algorithm optimization and acceleration,

3. Implementation on general purpose parallel architectures,

4. Use of contemporary off-the-shelf graphics hardware, and

5. Realization of special-purpose volume rendering engines.

Task and Data Decomposition

Since the work is essentially defined as "operations on data", the choice of task decomposition has a direct impact on data access patterns. On distributed memory architectures, where remote memory references are usually much more expensive than local memory references, the issues of task decomposition and data distribution are inseparable. Shared memory systems offer more flexibility, since all processors have an equal access to the data. While data locality is still important in achieving good caching performance, the penalties for global memory references tend to be less severe, and static assignment of data to processors is not generally required.

There are two main strategies for task decomposition. In an object-parallel approach, tasks are formed by partitioning either the geometric description of the scene or the associated object space. Rendering operations are then applied in parallel to subsets of the geometric data, producing pixel values which must then be integrated into a final image. In contrast, image-parallel algorithms reverse this mapping. Tasks are formed by partitioning the image space, and each task renders the geometric primitives which contribute to the pixels which it has been assigned. To achieve a better balance among the various overheads, some algorithms adopt a hybrid approach, incorporating features of both object- and image-parallel methods. These techniques partition both the object and image spaces, breaking the rendering pipeline in the middle and communicating intermediate results from object rendering tasks to image rendering tasks.

Volume rendering algorithms typically loops through the data, calculating the contribution of each volume sample to pixels on the image plane. This is a costly operation for moderate to large sized data, leading to rendering times that are non-interactive. Viewing the intermediate results in the image plane may be useful, but these partial image results are not always representatives of the final image. For the purpose of interaction, it is useful to be able to generate a lower quality image in a shorter amount of time, which is known as *data simplification*. For data sets with binary sample values, bits could be packed into bytes such that each byte represents a $2 \times 2 \times 2$ portion of the data. The data would be processed bit-by-bit to generate the full resolution image, but lower resolution image could be generated by processing the data byte-by-byte. If more than four bits of the byte are set, the byte is considered to represent an element of the object, otherwise it represents the background. This will produce an image with one-half the linear resolution in approximately one eighth the time.

Software-based Algorithm Optimization and Acceleration

Software based algorithm optimizations are divided into two broad groups according to the rendering methods they use, that is optimization methods for object-space rendering and image-space rendering. The methods that have been suggested to reduce the amount of computations needed for the transformation by exploiting the spatial coherency between voxels for object-space rendering are:

1. Recursive "divide and conquer",

2. Pre-calculated tables,

3. Incremental transformation, and

4. Shearing-based transforms.

The major algorithmic strategy for parallelizing volume rendering is the divide-and-conquer paradigm. The volume rendering problem can be subdivided either in data space or in image space. Data-space subdivision assigns the computation associated with particular sub volumes to processors, while image-space subdivision distributes the computation associated with particular portions of the image space. This method exploits coherency in voxel space by representing the 3D volume by an octree. A group of neighboring voxels having the same value may, under some restrictions, be grouped into a uniform cubic sub volume. This aggregate of voxels can be transformed and rendered as a uniform unit instead of processing each of its voxels.

The table-driven transformation method is based on the observation that volume transformation involves the multiplication of the matrix elements with integer values which are always in the range of volume resolution. Therefore, in a short preprocessing stage each matrix element is allocated a table. All the multiplication calculations required for the transformation matrix multiplication are stored into a look-up table. The transformation of a voxel can then be accomplished simply by accessing the look-up table, the entry accessed in the table depending on the xyz coordinates of the voxel. During the transformation stage, coordinate by matrix multiplication is replaced by table lookup.

The incremental transformation method is based on the observation that the transformation of a voxel can be incrementally computed given the transformed vector of the voxel. To employ this approach, all volume elements, including the empty ones, have to be transformed. This approach is especially attractive for vector processors since the transformations of the set of voxels can be computed from the transformation of the vector by adding, to each element in this vector.

Machiraju and Yagel exploit coherency within the volume to implement a novel incremental transformation scheme. A seed voxel is first transformed using the normal matrix-vector multiplication. All other voxels are then transformed in an incremental manner with just three extra additions per coordinate.

The shearing algorithm decomposes the 3D affine transformation into five 1D shearing transformations. The major advantage of this approach is its ability (using simple averaging techniques) to overcome some of the sampling problems causing the production of low quality images. In addition, this approach replaces the 3D transformation by five 1D transformations which require only one floating-point addition each.

The image-space optimization methods are based on the observation that most of the existing methods for speeding up the process of ray casting rely on one or more of the following principles:

1. Pixel-space coherency,

2. Object-space coherency,

3. Inter-ray coherency,

4. Frame coherency, and

5. Space-leaping.

Pixel-space coherency means that there is a high coherency between pixels in the image space. It is highly probable that between two pixels having identical or similar color we will find another pixel having the same or similar color. Therefore, it might be the case that we could avoid sending a ray for such obviously identical pixels.

Object-space coherency means that there is coherency between voxels in the object space. Therefore, it should be possible to avoid sampling in 3D regions having uniform or similar values. In this method the ray starts sampling the volume in a low frequency (i.e., large steps between sample points). If a large value difference is encountered between two adjacent samples, additional samples are taken between them to resolve ambiguities in these high frequency regions.

Inter-ray coherency means that, in parallel viewing, all rays have the same form and there is no need to reactivate the discrete line algorithm for each ray. Instead, we can compute the form of the ray once and store it in a data structure called the ray-template. Since all the rays are parallel, one ray can be discretized and used as a "template" for all other rays.

Frame coherency means that when an animation sequence is generated, in many cases, there is not much difference between successive images. Therefore, much of the work invested to produce one image may be used to expedite the generation of the next image.

The most prolific and effective branch of volume rendering acceleration techniques involve the utilization of the fifth principle: speeding up ray casting by providing efficient means to traverse the empty space, that is space leaping. The passage of a ray through the volume is two phased. In the first phase the ray advances through the empty space searching for an object. In the second phase the ray integrates colors and opacities as it penetrates the object. Since the passage of empty space does not contribute to the final image it is observed that skipping the empty space could provide a significant speed up without affecting the image quality.

Parallel and Distributed Architectures

The need for interactive or real-time response in many applications places additional demands on processing power. The only practical way to obtain the needed computational power is to exploit multiple processing units to speed up the rendering task, a concept which has become known as parallel rendering.

Several different types of parallelism can be applied in the rendering process. These include functional parallelism, data parallelism, and temporal parallelism. Some are more appropriate to specific applications or specific rendering methods, while others have a broader applicability. The basic types can also be combined into hybrid systems which exploit multiple forms of parallelism.

One way to obtain parallelism is to split the rendering process into several distinct functions which can be applied in series to individual data items. If a processing unit is assigned to each function (or group of functions) and a data path is provided from one unit to the next, a rendering pipeline is formed. As a processing unit completes work on one data item, it forwards it to the next unit, and receives a new item from its upstream neighbor. Once the pipeline is filled, the degree of parallelism achieved is proportional to the number of functional units. The functional approach works especially well for polygon and surface rendering applications.

Instead of performing a sequence of rendering functions on a single data stream, it may be preferable to split the data into multiple streams and operate on several items simultaneously by replicating a number of identical rendering units. The parallelism achievable with this approach is not limited by the number of stages in the rendering pipeline, but rather by economic and technical constraints on the number of processing units which can be incorporated into a single system.

In animation applications, where hundreds or thousands of high-quality images must be produced for a subsequent playback, the time to render individual frames may not be as important as the overall time required to render all of them. In this case, parallelism may be obtained by decomposing the problem in the time domain. The fundamental unit of work is a complete image, and each processor is assigned a number of frames to render, along with the data needed to produce those frames.

It is certainly possible to incorporate multiple forms of parallelism in a single system. For example, the functional- and data-parallel approaches may be combined by replicating all or a part of the rendering pipeline.

Commercial Graphics Hardware

One of the most common resources for rendering is off-the-shelf graphics hardware. However, these polygon rendering engines seem inherently unsuitable to the task. Recently, some new methods have tapped to this rendering power by either utilizing texture mapping capabilities for rendering splats, or by exploiting solid texturing capabilities to implement a slicing-based volume rendering

The commercially available solid texturing hardware allows mapping of volumes on polygons using these methods. These 3D texture maps are mapped on polygons in 3D space using either zero order or first order interpolation. By rendering polygons, slicing the volume and perpendicular to the view direction one generates a view of a rectangular volume data set.

Special Purpose Hardware

To fulfill the special requirements of high-speed volume visualization, several architectures have been proposed and a few have been built. The earliest proposed volume visualization system was the "Physician's Workstation" which proposed real-time medical volume viewing using a custom hardware accelerator. The Voxel Display Processor (VDP) was a set of parallel processing elements. A 64^3 prototype was constructed which generated 16 arbitrary projections each second by implementing depth-only-shading. Another system which presented a scalable method was SCOPE architecture. It was also implementing the depth-only-shading scheme.

The VOGUE architecture was developed at the University of Tübingen, Germany. A compact volume rendering accelerator, which implements the conventional volume rendering ray casting pipeline proposed in, originally called the Voxel Engine for Real-time Visualization and Examination (VERVE), achieved 2.5 frames/second for 256^3 datasets.

The design of VERVE was reconsidered in the context of a low cost PCI coprocessor board. This FPGA implementation called VIZARD was able to render 10 perspective, ray cast, grayscale 256 x 200 images of a 256^2 x 222 volume per second.

VIZARD II architecture is at the University of Tübingen to bring interactive ray casting into the realm of desktop computers and was designed to interface to a standard PC system using the PCI bus. It sustained a frame rate of 10 frames/second in a 256^3 volume.

VIZARD II co-processor card.

In DOGGETT system an array-based architecture for volume rendering is described. It performs ray casting by rotating planes of voxels with a warp array, then passing rays through it in the ray array. The estimated performance for an FPGA implementation is 15 frames/second yielding 384^2 images of 256^3 data sets.

The VIRIM architecture has been developed and assembled in the University of Mannheim which implements the Heidelberg ray tracing model, to achieve real-time visualization on moderate sized (256 x 256 x 128) datasets with a high image quality. VIRIM was capable of producing shadows and supports perspective projections. One VIRIM module with four boards has been assembled and achieved 2.5 Hz frame rates for 256 x 256 x 128 datasets. To achieve interactive frame rates, multiple rendering modules have to be used; however, dataset duplication was required. Four modules (16 boards) were estimated to achieve 10 Hz for the same dataset size, and eight modules (32 boards) were estimated to achieve 10 Hz for 256^3 datasets.

VIRIM II improved on VIRIM by reducing the memory bottleneck. The basic design of a single memory interface was unchanged. To achieve higher frame rates or to handle higher resolutions, multiple nodes must be connected on a ring network that scales with the number of nodes. It was predicted that using 512 nodes, a system could render 2048^3 datasets at 30 Hz.

The hierarchical, object order volume rendering architecture BELA, with eight projection processors and image assemblers, was capable of rendering a 256^3 volume into an imageat a 12 Hz rendering rate.

The Distributed Volume Visualization Architecture, DIV^{2}A, was an architecture that performed conventional ray casting with a linear array of custom processors. To achieve 20Hz frame rates with a 256^3 volume, 16 processing elements using several chips each were required.

The volume rendering architecture with the longest history is the Cube family. Beginning with Cube-1 and spanning to Cube-4 and beyond, the architecture provides a complete, real-time volume rendering visualization system. A mass market version of Cube-4 was introduced in 1998 providing real-time volume rendering of 256^3 volumes at 30 Hz for inclusion in a desktop personal computer.

The Cube-1 concept was proven with a wire-wrapped prototype. 2D projections were generated at a frame rate of 16 Hz for a 512^3 volume. The main problems with the implementation of Cube-1 were the large physical size and the long settling time. To improve these characteristics, Cube-2 was developed.

A 16^3 resolution prototype of Cube-1 architecture.

Cube-2 implemented a 16^3 VLSI version of Cube-1. A single chip contained all the memory and processing of a whole Cube-1 board.

A 16³ resolution Cube-2 VLSI implementation.

Although the prior Cube designs were fast, the foundations of volume sampling and rendering were not fully developed so the architecture was unable to provide higher order sampling and shading. Cube-3 improved the quality of rendering by supporting full 3D interpolation of samples along a ray, accurate gray-level gradient estimation, and flexible volumetric shading and provided real-time rendering of 512^3 volumes.

Due to the capability of providing real-time rendering, the cost and size of the Cube-3 was unreasonable. This prompted the development of Cube-4 which avoided all global communication, except at the pixel level and achieved rendering in 128^3 datasets in 0.65 seconds at 0.96 MHz processing frequency. There is also a new version Cube-4L which is currently being implemented by Japan Radio Co. as part of a real-time 3D ultrasound scanner.

EM-Cube is a commercial version of the high-performance Cube-4 volume rendering architecture that was originally developed at the State University of New York at Stony Brook, and is implemented as a PCI card for Windows NT computers. EM-Cube is a parallel projection engine with multiple rendering pipelines. Eight pipelines operating in parallel can process $8 \times 66 \times 10^6$ or approximately 533 million samples per second. This is sufficient to render 256^3 volumes at 30 frames per second. It does not support perspective projections.

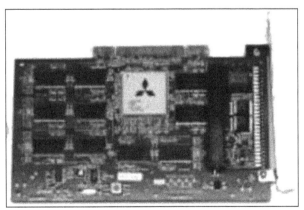

The VolumePro PCI card.

VolumePro, the first single chip rendering system is developed at SUNY Stony Brook and is based on the Cube-4 volume rendering architecture. VolumePro is the commercial implementation of

EM-Cube, and it makes several important enhancements to its architecture and design. Volume-Pro is now available on a low cost PCI board delivering the best price/performance ratio of any available volume rendering system.

Ray Tracing

In computer graphics, ray tracing is a rendering technique for generating an image by tracing the path of light as pixels in an image plane and simulating the effects of its encounters with virtual objects. The technique is capable of producing a very high degree of visual realism, usually higher than that of typical scanline rendering methods, but at a greater computational cost. This makes ray tracing best suited for applications where taking a relatively long time to render a frame can be tolerated, such as in still images and film and television visual effects, and more poorly suited for real-time applications such as video games where speed is critical. Ray tracing is capable of simulating a wide variety of optical effects, such as reflection and refraction, scattering, and dispersion phenomena (such as chromatic aberration).

This recursive ray tracing of a sphere demonstrates the effects of
shallow depth of field, area light sources and diffuse interreflection.

The idea of ray tracing comes from as early as 16th century when it was described by Albrecht Dürer, who is credited for its invention. In 1982, Scott Roth used the term ray casting in the context of computer graphics.

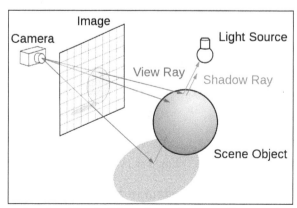

The ray tracing algorithm builds an image by extending rays into a scene.

Optical ray tracing describes a method for producing visual images constructed in 3D computer graphics environments, with more photorealism than either ray casting or scanline rendering techniques. It works by tracing a path from an imaginary eye through each pixel in a virtual screen, and calculating the color of the object visible through it.

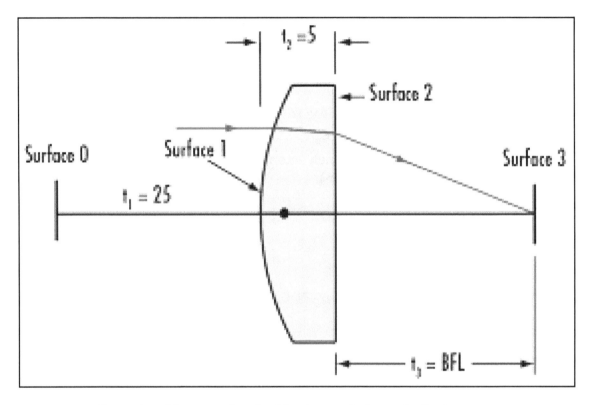

Illustration of the ray tracing algorithm for one pixel up to the first bounce.

Scenes in ray tracing are described mathematically by a programmer or by a visual artist (typically using intermediary tools). Scenes may also incorporate data from images and models captured by means such as digital photography.

Typically, each ray must be tested for intersection with some subset of all the objects in the scene. Once the nearest object has been identified, the algorithm will estimate the incoming light at the point of intersection, examine the material properties of the object, and combine this information to calculate the final color of the pixel. Certain illumination algorithms and reflective or translucent materials may require more rays to be re-cast into the scene.

It may at first seem counterintuitive or "backward" to send rays *away* from the camera, rather than *into* it (as actual light does in reality), but doing so is many orders of magnitude more efficient. Since the overwhelming majority of light rays from a given light source do not make it directly into the viewer's eye, a "forward" simulation could potentially waste a tremendous amount of computation on light paths that are never recorded.

Therefore, the shortcut taken in raytracing is to presuppose that a given ray intersects the view frame. After either a maximum number of reflections or a ray traveling a certain distance without intersection, the ray ceases to travel and the pixel's value is updated.

Calculate Rays for Rectangular Viewport

On input we have (in calculation we use vector normalization and cross product):

- $E \in \mathbb{R}^3$ eye position

- $T \in \mathbb{R}^3$ target position

- $\theta \in [0, \pi]$ field of view - for human we can assume $\approx \pi / 2$ rad $= 90°$

- $m, k \in \mathbb{N}$ numbers of square pixels on viewport vertical and horizontal direction

- $i, j \in \mathbb{N}, 1 \leq i \leq k \wedge 1 \leq j \leq m$ numbers of actual pixel

- $\vec{w} \in \mathbb{R}^3$ vertical vector which indicates where is up and down, usually $\vec{w} = [0, 1, 0]$ (not visible on picture) - roll component which determine viewport rotation around point C (where the axis of rotation is the ET section).

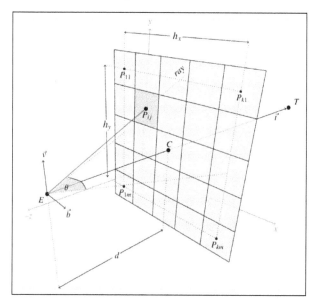

The idea is to find the position of each viewport pixel center P_{ij} which allows us to find the line going from eye E through that pixel and finally get the ray described by point E and vector $\vec{R}_{ij} = P_{ij} - E$ (or its normalisation $_{ij}$). First we need to find the coordinates of the bottom left viewport pixel P_{1m} and find the next pixel by making a shift along directions parallel to viewport (vectors $\vec{b}_n$ i $\vec{v}_n$) multiplied by the size of the pixel. Below we introduce formulas which include distance d between the eye and the viewport. However, this value will be reduced during ray normalization $\vec{r}_{ij}$ (so you might as well accept that $d = 1$ and remove it from calculations).

Pre-calculations: let's find and normalise vector $\vec{t}$ and vectors $\vec{b}, \vec{v}$ which are parallel to the viewport:

$$\vec{t} = T - E, \qquad \vec{b} = \vec{w} \times \vec{t}$$

$$\vec{t}_n = \frac{\vec{t}}{\| \vec{t} \|}, \qquad \vec{b}_n = \frac{\vec{b}}{\| \vec{b} \|}, \qquad \vec{v}_n = \vec{t}_n \times \vec{b}_n$$

note that viewport center $C = E + \vec{t}_n d$, next we calculate viewport sizes h_x, h_y divided by 2 including aspect ratio $\dfrac{m}{k}$:

$$g_x = \frac{h_x}{2} = d \tan\frac{\theta}{2}, \qquad g_y = \frac{h_y}{2} = g_x \frac{m}{k}$$

and then we calculate next-pixel shifting vectors q_x, q_y along directions parallel to viewport $(\vec{b}, \vec{v})$, and left bottom pixel center p_{1m} :

$$\vec{q}_x = \frac{2g_x}{k-1}\vec{b}_n, \qquad \vec{q}_y = \frac{2g_y}{m-1}\vec{v}_n, \qquad \vec{p}_{1m} = \vec{t}_n d - g_x\vec{b}_n - g_y\vec{v}_n$$

Calculations: note $P_{ij} = E + \vec{p}_{ij}$ and ray $\vec{R}_{ij} = P_{ij} - E = \vec{p}_{ij}$ so:

$$\vec{p}_{ij} = \vec{p}_{1m} + \vec{q}_x(i-1) + \vec{q}_y(j-1)$$

$$\vec{r}_{ij} = \frac{\vec{R}_{ij}}{\| \vec{R}_{ij} \|} = \frac{\vec{p}_{ij}}{\| \vec{p}_{ij} \|}$$

Ray Tracing Computer Algorithm and its Genesis

In nature, a light source emits a ray of light which travels, eventually, to a surface that interrupts its progress. One can think of this "ray" as a stream of photons traveling along the same path. In a perfect vacuum this ray will be a straight line (ignoring relativistic effects). Any combination of four things might happen with this light ray: absorption, reflection, refraction and fluorescence. A surface may absorb part of the light ray, resulting in a loss of intensity of the reflected and/or refracted light. It might also reflect all or part of the light ray, in one or more directions. If the surface has any transparent or translucent properties, it refracts a portion of the light beam into itself in a different direction while absorbing some (or all) of the spectrum (and possibly altering the color). Less commonly, a surface may absorb some portion of the light and fluorescently re-emit the light at a longer wavelength color in a random direction, though this is rare enough that it can be discounted from most rendering applications. Between absorption, reflection, refraction and fluorescence, all of the incoming light must be accounted for, and no more. A surface cannot, for instance, reflect 66% of an incoming light ray, and refract 50%, since the two would add up to be 116%. From here, the reflected and/or refracted rays may strike other surfaces, where their absorptive, refractive, reflective and fluorescent properties again affect the progress of the incoming rays. Some of these rays travel in such a way that they hit our eye, causing us to see the scene and so contribute to the final rendered image.

Ray Casting Algorithm

The first ray tracing algorithm used for rendering was presented by Arthur Appel in 1968. This algorithm has since been termed "ray casting". The idea behind ray casting is to shoot rays from the eye, one per pixel, and find the closest object blocking the path of that ray. Think of an image as a screen-door, with each square in the screen being a pixel. This is then the object the eye sees through that pixel. Using the material properties and the effect of the lights in the scene, this algorithm can determine the shading of this object. The simplifying assumption is made that if a surface faces a light, the light will reach that surface and not be blocked or in shadow. The shading of the surface is computed using traditional 3D computer graphics shading models. One important advantage ray casting offered over older scanline algorithms was its ability to easily deal with non-planar surfaces and solids, such as cones and spheres. If a mathematical surface can be intersected by a ray, it can be rendered using ray casting. Elaborate objects can be created by using solid modeling techniques and easily rendered.

Recursive Ray Tracing Algorithm

The number of reflections a "ray" can take and how it is affected each time it encounters a surface is all controlled via software settings during ray tracing.

In addition to the high degree of realism, ray tracing can simulate the effects of a camera due to depth of field and aperture shape (in this case a hexagon).

The next important research breakthrough came from Turner Whitted in 1979. Previous algorithms traced rays from the eye into the scene until they hit an object, but determined the ray color without recursively tracing more rays. Whitted continued the process. When a ray hits a surface, it can generate up to three new types of rays: reflection, refraction, and shadow. A reflection ray is traced in the mirror-reflection direction. The closest object it intersects is what will be seen in the reflection. Refraction rays traveling through transparent material work similarly, with the addition that a refractive ray could be entering or exiting a material. A shadow ray is traced toward each light. If any opaque object is found between the surface and the light, the surface is in shadow and the light does not illuminate it. This recursive ray tracing added more realism to ray traced images.

The number of refractions a "ray" can take and how it is affected each time it encounters a surface is all controlled via software settings during ray tracing. Here, each ray was allowed to refract and reflect up to 9 times. Fresnel reflections were used.

Advantages over other Rendering Methods

Ray tracing's popularity stems from its basis in a realistic simulation of lighting over other rendering methods (such as scanline rendering or ray casting). Effects such as reflections and shadows, which are difficult to simulate using other algorithms, are a natural result of the ray tracing algorithm. The computational independence of each ray makes ray tracing amenable to parallelization.

Disadvantages

A serious disadvantage of ray tracing is performance (though it can in theory be faster than traditional scanline rendering depending on scene complexity vs. number of pixels on-screen). Scanline algorithms and other algorithms use data coherence to share computations between pixels, while ray tracing normally starts the process anew, treating each eye ray separately. However, this separation offers other advantages, such as the ability to shoot more rays as needed to perform spatial anti-aliasing and improve image quality where needed.

Although it does handle interreflection and optical effects such as refraction accurately, traditional ray tracing is also not necessarily photorealistic. True photorealism occurs when the rendering equation is closely approximated or fully implemented. Implementing the rendering equation gives true photorealism, as the equation describes every physical effect of light flow. However, this is usually infeasible given the computing resources required.

The realism of all rendering methods can be evaluated as an approximation to the equation. Ray tracing, if it is limited to Whitted's algorithm, is not necessarily the most realistic. Methods that trace rays, but include additional techniques (photon mapping, path tracing), give a far more accurate simulation of real-world lighting.

Reversed Direction of Traversal of Scene by the Rays

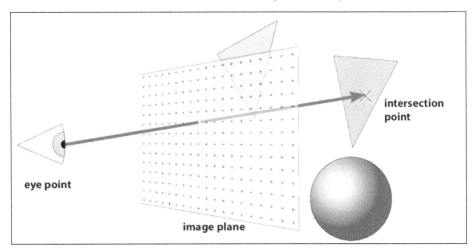

The process of shooting rays from the eye to the light source to render an image is sometimes called backwards ray tracing, since it is the opposite direction photons actually travel. However, there is confusion with this terminology. Early ray tracing was always done from the eye, and early researchers such as James Arvo used the term backwards ray tracing to mean shooting rays from the lights and gathering the results. Therefore, it is clearer to distinguish eye-based versus light-based ray tracing.

While the direct illumination is generally best sampled using eye-based ray tracing, certain indirect effects can benefit from rays generated from the lights. Caustics are bright patterns caused by the focusing of light off a wide reflective region onto a narrow area of (near-)diffuse surface. An algorithm that casts rays directly from lights onto reflective objects, tracing their paths to the eye, will better sample this phenomenon. This integration of eye-based and light-based rays is often expressed as bidirectional path tracing, in which paths are traced from both the eye and lights, and the paths subsequently joined by a connecting ray after some length.

Photon mapping is another method that uses both light-based and eye-based ray tracing; in an initial pass, energetic photons are traced along rays from the light source so as to compute an estimate of radiant flux as a function of 3-dimensional space (the eponymous photon map itself). In a subsequent pass, rays are traced from the eye into the scene to determine the visible surfaces, and the photon map is used to estimate the illumination at the visible surface points. The advantage of photon mapping versus bidirectional path tracing is the ability to achieve significant reuse of photons, reducing computation, at the cost of statistical bias.

An additional problem occurs when light must pass through a very narrow aperture to illuminate the scene (consider a darkened room, with a door slightly ajar leading to a brightly lit room), or a scene in which most points do not have direct line-of-sight to any light source (such as with ceiling-directed light fixtures or torchieres). In such cases, only a very small subset of paths will transport energy; Metropolis light transport is a method which begins with a random search of the path space, and when energetic paths are found, reuses this information by exploring the nearby space of rays.

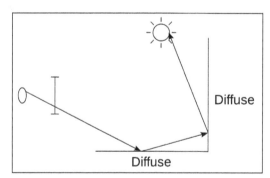

To the right is an image showing a simple example of a path of rays recursively generated from the camera (or eye) to the light source using the above algorithm. A diffuse surface reflects light in all directions.

First, a ray is created at an eyepoint and traced through a pixel and into the scene, where it hits a diffuse surface. From that surface the algorithm recursively generates a reflection ray, which is traced through the scene, where it hits another diffuse surface. Finally, another reflection ray is generated and traced through the scene, where it hits the light source and is absorbed. The color of the pixel now depends on the colors of the first and second diffuse surface and the color of the light emitted from the light source. For example, if the light source emitted white light and the two diffuse surfaces were blue, then the resulting color of the pixel is blue.

Example:

As a demonstration of the principles involved in raytracing, consider how one would find the intersection between a ray and a sphere. This is merely the math behind the line–sphere intersection and the subsequent determination of the colour of the pixel being calculated. There is, of course, far more to the general process of raytracing, but this demonstrates an example of the algorithms used.

In vector notation, the equation of a sphere with center c and radius r is:

$$\|x-c\|^2 = r^2.$$

Any point on a ray starting from point s with direction d (here d is a unit vector) can be written as:

$$x = s + td,$$

where t is its distance between x and s. In our problem, we know c, r ,s (e.g. the position of a light source) and , and we need to find t. Therefore, we substitute for x:

$$\|s+td-c\|^2 = r^2.$$

Let $v \overset{\text{def}}{=} s-c$ for simplicity; then:

$$\| v + td \|^2 = r^2$$
$$v^2 + t^2 d^2 + 2v{\cdot}td = r^2$$
$$(d^2)t^2 + (2v{\cdot}d)t + (v^2 - r^2) = 0.$$

Knowing that d is a unit vector allows us this minor simplification:

$$t^2 + (2\,v{\cdot}d)\,t + (v^2 - r^2) = 0.$$

This quadratic equation has solutions:

$$t = \frac{-(2\,v{\cdot}d) \pm \sqrt{(2\,v{\cdot}d)^2 - 4(v^2 - r^2)}}{2} = -(v \times d) \pm \sqrt{(v \times d)^2 - (v^2 - r^2)}.$$

The two values of t found by solving this equation are the two ones such that $s + td$ are the points where the ray intersects the sphere.

Any value which is negative does not lie on the ray, but rather in the opposite half-line (i.e. the one starting from s with opposite direction).

If the quantity under the square root (the discriminant) is negative, then the ray does not intersect the sphere.

Let us suppose now that there is at least a positive solution, and let t be the minimal one. In addition, let us suppose that the sphere is the nearest object on our scene intersecting our ray, and that it is made of a reflective material. We need to find in which direction the light ray is reflected. The laws of reflection state that the angle of reflection is equal and opposite to the angle of incidence between the incident ray and the normal to the sphere.

The normal to the sphere is simply:

$$n = \frac{y-c}{\|y-c\|},$$

where $y = s + td$ is the intersection point found before. The reflection direction can be found by a reflection of d with respect to n , that is:

$$r = d - 2(n \cdot d)n.$$

Thus the reflected ray has equation:

$$x = y + ur.$$

Now we only need to compute the intersection of the latter ray with our field of view, to get the pixel which our reflected light ray will hit. Lastly, this pixel is set to an appropriate color, taking into account how the color of the original light source and the one of the sphere are combined by the reflection.

Adaptive Depth Control

Adaptive depth control means that the renderer stops generating reflected/transmitted rays when the computed intensity becomes less than a certain threshold. There must always be a set maximum depth or else the program would generate an infinite number of rays. But it is not always necessary to go to the maximum depth if the surfaces are not highly reflective. To test for this the ray tracer must compute and keep the product of the global and reflection coefficients as the rays are traced.

Example: let Kr = 0.5 for a set of surfaces. Then from the first surface the maximum contribution is 0.5, for the reflection from the second: 0.5 * 0.5 = 0.25, the third: 0.25 * 0.5 = 0.125, the fourth: 0.125 * 0.5 = 0.0625, the fifth: 0.0625 * 0.5 = 0.03125, etc. In addition we might implement a distance attenuation factor such as $1/D2$, which would also decrease the intensity contribution.

For a transmitted ray we could do something similar but in that case the distance traveled through the object would cause even faster intensity decrease. As an example of this, Hall & Greenberg found that even for a very reflective scene, using this with a maximum depth of 15 resulted in an average ray tree depth of 1.7.

Bounding Volumes

We enclose groups of objects in sets of hierarchical bounding volumes and first test for intersection with the bounding volume, and then only if there is an intersection, against the objects enclosed by the volume.

Bounding volumes should be easy to test for intersection, for example a sphere or box (slab). The best bounding volume will be determined by the shape of the underlying object or objects. For example, if the objects are long and thin then a sphere will enclose mainly empty space and a box is much better. Boxes are also easier for hierarchical bounding volumes.

Note that using a hierarchical system like this (assuming it is done carefully) changes the intersection computational time from a linear dependence on the number of objects to something between linear and a logarithmic dependence. This is because, for a perfect case, each intersection test would divide the possibilities by two, and we would have a binary tree type structure. Spatial subdivision methods, discussed below, try to achieve this.

Kay & Kajiya give a list of desired properties for hierarchical bounding volumes:

- Subtrees should contain objects that are near each other and the further down the tree the closer should be the objects.

- The volume of each node should be minimal.

- The sum of the volumes of all bounding volumes should be minimal.

- Greater attention should be placed on the nodes near the root since pruning a branch near the root will remove more potential objects than one farther down the tree.

- The time spent constructing the hierarchy should be much less than the time saved by using it.

In Real Time

The first implementation of a "real-time" ray-tracer was the LINKS-1 Computer Graphics System built in 1982 at Osaka University's School of Engineering, by professors Ohmura Kouichi, Shirakawa Isao and Kawata Toru with 50 students. It was a massively parallel processing computer system with 514 microprocessors (257 Zilog Z8001's and 257 iAPX 86's), used for rendering realistic 3D computer graphics with high-speed ray tracing. According to the Information Processing Society of Japan: "The core of 3D image rendering is calculating the luminance of each pixel making up a rendered surface from the given viewpoint, light source, and object position. The LINKS-1 system was developed to realize an image rendering methodology in which each pixel could be parallel processed independently using ray tracing. By developing a new software methodology specifically for high-speed image rendering, LINKS-1 was able to rapidly render highly realistic images." It was "used to create the world's first 3D planetarium-like video of the entire heavens that was made completely with computer graphics. The video was presented at the Fujitsu pavilion at the 1985 International Exposition in Tsukuba." The LINKS-1 was the world's most powerful computer at the time, as of 1984.

The earliest public record of "real-time" ray tracing with interactive rendering (i.e., updates greater than a frame per second) was credited at the 2005 SIGGRAPH computer graphics conference as being the REMRT/RT tools developed in 1986 by Mike Muuss for the BRL-CAD solid modeling system. Initially published in 1987 at USENIX, the BRL-CAD ray-tracer was an early implementation of a parallel network distributed ray-tracing system that achieved several frames per second in rendering performance. This performance was attained by means of the highly optimized yet platform independent LIBRT ray-tracing engine in BRL-CAD and by using solid implicit CSG geometry on several shared memory parallel machines over a commodity network. BRL-CAD's ray-tracer, including the REMRT/RT tools, continue to be available and developed today as Open source software.

Since then, there have been considerable efforts and research towards implementing ray tracing in real-time speeds for a variety of purposes on stand-alone desktop configurations. These purposes include interactive 3D graphics applications such as demoscene productions, computer and video games, and image rendering. Some real-time software 3D engines based on ray tracing have been developed by hobbyist demo programmers since the late 1990s.

The OpenRT project includes a highly optimized software core for ray tracing along with an Open-GL-like API in order to offer an alternative to the current rasterisation based approach for interactive 3D graphics. Ray tracing hardware, such as the experimental Ray Processing Unit developed at the Saarland University, has been designed to accelerate some of the computationally intensive operations of ray tracing. In 2007, the University of Saarland revealed an implementation of a high-performance ray tracing engine that allowed computer games to be rendered via ray tracing without intensive resource usage.

In 2008 Intel demonstrated a special version of Enemy Territory: Quake Wars, titled Quake Wars: Ray Traced, using ray tracing for rendering, running in basic HD (720p) resolution. ETQW operated at 14-29 frames per second. The demonstration ran on a 16-core (4 socket, 4 core) Xeon Tigerton system running at 2.93 GHz.

At SIGGRAPH 2009, Nvidia announced OptiX, a free API for real-time ray tracing on Nvidia GPUs. The API exposes seven programmable entry points within the ray tracing pipeline, allowing for custom cameras, ray-primitive intersections, shaders, shadowing, etc. This flexibility enables bidirectional path tracing, Metropolis light transport, and many other rendering algorithms that cannot be implemented with tail recursion. Nvidia has shipped over 350,000,000 OptiX capable GPUs as of April 2013. OptiX-based renderers are used in Adobe AfterEffects, Bunkspeed Shot, Autodesk Maya, 3ds max, and many other renderers.

AMD enabled real-time ray-tracing on Vega graphics cards through GPUOpen Radeon ProRender. The company is reportedly planning to release the second generation Navi GPUs with hardware accelerated ray tracing in 2020. Nvidia has announced real-time ray-tracing on their Quadro RTX workstation graphics cards. The Nvidia GeForce 20 series of video cards have real-time ray tracing capabilities.

Imagination Technologies offers a free API called OpenRL which accelerates tail recursive ray tracing-based rendering algorithms and, together with their proprietary ray tracing hardware, works with Autodesk Maya to provide what 3D World calls "real-time raytracing to the everyday artist".

In 2014, a demo of the PlayStation 4 video game The Tomorrow Children, developed by Q-Games and SIE Japan Studio, demonstrated new lighting techniques developed by Q-Games, notably cascaded voxel cone ray tracing, which simulates lighting in real-time and uses more realistic reflections rather than screen space reflections.

The upcoming game MechWarrior 5: Mercenaries is stated to feature ray tracing. As of 2018, the option is admitted to be a strain even on the highest-end graphic cards.

Computational Complexity

Various complexity results have been proven for certain formulations of the ray tracing problem. In particular, if the decision version of the ray tracing problem is defined as follows – given a light ray's initial position and direction and some fixed point, does the ray eventually reach that point, then the referenced paper proves the following results:

- Ray tracing in 3D optical systems with a finite set of reflective or refractive objects represented by a system of rational quadratic inequalities is undecidable.

- Ray tracing in 3D optical systems with a finite set of refractive objects represented by a system of rational linear inequalities is undecidable.

- Ray tracing in 3D optical systems with a finite set of rectangular reflective or refractive objects is undecidable.

- Ray tracing in 3D optical systems with a finite set of reflective or partially reflective objects represented by a system of linear inequalities, some of which can be irrational is undecidable.

- Ray tracing in 3D optical systems with a finite set of reflective or partially reflective objects represented by a system of rational linear inequalities is PSPACE-hard.

- For any dimension equal to or greater than 2, ray tracing with a finite set of parallel and perpendicular reflective surfaces represented by rational linear inequalities is in PSPACE.

Texture Filtering

In computer graphics, texture filtering or texture smoothing is the method used to determine the texture color for a texture mapped pixel, using the colors of nearby texels (pixels of the texture). There are two main categories of texture filtering, magnification filtering and minification filtering. Depending on the situation texture filtering is either a type of reconstruction filter where sparse data is interpolated to fill gaps (magnification), or a type of anti-aliasing (AA), where texture samples exist at a higher frequency than required for the sample frequency needed for texture fill (minification). Put simply, filtering describes how a texture is applied at many different shapes, size, angles and scales. Depending on the chosen filter algorithm the result will show varying degrees of blurriness, detail, spatial aliasing, temporal aliasing and blocking. Depending on the circumstances filtering can be performed in software (such as a software rendering package) or in hardware for real time or GPU accelerated rendering or in a mixture of both. For most common interactive graphical applications modern texture filtering is performed by dedicated hardware which optimizes memory access through memory cacheing and pre-fetch and implements a selection of algorithms available to the user and developer.

There are many methods of texture filtering, which make different trade-offs between computational complexity, memory bandwidth and image quality.

The Need for Filtering

During the texture mapping process for any arbitrary 3D surface, a *texture lookup* takes place to find out where on the texture each pixel center falls. For texture-mapped polygonal surfaces composed of triangles typical of most surfaces in 3D games and movies, every pixel (or subordinate pixel sample) of that surface will be associated with some triangle(s) and a set of barycentric coordinates, which are used to provide a position within a texture. Such a position may not lie perfectly on the "pixel grid," necessitating some function to account for these cases. In other words, since the textured surface may be at an arbitrary distance and orientation relative to the viewer, one pixel does not usually correspond directly to one texel. Some form of filtering has to be applied to determine the best color for the pixel. Insufficient or incorrect filtering will show up in the image as artifacts (errors in the image), such as 'blockiness', jaggies, or shimmering.

There can be different types of correspondence between a pixel and the texel/texels it represents on the screen. These depend on the position of the textured surface relative to the viewer, and different forms of filtering are needed in each case. Given a square texture mapped on to a square surface in the world, at some viewing distance the size of one screen pixel is exactly the same as one texel. Closer than that, the texels are larger than screen pixels, and need to be scaled up appropriately - a process known as texture magnification. Farther away, each texel is smaller than a pixel, and so one pixel covers multiple texels. In this case an appropriate color has to be picked based on the covered texels, via texture minification. Graphics APIs such as OpenGL allow the programmer to set different choices for minification and magnification filters.

Note that even in the case where the pixels and texels are exactly the same size, one pixel will not necessarily match up exactly to one texel. It may be misaligned or rotated, and cover parts of up to four neighboring texels. Hence some form of filtering is still required.

Mipmapping

Mipmapping is a standard technique used to save some of the filtering work needed during texture minification. It is also highly beneficial for cache coherency - without it the memory access pattern during sampling from distant textures will exhibit extremely poor locality, adversely affecting performance even if no filtering is performed.

During texture magnification, the number of texels that need to be looked up for any pixel is always four or fewer; during minification, however, as the textured polygon moves farther away potentially the entire texture might fall into a single pixel. This would necessitate reading all of its texels and combining their values to correctly determine the pixel color, a prohibitively expensive operation. Mipmapping avoids this by prefiltering the texture and storing it in smaller sizes down to a single pixel. As the textured surface moves farther away, the texture being applied switches to the prefiltered smaller size. Different sizes of the mipmap are referred to as 'levels', with Level 0 being the largest size (used closest to the viewer), and increasing levels used at increasing distances.

Filtering Methods

The most common texture filtering methods, in increasing order of computational cost and image quality.

Nearest-neighbor Interpolation

Nearest-neighbor interpolation is the simplest and crudest filtering method — it simply uses the color of the texel closest to the pixel center for the pixel color. While simple, this results in a large number of artifacts - texture 'blockiness' during magnification, and aliasing and shimmering during minification. This method is fast during magnification but during minification the stride through memory becomes arbitrarily large and it can often be less efficient than MIP-mapping due to the lack of spatially coherent texture access and cache-line reuse.

Nearest-neighbor with Mipmapping

This method still uses nearest neighbor interpolation, but adds mipmapping — first the nearest mipmap level is chosen according to distance, then the nearest texel center is sampled to get the pixel color. This reduces the aliasing and shimmering significantly during minification but does not eliminate it entirely. In doing so it improves texture memory access and cache-line reuse through avoiding arbitrarily large access strides through texture memory during rasterization. This does not help with blockiness during magnification as each magnified texel will still appear as a large rectangle.

Linear Mipmap Filtering

Less commonly used, OpenGL and other APIs support nearest-neighbor sampling from individual mipmaps whilst linearly interpolating the two nearest mipmaps relevant to the sample.

Bilinear Filtering

Bilinear filtering is the next step up. In this method the four nearest texels to the pixel center are sampled (at the closest mipmap level), and their colors are combined by weighted average according to distance. This removes the 'blockiness' seen during magnification, as there is now a smooth gradient of color change from one texel to the next, instead of an abrupt jump as the pixel center crosses the texel boundary. Bilinear filtering for magnification filtering is common. When used for minification it is often used with mipmapping; though it can be used without, it would suffer the same aliasing and shimmering problems as nearest-neighbor filtering when minified too much. For modest minification ratios, however, it can be used as an inexpensive hardware accelerated weighted texture supersample.

Trilinear Filtering

Trilinear filtering is a remedy to a common artifact seen in mipmapped bilinearly filtered images: an abrupt and very noticeable change in quality at boundaries where the renderer switches from one mipmap level to the next. Trilinear filtering solves this by doing a texture lookup and bilinear filtering on the *two* closest mipmap levels (one higher and one lower quality), and then linearly interpolating the results. This results in a smooth degradation of texture quality as distance from the viewer increases, rather than a series of sudden drops. Of course, closer than Level 0 there is only one mipmap level available, and the algorithm reverts to bilinear filtering.

Anisotropic Filtering

Anisotropic filtering is the highest quality filtering available in current consumer 3D graphics cards. Simpler, "isotropic" techniques use only square mipmaps which are then interpolated using bi– or trilinear filtering. (*Isotropic* means same in all directions, and hence is used to describe a system in which all the maps are squares rather than rectangles or other quadrilaterals.)

When a surface is at a high angle relative to the camera, the fill area for a texture will not be approximately square. Consider the common case of a floor in a game: the fill area is far wider than it is tall. In this case, none of the square maps are a good fit. The result is blurriness and/or shimmering, depending on how the fit is chosen. Anisotropic filtering corrects this by sampling the texture as a non-square shape. The goal is to sample a texture to match the pixel footprint as projected into texture space, and such a footprint is not always axis aligned to the texture. Further, when dealing with sample theory a pixel is not a little square therefore its footprint would not be a projected square. Footprint assembly in texture space samples some approximation of the computed function of a projected pixel in texture space but the details are often approximate, highly proprietary and steeped in opinions about sample theory. Conceptually though the goal is to sample a more correct anisotropic sample of appropriate orientation to avoid the conflict between aliasing on one axis vs. blurring on the other when projected size differs.

In anisotropic implementations, the filtering may incorporate the same filtering algorithms used to filter the square maps of traditional mipmapping during the construction of the intermediate or final result.

Percentage Closer Filtering

Depth based Shadow mapping can use an interesting Percentage Closer Filter (PCF) with depth mapped textures that broadens one's perception of the kinds of texture filters that might be applied. In PCF a depth map of the scene is rendered from the light source. During the subsequent rendering of the scene this depth map is then projected back into the scene from the position of the light and a comparison is performed between the projective depth coordinate and the fetched texture sample depth. The projective coordinate will be the scene pixels depth from the light but the fetched depth from the depth map will represent the depth of the scene along that projected direction. In this way a determination of visibility to the light and therefore illumination by the light can be made for the rendered pixel. So this texturing operation is a boolean test of whether the pixel is lit, however multiple samples can be tested for a given pixel and the boolean results summed and averaged. In this way in combination with varying parameters like sampled texel location and even jittered depth map projection location a post-depth-comparison average or percentage of samples closer and therefore illuminated can be computed for a pixel. Critically, the summation of boolean results and generation of a percentage value must be performed after the depth comparison of projective depth and sample fetch, so this depth comparison becomes an integral part of the texture filter. This percentage can then be used to weight an illumination calculation and provide not just a boolean illumination or shadow value but a soft shadow penumbra result. A version of this is supported in modern hardware where a comparison is performed and a post boolean comparison bilinear filter by distance is applied.

Visualization

Visualization or visualisation is any technique for creating images, diagrams, or animations to communicate a message. Visualization through visual imagery has been an effective way to communicate both abstract and concrete ideas since the dawn of humanity. Examples from history include cave paintings, Egyptian hieroglyphs, Greek geometry, and Leonardo da Vinci's revolutionary methods of technical drawing for engineering and scientific purposes.

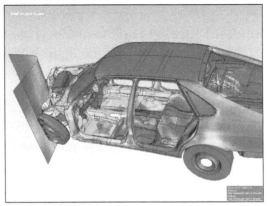

Visualization of how a car deforms in an
asymmetrical crash using finite element analysis.

Visualization today has ever-expanding applications in science, education, engineering (e.g., product visualization), interactive multimedia, medicine, etc. Typical of a visualization application is the field of computer graphics. The invention of computer graphics may be the most important development in visualization since the invention of central perspective in the Renaissance period. The development of animation also helped advance visualization.

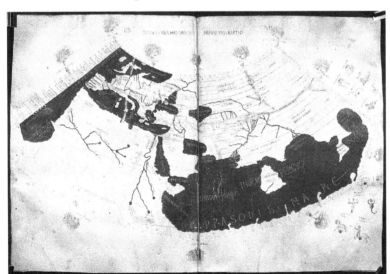

The Ptolemy world map, reconstituted from Ptolemy's *Geographia* (circa 150), indicating
the countries of "Serica" and "Sinae" (China) at the extreme right, beyond the island of
"Taprobane" (Sri Lanka, oversized) and the "Aurea Chersonesus" (Southeast Asian peninsula).

The use of visualization to present information is not a new phenomenon. It has been used in maps, scientific drawings, and data plots for over a thousand years. Examples from cartography include Ptolemy's Geographia (2nd Century AD), a map of China (1137 AD), and Minard's map (1861) of Napoleon's invasion of Russia a century and a half ago. Most of the concepts learned in devising these images carry over in a straightforward manner to computer visualization. Edward Tufte has written three critically acclaimed books that explain many of these principles.

Computer graphics has from its beginning been used to study scientific problems. However, in its early days the lack of graphics power often limited its usefulness. The recent emphasis on visualization started in 1987 with the publication of Visualization in Scientific Computing, a special issue of Computer Graphics.

Most people are familiar with the digital animations produced to present meteorological data during weather reports on television, though few can distinguish between those models of reality and the satellite photos that are also shown on such programs. TV also offers scientific visualizations when it shows computer drawn and animated reconstructions of road or airplane accidents. Some of the most popular examples of scientific visualizations are computer-generated images that show real spacecraft in action, out in the void far beyond Earth, or on other planets. Dynamic forms of visualization, such as educational animation or timelines, have the potential to enhance learning about systems that change over time.

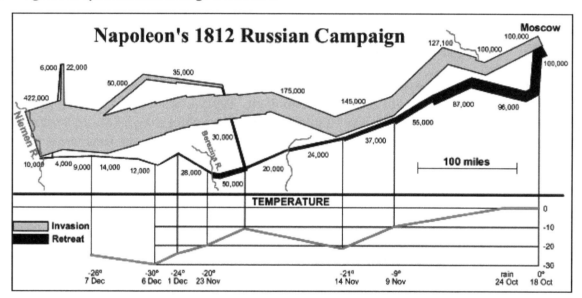

Charles Minard's information graphic of Napoleon's march.

Apart from the distinction between interactive visualizations and animation, the most useful categorization is probably between abstract and model-based scientific visualizations. The abstract visualizations show completely conceptual constructs in 2D or 3D. These generated shapes are completely arbitrary. The model-based visualizations either place overlays of data on real or digitally constructed images of reality or make a digital construction of a real object directly from the scientific data.

Scientific visualization is usually done with specialized software, though there are a few exceptions, noted below. Some of these specialized programs have been released as open source software, having very often its origins in universities, within an academic environment where sharing software tools and giving access to the source code is common. There are also many proprietary software packages of scientific visualization tools.

Models and frameworks for building visualizations include the data flow models popularized by systems such as AVS, IRIS Explorer, and VTK toolkit, and data state models in spreadsheet systems such as the Spreadsheet for Visualization and Spreadsheet for Images.

Applications

Scientific Visualization

Simulation of a Raleigh–Taylor instability
caused by two mixing fluids.

As a subject in computer science, scientific visualization is the use of interactive, sensory representations, typically visual, of abstract data to reinforce cognition, hypothesis building, and reasoning. Data visualization is a related subcategory of visualization dealing with statistical graphics and geographic or spatial data (as in thematic cartography) that is abstracted in schematic form.

Scientific visualization is the transformation, selection, or representation of data from simulations or experiments, with an implicit or explicit geometric structure, to allow the exploration, analysis, and understanding of the data. Scientific visualization focuses and emphasizes the representation of higher order data using primarily graphics and animation techniques. It is a very important part of visualization and maybe the first one, as the visualization of experiments and phenomena is as old as science itself. Traditional areas of scientific visualization are flow visualization, medical visualization, astrophysical visualization, and chemical visualization. There are several different techniques to visualize scientific data, with isosurface reconstruction and direct volume rendering being the more common.

Educational Visualization

Educational visualization is using a simulation to create an image of something so it can be taught about. This is very useful when teaching about a topic that is difficult to otherwise see, for example, atomic structure, because atoms are far too small to be studied easily without expensive and difficult to use scientific equipment.

Information Visualization

Information visualization concentrates on the use of computer-supported tools to explore large amount of abstract data. The term "information visualization" was originally coined by the User Interface Research Group at Xerox PARC and included Jock Mackinlay. Practical application of information visualization in computer programs involves selecting, transforming, and representing abstract data in a form that facilitates human interaction for exploration and understanding.

Important aspects of information visualization are dynamics of visual representation and the interactivity. Strong techniques enable the user to modify the visualization in real-time, thus affording unparalleled perception of patterns and structural relations in the abstract data in question.

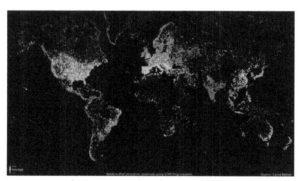

Relative average utilization of IPv4.

Knowledge Visualization

The use of visual representations to transfer knowledge between at least two persons aims to improve the transfer of knowledge by using computer and non-computer-based visualization methods complementarily. Examples of such visual formats are sketches, diagrams, images, objects, interactive visualizations, information visualization applications, and imaginary visualizations as in stories. While information visualization concentrates on the use of computer-supported tools to derive new insights, knowledge visualization focuses on transferring insights and creating new knowledge in groups. Beyond the mere transfer of facts, knowledge visualization aims to further transfer insights, experiences, attitudes, values, expectations, perspectives, opinions, and predictions by using various complementary visualizations.

Product Visualization

Product visualization involves visualization software technology for the viewing and manipulation of 3D models, technical drawing and other related documentation of manufactured components and large assemblies of products. It is a key part of product lifecycle management. Product visualization software typically provides high levels of photorealism so that a product can be viewed before it is actually manufactured. This supports functions ranging from design and styling to sales and marketing. *Technical visualization* is an important aspect of product development. Originally technical drawings were made by hand, but with the rise of advanced computer graphics the drawing board has been replaced by computer-aided design (CAD). CAD-drawings and models have several advantages over hand-made drawings such as the possibility of 3-D modeling, rapid prototyping, and simulation.

Visual Communication

Visual communication is the communication of ideas through the visual display of information. Primarily associated with two dimensional images, it includes: alphanumerics, art, signs, and electronic resources. Recent research in the field has focused on web design and graphically-oriented usability.

Visual Analytics

Visual analytics focuses on human interaction with visualization systems as part of a larger process of data analysis. Visual analytics has been defined as "the science of analytical reasoning supported by the interactive visual interface".

Its focus is on human information discourse (interaction) within massive, dynamically changing information spaces. Visual analytics research concentrates on support for perceptual and cognitive operations that enable users to detect the expected and discover the unexpected in complex information spaces.

Technologies resulting from visual analytics find their application in almost all fields, but are being driven by critical needs (and funding) in biology and national security.

Fluid Animation

Fluid animation refers to computer graphics techniques for generating realistic animations of fluids such as water and smoke. Fluid animations are typically focused on emulating the qualitative visual behavior of a fluid, with less emphasis placed on rigorously correct physical results, although they often still rely on approximate solutions to the Euler equations or Navier–Stokes equations that govern real fluid physics. Fluid animation can be performed with different levels of complexity, ranging from time-consuming, high-quality animations for films or visual effects, to simple and fast animations for real-time animations like computer games.

Relationship to Computational Fluid Dynamics

Fluid animation differs from computational fluid dynamics (CFD) in that fluid animation is used primarily for visual effects, whereas computational fluid dynamics is used to study the behavior of fluids in a scientifically rigorous way.

Development

The development of fluid animation techniques based on the Navier–Stokes equations began in 1996, when Nick Foster and Dimitris Metaxas implemented solutions to 3D Navier-Stokes equations in a computer graphics context, basing their work on a scientific CFD paper by Harlow and Welch from 1965. Up to that point, a variety of simpler methods had primarily been used, including ad-hoc particle systems, lower dimensional techniques such as height fields, and semi-random turbulent noise fields. In 1999, Jos Stam published the "Stable Fluids" method, which exploited a semi-Lagrangian advection technique and implicit integration of viscosity to provide unconditionally stable behaviour. This allowed for much larger time steps and therefore faster simulations. This general technique was extended by Ronald Fedkiw and co-authors to handle more realistic smoke and fire, as well as complex 3D water simulations using variants of the level-set method.

Some notable academic researchers in this area include Jerry Tessendorf, James F. O'Brien, Ron Fedkiw, Mark Carlson, Greg Turk, Robert Bridson, Ken Museth and Jos Stam.

Software

Many 3D computer graphics programs implement fluid animation techniques. RealFlow is a standalone commercial package that has been used to produce visual effects in movies, television shows, commercials, and games. RealFlow implements a fluid-implicit particle (FLIP) solver, a hybrid grid, and a particle method that allows for advanced features such as foam and spray. Maya and Houdini are two other 3D computer graphics programs that enable fluid animation. Blender is an open-source 3D computer graphics program that utilizes a particle-based Lattice Boltzmann method for animating fluids.

Multiview Projection

In technical drawing and computer graphics, a multiview projection is a technique of illustration by which a standardized series of orthographic two-dimensional pictures is constructed to represent the form of a three-dimensional object. Up to six pictures of an object are produced (called primary views), with each projection plane parallel to one of the coordinate axes of the object. The views are positioned relative to each other according to either of two schemes: first-angle or third-angle projection. In each, the appearances of views may be thought of as being projected onto planes that form a six-sided box around the object. Although six different sides can be drawn, usually three views of a drawing give enough information to make a three-dimensional object. These views are known as front view, top view and end view. Other names for these views include plan, elevation and section.

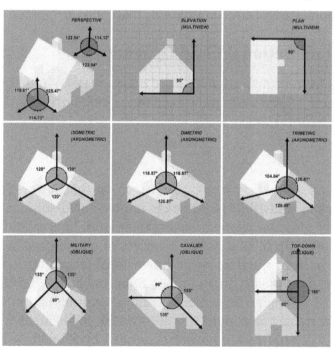

Comparison of several types of graphical projection, including *elevation* and *plan* views.

The terms orthographic projection and orthogonal projection are sometimes reserved specifically for multiview. However, orthographic and orthogonal more correctly refer to the right angle formed between the projection rays and the projection plane, versus the angle formed between the subject of the drawing and the projection plane. Thus, orthographic projections include axonometric or auxiliary views in addition to multiviews.

To render each such picture, a ray of sight (also called a projection line, projection ray or line of sight) towards the object is chosen, which determines on the object various points of interest (for instance, the points that are visible when looking at the object along the ray of sight); those points of interest are mapped by an orthographic projection to points on some geometric plane (called a projection plane or image plane) that is perpendicular to the ray of sight, thereby creating a 2D representation of the 3D object.

Customarily, two rays of sight are chosen for each of the three axes of the object's coordinate system; that is, parallel to each axis, the object may be viewed in one of 2 opposite directions, making for a total of 6 orthographic projections (or "views") of the object:

- Along the x-axis: The left and right views, which are known as elevations (because they often show the features along the "vertical" length of an object such as a building).

- Along the y-axis: The top and bottom views, which are known as plans (because they often show the features within a cross section of the object, such as a floor in a building).

- Along the z-axis: The front and back views, which are also known as elevations, following the same reasoning.

These six planes of projection intersect each other, forming a box around the object, the most uniform construction of which is a cube; traditionally, these six views are presented together by first projecting the 3D object onto the 2D faces of a cube, and then "unfolding" the faces of the cube such that all of them are contained within the same plane (namely, the plane of the medium on which all of the images will be presented together, such as a piece of paper, or a computer monitor, etc.). However, even if the faces of the box are unfolded in one standardized way, there is ambiguity as to which projection is being displayed by a particular face; the cube has two faces that are perpendicular to a ray of sight, and the points of interest may be projected onto either one of them, a choice which has resulted in two predominant standards of projection:

- First-angle projection: In this, the object is imagined to be in the first quadrant. Because the observer normally looks from the right side of the quadrant to obtain the front view. The objects will come in between the observer and the plane of projection. Therefore, in this case, the object is to be transparent, and the projectors are imagined ta be extended from various points of the object to meet the projection plane. These meeting points when joined in the order form an image First plane Principle first angle projection view This is the principle of the first angle projection. Thus in the first angle projection, any view is so placed that it represents the side of the object away from it. First angle projection is measurably used throughout all parts of Europe so that called European projection.

- Third-angle projection: In this, the object is imagined to be placed in the third quadrant. Again, as the observer is normally supposed to look from the right side of the quadrant to obtain the front view, in this method, the projection plane comes in between the observer and the object. Therefore, the plane of projection has to be assumed to be transparent. The intersection of this plan with the projectors from all the points of the object would form an image on the transparent plane. Thus it is seen that in the third angle projection any view is so placed that it represents the side from the object nearest to it.

Primary Views

Multiview projections show the primary views of an object, each viewed in a direction parallel to one of the main coordinate axes. These primary views are called plans and elevations. Sometimes they are shown as if the object has been cut across or sectioned to expose the interior: these views are called sections.

Plan

A plan is a view of a 3-dimensional object seen from vertically above (or sometimes below). It may be drawn in the position of a horizontal plane passing through, above, or below the object. The outline of a shape in this view is sometimes called its planform, for example with aircraft wings.

The plan view from above a building is called its roof plan. A section seen in a horizontal plane through the walls and showing the floor beneath is called a *floor plan*.

Elevation

Elevation is the view of a 3-dimensional object from the position of a vertical plane beside an object. In other words, an elevation is a side view as viewed from the front, back, left or right (and referred to as a front elevation, [left/ right] side elevation, and a rear elevation).

An elevation is a common method of depicting the external configuration and detailing of a 3-dimensional object in two dimensions. Building façades are shown as elevations in architectural drawings and technical drawings.

Principal façade of the Panthéon, Paris,
by Jacques-Germain Soufflot.

Elevations are the most common orthographic projection for conveying the appearance of a building from the exterior. Perspectives are also commonly used for this purpose. A building elevation is typically labeled in relation to the compass direction it faces; the direction from which a person views it. E.g. the North Elevation of a building is the side that most closely faces true north on the compass.

Interior elevations are used to show details such as millwork and trim configurations.

In the building industry elevations is a non-perspective view of the structure. These are drawn to scale so that measurements can be taken for any aspect necessary. Drawing sets include front, rear, and both side elevations. The elevations specify the composition of the different facades of the building, including ridge heights, the positioning of the final fall of the land, exterior finishes, roof pitches, and other architectural details.

Developed Elevation

A developed elevation is a variant of a regular elevation view in which several adjacent non-parallel sides may be shown together as if they have been unfolded. For example, the north and west views may be shown side-by-side, sharing an edge, even though this does not represent a proper orthographic projection.

Section

A section, or cross-section, is a view of a 3-dimensional object from the position of a plane through the object.

A section is a common method of depicting the internal arrangement of a 3-dimensional object in two dimensions. It is often used in technical drawing and is traditionally crosshatched. The style of crosshatching often indicates the type of material the section passes through.

With computed axial tomography, computers construct cross-sections from x-ray data.

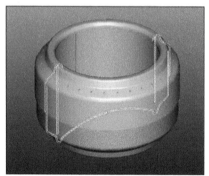

A 3-D view of a beverage-can stove with a cross-section in yellow.

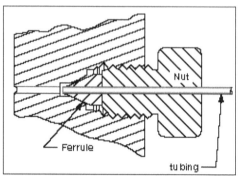

A 2-D cross-sectional view of a compression seal.

Cutaway of a Porsche 996.

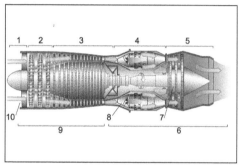

Cross-section of a jet engine.

Auxiliary Views

An auxiliary view or pictorial, is an orthographic view that is projected into any plane other than one of the six primary views. These views are typically used when an object has a surface in an oblique plane. By projecting into a plane parallel with the oblique surface, the true size and shape of the surface are shown. Auxiliary views tend to make use of axonometric projection.

Multiviews

Quadrants in Descriptive Geometry

Modern orthographic projection is derived from Gaspard Monge's descriptive geometry. Monge defined a reference system of two viewing planes, horizontal H ("ground") and vertical V ("backdrop"). These two planes intersect to partition 3D space into 4 quadrants, which he labeled:

- I: above H, in front of V

- II: above H, behind V

- III: below H, behind V

- IV: below H, in front of V

These quadrant labels are the same as used in 2D planar geometry, as seen from infinitely far to the "left", taking H and V to be the X-axis and Y-axis, respectively.

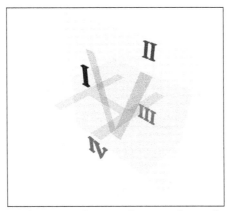

Gaspard Monge's four quadrants and two planes.

The 3D object of interest is then placed into either quadrant I or III (equivalently, the position of the intersection line between the two planes is shifted), obtaining first- and third-angle projections, respectively. Quadrants II and IV are also mathematically valid, but their use would result in one view "true" and the other view "flipped" by 180° through its vertical centerline, which is too confusing for technical drawings. (In cases where such a view is useful, e.g. a ceiling viewed from above, a reflected view is used, which is a mirror image of the true orthographic view.)

Monge's original formulation uses two planes only and obtains the top and front views only. The addition of a third plane to show a side view (either left or right) is a modern extension. The terminology of quadrant is a mild anachronism, as a modern orthographic projection with three views corresponds more precisely to an octant of 3D space.

First-angle Projection

In first-angle projection, the object is conceptually located in quadrant I, i.e. it floats above and before the viewing planes, the planes are opaque, and each view is pushed through the object onto the plane furthest from it. (Mnemonic: an "actor on a stage".) Extending to the 6-sided box, each view of the object is projected in the direction (sense) of sight of the object, onto the (opaque) interior walls of the box; that is, each view of the object is drawn on the opposite side of the box. A two-dimensional representation of the object is then created by "unfolding" the box, to view all of the interior walls. This produces two plans and four elevations. A simpler way to visualize this is to place the object on top of an upside-down bowl. Sliding the object down the right edge of the bowl reveals the right side view.

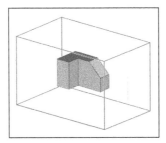

- An image of an object in a box.

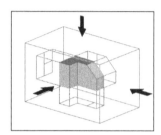

- The same image, with views of the object projected in the direction of sight onto walls using first-angle projection.

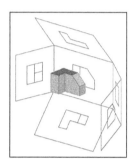

- Similar image showing the box unfolding from around the object.

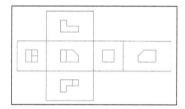

- Image showing orthographic views located relative to each other in accordance with first-angle projection.

Third-angle Projection

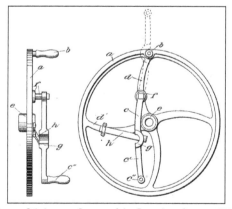

An example of a multiview orthographic drawing from a US Patent (1913), showing two views of the same object.

In third-angle projection, the object is conceptually located in quadrant III, i.e. it is positioned below and behind the viewing planes, the planes are transparent, and each view is pulled onto the plane closest to it. (Mnemonic: a "shark in a tank", esp. that is sunken into the floor.) Using the 6-sided viewing box, each view of the object is projected opposite to the direction (sense) of sight, onto the (transparent) exterior walls of the box; that is, each view of the object is drawn on the same side of the box. The box is then unfolded to view all of its exterior walls. A simpler way to visualize this is to place the object in the bottom of a bowl. Sliding the object up the right edge of the bowl reveals the right side view.

Here is the construction of third angle projections of the same object as above. Note that the individual views are the same, just arranged differently.

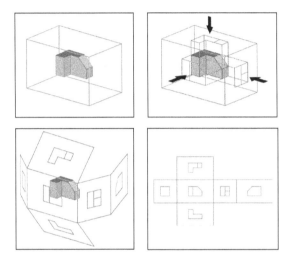

Multiviews without Rotation

Orthographic multiview projection is derived from the principles of descriptive geometry and may produce an image of a specified, imaginary object as viewed from any direction of space. Orthographic projection is distinguished by parallel projectors emanating from all points of the imaged object and which intersect of projection at right angles. Above, a technique is described that obtains varying views by projecting images after the object is rotated to the desired position.

Descriptive geometry customarily relies on obtaining various views by imagining an object to be stationary and changing the direction of projection (viewing) in order to obtain the desired view.

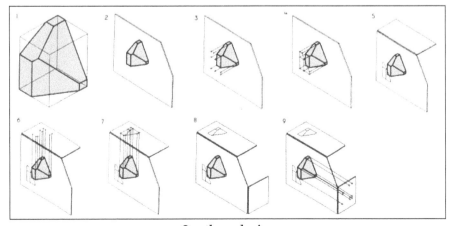

One through nine.

Using the rotation technique above, note that no orthographic view is available looking perpendicularly at any of the inclined surfaces. Suppose a technician desired such a view to, say, look through a hole to be drilled perpendicularly to the surface. Such a view might be desired for calculating clearances or for dimensioning purposes. To obtain this view without multiple rotations requires the principles of Descriptive Geometry. The steps below describe the use of these principles in third angle projection.

- Figure 1: Pictorial of the imaginary object that the technician wishes to image.

- Figure 2: The object is imagined behind a vertical plane of projection. The angled corner of the plane of projection is addressed later.

- Figure 3: Projectors emanate parallel from all points of the object, perpendicular to the plane of projection.

- Figure 4: An image is created thereby.

- Figure 5: A second, horizontal plane of projection is added, perpendicular to the first.

- Figure 6: Projectors emanate parallel from all points of the object perpendicular to the second plane of projection.

- Figure 7: An image is created thereby.

- Figure 8: The third plane of projection is added, perpendicular to the previous two.

- Figure 9: Projectors emanate parallel from all points of the object perpendicular to the third plane of projection.

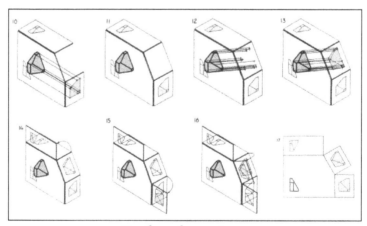

Ten through seventeen.

- Figure 10: An image is created thereby.

- Figure 11: The fourth plane of projection is added parallel to the chosen inclined surface, and perforce, perpendicular to the first (Frontal) plane of projection.

- Figure 12: Projectors emanate parallel from all points of the object perpendicularly from the inclined surface, and perforce, perpendicular to the fourth (Auxiliary) plane of projection.

- Figure 13: An image is created thereby.

- Figure 14-16: The various planes of projection are unfolded to be planar with the Frontal plane of projection.

- Figure 17: The final appearance of an orthographic multiview projection and which includes an "Auxiliary view" showing the true shape of an inclined surface.

Shaders

In computer graphics, a shader is a type of computer program that was originally used for shading (the production of appropriate levels of light, darkness, and color within an image), but which now performs a variety of specialized functions in various fields of computer graphics special effects, or does video post-processing unrelated to shading, or even performs functions unrelated to graphics at all.

Shaders calculate rendering effects on graphics hardware with a high degree of flexibility. Most shaders are coded for a graphics processing unit (GPU), though this is not a strict requirement. Shading languages are usually used to program the GPU rendering pipeline, which has mostly superseded the fixed-function pipeline that only allowed for common geometry transformation and pixel-shading functions; with shaders, customized effects can be used. The position, hue, saturation, brightness, and contrast of all pixels, vertices, and/or textures used to construct a final image can be altered on the fly using algorithms defined in the shader, and can be modified by external variables or textures introduced by the program calling the shader.

Shaders are used widely in cinema postprocessing, computer-generated imagery, and video games to produce a very wide range of effects. Beyond just simple lighting models, more complex uses include: altering the hue, saturation, brightness or contrast of an image; producing blur, light bloom, volumetric lighting, normal mapping (for depth effects), bokeh, cel shading, posterization, bump mapping, distortion, chroma keying (so-called "bluescreen/greenscreen" effects), edge detection and motion detection, and psychedelic effects.

This use of the term "shader" was introduced to the public by Pixar with version 3.0 of their RenderMan Interface Specification, originally published in May 1988.

As graphics processing units evolved, major graphics software libraries such as OpenGL and Direct3D began to support shaders. The first shader-capable GPUs only supported pixel shading, but vertex shaders were quickly introduced once developers realized the power of shaders. The first video card with a programmable pixel shader was the Nvidia GeForce 3 (NV20), released in 2001. Geometry shaders were introduced with Direct3D 10 and OpenGL 3.2. Eventually, graphics hardware evolved toward a unified shader model.

Design

Shaders are simple programs that describe the traits of either a vertex or a pixel. Vertex shaders describe the traits (position, texture coordinates, colors, etc.) of a vertex, while pixel shaders describe the traits (color, z-depth and alpha value) of a pixel. A vertex shader is called for each vertex in a primitive (possibly after tessellation); thus one vertex in, one (updated) vertex out. Each vertex is then rendered as a series of pixels onto a surface (block of memory) that will eventually be sent to the screen.

Shaders replace a section of the graphics hardware typically called the Fixed Function Pipeline (FFP), so-called because it performs lighting and texture mapping in a hard-coded manner. Shaders provide a programmable alternative to this hard-coded approach.

The basic graphics pipeline is as follows:

- The CPU sends instructions (compiled shading language programs) and geometry data to the graphics processing unit, located on the graphics card.

- Within the vertex shader, the geometry is transformed.

- If a geometry shader is in the graphic processing unit and active, some changes of the geometries in the scene are performed.

- If a tessellation shader is in the graphic processing unit and active, the geometries in the scene can be subdivided.

- The calculated geometry is triangulated (subdivided into triangles).

- Triangles are broken down into fragment quads (one fragment quad is a 2 × 2 fragment primitive).

- Fragment quads are modified according to the fragment shader.

- The depth test is performed, fragments that pass will get written to the screen and might get blended into the frame buffer.

The graphic pipeline uses these steps in order to transform three-dimensional (or two-dimensional) data into useful two-dimensional data for displaying. In general, this is a large pixel matrix or "frame buffer".

Types

There are three types of shaders in common use, with one more recently added. While older graphics cards utilize separate processing units for each shader type, newer cards feature unified shaders which are capable of executing any type of shader. This allows graphics cards to make more efficient use of processing power.

2D Shaders

2D shaders act on digital images, also called *textures* in the field of computer graphics. They modify attributes of pixels. 2D shaders may take part in rendering 3D geometry. Currently the only type of 2D shader is a pixel shader.

Pixel Shaders

Pixel shaders, also known as fragment shaders, compute color and other attributes of each "fragment": a unit of rendering work affecting at most a single output pixel. The simplest kinds of pixel shaders output one screen pixel as a color value; more complex shaders with multiple inputs/ outputs are also possible. Pixel shaders range from simply always outputting the same color, to applying a lighting value, to doing bump mapping, shadows, specular highlights, translucency and other phenomena. They can alter the depth of the fragment (for Z-buffering), or output more than one color if multiple render targets are active. In 3D graphics, a pixel shader alone cannot produce some kinds of complex effects because it operates only on a single fragment, without knowledge of a scene's geometry (i.e. vertex data). However, pixel shaders do have knowledge of the screen coordinate being drawn, and can sample the screen and nearby pixels if the contents of the entire screen are passed as a texture to the shader. This technique can enable a wide variety of two-dimensional postprocessing effects such as blur, or edge detection/enhancement for cartoon/cel shaders. Pixel shaders may also be applied in intermediate stages to any two-dimensional images—sprites or textures—in the pipeline, whereas vertex shaders always require a 3D scene. For instance, a pixel shader is the only kind of shader that can act as a postprocessor or filter for a video stream after it has been rasterized.

3D Shaders

3D shaders act on 3D models or other geometry but may also access the colors and textures used to draw the model or mesh. Vertex shaders are the oldest type of 3D shader, generally making modifications on a per-vertex basis. Newer geometry shaders can generate new vertices from within the shader. Tessellation shaders are the newest 3D shaders; they act on batches of vertices all at once to add detail—such as subdividing a model into smaller groups of triangles or other primitives at runtime, to improve things like curves and bumps, or change other attributes.

Vertex Shaders

Vertex shaders are the most established and common kind of 3D shader and are run once for each vertex given to the graphics processor. The purpose is to transform each vertex's 3D position in virtual space to the 2D coordinate at which it appears on the screen (as well as a depth value for the Z-buffer). Vertex shaders can manipulate properties such as position, color and texture coordinates, but cannot create new vertices. The output of the vertex shader goes to the next stage in the pipeline, which is either a geometry shader if present, or the rasterizer. Vertex shaders can enable powerful control over the details of position, movement, lighting, and color in any scene involving 3D models.

Geometry Shaders

Geometry shaders are a relatively new type of shader, introduced in Direct3D 10 and OpenGL 3.2; formerly available in OpenGL 2.0+ with the use of extensions. This type of shader can generate new graphics primitives, such as points, lines, and triangles, from those primitives that were sent to the beginning of the graphics pipeline.

Geometry shader programs are executed after vertex shaders. They take as input a whole primitive, possibly with adjacency information. For example, when operating on triangles, the three vertices are the geometry shader's input. The shader can then emit zero or more primitives, which are rasterized and their fragments ultimately passed to a pixel shader.

Typical uses of a geometry shader include point sprite generation, geometry tessellation, shadow volume extrusion, and single pass rendering to a cube map. A typical real-world example of the benefits of geometry shaders would be automatic mesh complexity modification. A series of line strips representing control points for a curve are passed to the geometry shader and depending on the complexity required the shader can automatically generate extra lines each of which provides a better approximation of a curve.

Tessellation Shaders

As of OpenGL 4.0 and Direct3D 11, a new shader class called a tessellation shader has been added. It adds two new shader stages to the traditional model: tessellation control shaders (also known as hull shaders) and tessellation evaluation shaders (also known as Domain Shaders), which together allow for simpler meshes to be subdivided into finer meshes at run-time according to a mathematical function. The function can be related to a variety of variables, most notably the distance from the viewing camera to allow active level-of-detail scaling. This allows objects close to the camera to have fine detail, while further away ones can have more coarse meshes, yet seem comparable in quality. It also can drastically reduce required mesh bandwidth by allowing meshes to be refined once inside the shader units instead of downsampling very complex ones from memory. Some algorithms can upsample any arbitrary mesh, while others allow for "hinting" in meshes to dictate the most characteristic vertices and edges.

Primitive Shaders

AMD Vega microarchitecture added support for a new shader stage - primitive shaders.

Compute Shaders

Compute shaders are not limited to graphics applications, but use the same execution resources for GPGPU. They may be used in graphics pipelines e.g. for additional stages in animation or lighting algorithms, (e.g. tiled forward rendering). Some rendering APIs allow compute shaders to easily share data resources with the graphics pipeline.

Parallel Processing

Shaders are written to apply transformations to a large set of elements at a time, for example, to each pixel in an area of the screen, or for every vertex of a model. This is well suited to parallel processing, and most modern GPUs have multiple shader pipelines to facilitate this, vastly improving computation throughput.

A programming model with shaders is similar to a higher order function for rendering, taking the shaders as arguments, and providing a specific dataflow between intermediate results, enabling both data parallelism (across pixels, vertices etc.) and pipeline parallelism (between stages).

Programming

The language in which shaders are programmed depends on the target environment. The official OpenGL and OpenGL ES shading language is OpenGL Shading Language, also known as GLSL, and the official Direct3D shading language is High Level Shader Language, also known as HLSL.

However, Cg is a deprecated third-party shading language developed by Nvidia that outputs both OpenGL and Direct3D shaders. Apple released its own shading language called Metal Shading Language as part of the Metal framework.

GUI Shader Editors

Modern videogame development platforms such as Unity and Unreal Engine increasingly include node-based editors that can create shaders without the need for actual code; the user is instead presented with a directed graph of connected nodes that allow users to direct various textures, maps, and mathematical functions into output values like the diffuse color, the specular color and intensity, roughness/metalness, height, normal, and so on. Automatic compilation then turns the graph into an actual, compiled shader.

3D Modeling

In 3D computer graphics, 3D modeling is the process of developing a mathematical representation of any *surface* of an object (either inanimate or living) in three dimensions via specialized software. The product is called a 3D model. Someone who works with 3D models may be referred to as a 3D artist. It can be displayed as a two-dimensional image through a process called *3D rendering* or used in a computer simulation of physical phenomena. The model can also be physically created using 3D printing devices.

Models may be created automatically or manually. The manual modeling process of preparing geometric data for 3D computer graphics is similar to plastic arts such as sculpting.

3D modeling software is a class of 3D computer graphics software used to produce 3D models. Individual programs of this class are called modeling applications or modelers.

Models

Three-dimensional (3D) models represent a physical body using a collection of points in 3D space, connected by various geometric entities such as triangles, lines, curved surfaces, etc. Being a collection of data (points and other information), 3D models can be created by hand, algorithmically (procedural modeling), or scanned. Their surfaces may be further defined with texture mapping.

3D models are widely used anywhere in 3D graphics and CAD. Their use predates the widespread use of 3D graphics on personal computers. Many computer games used pre-rendered images of 3D models as sprites before computers could render them in real-time. The designer can then see the model in various directions and views, this can help the designer see if the object is created as intended to compared to their original vision. Seeing the design this way can help the designer/company figure out changes or improvements needed to the product.

Today, 3D models are used in a wide variety of fields. The medical industry uses detailed models of organs; these may be created with multiple 2-D image slices from an MRI or CT scan. The movie industry uses them as characters and objects for animated and real-life motion pictures. The video game industry uses them as assets for computer and video games. The science sector uses them as highly detailed models of chemical compounds. The architecture industry uses them to demonstrate proposed buildings and landscapes in lieu of traditional, physical architectural models. The engineering community uses them as designs of new devices, vehicles and structures as well as a host of other uses. In recent decades the earth science community has started to construct 3D geological models as a standard practice. 3D models can also be the basis for physical devices that are built with 3D printers or CNC machines.

Representation

A modern render of the iconic Utah teapot model developed
by Martin Newell. The Utah teapot is one of the most
common models used in 3D graphics education.

Almost all 3D models can be divided into two categories.

- Solid – These models define the volume of the object they represent (like a rock). Solid models are mostly used for engineering and medical simulations, and are usually built with constructive solid geometry.

- Shell/boundary – These models represent the surface, e.g. the boundary of the object, not its volume (like an infinitesimally thin eggshell). Almost all visual models used in games and film are shell models.

Solid and shell modeling can create functionally identical objects. Differences between them are mostly variations in the way they are created and edited and conventions of use in various fields and differences in types of approximations between the model and reality.

Shell models must be manifold (having no holes or cracks in the shell) to be meaningful as a real object. Polygonal meshes (and to a lesser extent subdivision surfaces) are by far the most common representation. Level sets are a useful representation for deforming surfaces which undergo many topological changes such as fluids.

The process of transforming representations of objects, such as the middle point coordinate of a sphere and a point on its circumference into a polygon representation of a sphere, is called tessellation. This step is used in polygon-based rendering, where objects are broken down from abstract representations ("primitives") such as spheres, cones etc., to so-called *meshes*, which are nets of interconnected triangles. Meshes of triangles (instead of e.g. squares) are popular as they have proven to be easy to rasterise (the surface described by each triangle is planar, so the projection is always convex); . Polygon representations are not used in all rendering techniques, and in these cases the tessellation step is not included in the transition from abstract representation to rendered scene.

Modeling Process

There are three popular ways to represent a model:

- Polygonal modeling – Points in 3D space, called vertices, are connected by line segments to form a polygon mesh. The vast majority of 3D models today are built as textured polygonal models, because they are flexible and because computers can render them so quickly. However, polygons are planar and can only approximate curved surfaces using many polygons.

- Curve modeling – Surfaces are defined by curves, which are influenced by weighted control points. The curve follows (but does not necessarily interpolate) the points. Increasing the weight for a point will pull the curve closer to that point. Curve types include nonuniform rational B-spline (NURBS), splines, patches, and geometric primitives.

- Digital sculpting – Still a fairly new method of modeling, 3D sculpting has become very popular in the few years it has been around. There are currently three types of digital sculpting: Displacement, which is the most widely used among applications at this moment, uses a dense model (often generated by subdivision surfaces of a polygon control mesh) and stores new locations for the vertex positions through use of an image map that stores the adjusted locations. Volumetric, loosely based on voxels, has similar capabilities as displacement but does not suffer from polygon stretching when there are not enough polygons in a region to achieve a deformation. Dynamic tessellation is similar to voxel but divides the surface using triangulation to maintain a smooth surface and allow finer details. These methods allow for very artistic exploration as the model will have a new topology created over it once the models form and possibly details have been sculpted. The new mesh will usually have the original high resolution mesh information transferred into displacement data or normal map data if for a game engine.

A 3D fantasy fish composed of organic surfaces generated using LAI4D.

The modeling stage consists of shaping individual objects that are later used in the scene. There are a number of modeling techniques, including:

- Constructive solid geometry.

- Implicit surfaces.

- Subdivision surfaces.

Modeling can be performed by means of a dedicated program (e.g., Cinema 4D, Maya, 3ds Max, Blender, LightWave, Modo) or an application component (Shaper, Lofter in 3ds Max) or some scene description language (as in POV-Ray). In some cases, there is no strict distinction between these phases; in such cases modeling is just part of the scene creation process (this is the case, for example, with Caligari trueSpace and Realsoft 3D).

3D models can also be created using the technique of Photogrammetry with dedicated programs such as RealityCapture, Metashape, 3DF Zephyr, and Meshroom, and cleanup applications such as MeshLab, netfabb or MeshMixer. Photogrammetry creates models using algorithms to interpret the shape and texture of real-world objects and environments based on photographs taken from many angles of the subject.

Complex materials such as blowing sand, clouds, and liquid sprays are modeled with particle systems, and are a mass of 3D coordinates which have either points, polygons, texture splats, or sprites assigned to them.

Human Models

The first widely available commercial application of human virtual models appeared in 1998 on the Lands' End web site. The human virtual models were created by the company My Virtual Mode Inc. and enabled users to create a model of themselves and try on 3D clothing. There are several modern programs that allow for the creation of virtual human models (Poser being one example).

3D Clothing

Dynamic 3D Clothing Model made in Marvelous Designer.

The development of cloth simulation software such as Marvelous Designer, CLO3D and Optitex, has enabled artists and fashion designers to model dynamic 3D clothing on the computer. Dynamic 3D clothing is used for virtual fashion catalogs, as well as for dressing 3D characters for video games, 3D animation movies, for digital doubles in movies as well as for making clothes for avatars in virtual worlds such as SecondLife.

Compared to 2D Methods

3D photorealistic effects are often achieved without wireframe modeling and are sometimes indistinguishable in the final form. Some graphic art software includes filters that can be applied to 2D vector graphics or 2D raster graphics on transparent layers.

A fully textured and lit rendering of a 3D model.

Advantages of wireframe 3D modeling over exclusively 2D methods include:

- Flexibility, ability to change angles or animate images with quicker rendering of the changes;

- Ease of rendering, automatic calculation and rendering photorealistic effects rather than mentally visualizing or estimating;

- Accurate photorealism, less chance of human error in misplacing, overdoing, or forgetting to include a visual effect.

Disadvantages compare to 2D photorealistic rendering may include a software learning curve and difficulty achieving certain photorealistic effects. Some photorealistic effects may be achieved with special rendering filters included in the 3D modeling software. For the best of both worlds, some artists use a combination of 3D modeling followed by editing the 2D computer-rendered images from the 3D model.

3D Model Market

A large market for 3D models (as well as 3D-related content, such as textures, scripts, etc.) still exists – either for individual models or large collections. Several online marketplaces for 3D content allow individual artists to sell content that they have created, including TurboSquid, CGStudio, CreativeMarket, Sketchfab, CGTrader and Cults. Often, the artists' goal is to get additional value out of assets they have previously created for projects. By doing so, artists can earn more money out of their old content, and companies can save money by buying pre-made models instead of paying an employee to create one from scratch. These marketplaces typically split the sale between themselves and the artist that created the asset, artists get 40% to 95% of the sales according to the marketplace. In most cases, the artist retains ownership of the 3d model; the customer only buys the right to use and present the model. Some artists sell their products directly in its own stores offering their products at a lower price by not using intermediaries.

Over the last several years numerous marketplaces specialized in 3D printing models have emerged. Some of the 3D printing marketplaces are combination of models sharing sites, with or without a built in e-com capability. Some of those platforms also offer 3D printing services on demand, software for model rendering and dynamic viewing of items, etc. 3D printing file sharing platforms include Shapeways, Sketchfab, Pinshape, Thingiverse, TurboSquid, CGTrader, Threeding, MyMiniFactory, and GrabCAD.

3D Printing

3D printing is a form of additive manufacturing technology where a three dimensional object is created by laying down or build from successive layers of material.

3D printing is a great way to create objects because you can create objects that you couldn't make otherwise without having complex expensive molds created or by having the objects made with multiple parts. A 3D printed part can be edited by simply editing the 3D model. That avoids having to do any additional tooling which can save time and money. 3D printing is great for testing out an idea without having to go through the production process which is great for getting a physical form of the person/company's idea.

In recent years, there has been an upsurge in the number of companies offering personalized 3D printed models of objects that have been scanned, designed in CAD software, and then printed to the customer's requirements. As previously mentioned, 3D models can be purchased from online marketplaces and printed by individuals or companies using commercially available 3D printers, enabling the home-production of objects such as spare parts, mathematical models, and even medical equipment.

Uses

Steps of forensic facial reconstruction of a mummy made in Blender by the Brazilian 3D designer Cícero Moraes.

3D modeling is used in various industries like film, animation and gaming, interior design and architecture. They are also used in the medical industry to create interactive representations of anatomy. A wide number of 3D software are also used in constructing digital representation of mechanical models or parts before they are actually manufactured. CAD/CAM related software are used in such fields, and with these software, not only can you construct the parts, but also assemble them, and observe their functionality.

3D modeling is also used in the field of Industrial Design, wherein products are 3D modeled before representing them to the clients. In Media and Event industries, 3D modeling is used in Stage/Set Design.

The OWL 2 translation of the vocabulary of X3D can be used to provide semantic descriptions for 3D models, which is suitable for indexing and retrieval of 3D models by features such as geometry, dimensions, material, texture, diffuse reflection, transmission spectra, transparency, reflectivity, opalescence, glazes, varnishes, and enamels (as opposed to unstructured textual descriptions or 2.5D virtual museums and exhibitions using Google Street View on Google Arts & Culture, for example). The RDF representation of 3D models can be used in reasoning, which enables intelligent 3D applications which, for example, can automatically compare two 3D models by volume.

Testing a 3D Solid Model

3D solid models can be tested in different ways depending on what is needed by using simulation, mechanism design, and analysis. If a motor is designed and assembled correctly (this can be done differently depending on what 3D modeling program is being used), using the mechanism tool the user should be able to tell if the motor or machine is assembled correctly by how it operates. Different design will need to be tested in different ways. For example; a pool pump would need a simulation ran of the water running through the pump to see how the water flows through the pump. These test verify if a product is developed correctly or if it needs to me modified to meet its requirements.

Reflection Mapping

An example of reflection mapping.

In computer graphics, environment mapping, or reflection mapping, is an efficient image-based lighting technique for approximating the appearance of a reflective surface by means of a precomputed texture image. The texture is used to store the image of the distant environment surrounding the rendered object.

Several ways of storing the surrounding environment are employed. The first technique was sphere mapping, in which a single texture contains the image of the surroundings as reflected on a mirror ball. It has been almost entirely surpassed by cube mapping, in which the environment is projected onto the six faces of a cube and stored as six square textures or unfolded into six square regions of a single texture. Other projections that have some superior mathematical or computational properties include the paraboloid mapping, the pyramid mapping, the octahedron mapping, and the HEALPix mapping.

The reflection mapping approach is more efficient than the classical ray tracing approach of computing the exact reflection by tracing a ray of light and following its optical path. The reflection color used in the shading computation at a pixel is determined by calculating the reflection vector at the point on the object and mapping it to the texel in the environment map. This technique often produces results that are superficially similar to those generated by raytracing, but is less computationally expensive since the radiance value of the reflection comes from calculating the angles of incidence and reflection, followed by a texture lookup, rather than followed by tracing a ray against the scene geometry and computing the radiance of the ray, simplifying the GPU workload.

However, in most circumstances a mapped reflection is only an approximation of the real reflection. Environment mapping relies on two assumptions that are seldom satisfied:

1. All radiance incident upon the object being shaded comes from an infinite distance. When this is not the case the reflection of nearby geometry appears in the wrong place on the reflected object. When this is the case, no parallax is seen in the reflection.

2. The object being shaded is convex, such that it contains no self-interreflections. When this is not the case the object does not appear in the reflection; only the environment does.

Reflection mapping is also a traditional image-based lighting technique for creating reflections of real-world backgrounds on synthetic objects.

Environment mapping is generally the fastest method of rendering a reflective surface. To further increase the speed of rendering, the renderer may calculate the position of the reflected ray at each vertex. Then, the position is interpolated across polygons to which the vertex is attached. This eliminates the need for recalculating every pixel's reflection direction.

If normal mapping is used, each polygon has many face normals (the direction a given point on a polygon is facing), which can be used in tandem with an environment map to produce a more realistic reflection. In this case, the angle of reflection at a given point on a polygon will take the normal map into consideration. This technique is used to make an otherwise flat surface appear textured, for example corrugated metal, or brushed aluminium.

Types

Sphere Mapping

Sphere mapping represents the sphere of incident illumination as though it were seen in the reflection of a reflective sphere through an orthographic camera. The texture image can be created by approximating this ideal setup, or using a fisheye lens or via prerendering a scene with a spherical mapping.

The spherical mapping suffers from limitations that detract from the realism of resulting renderings. Because spherical maps are stored as azimuthal projections of the environments they represent, an abrupt point of singularity (a "black hole" effect) is visible in the reflection on the object where texel colors at or near the edge of the map are distorted due to inadequate resolution to represent the points accurately. The spherical mapping also wastes pixels that are in the square but not in the sphere.

The artifacts of the spherical mapping are so severe that it is effective only for viewpoints near that of the virtual orthographic camera.

Cube Mapping

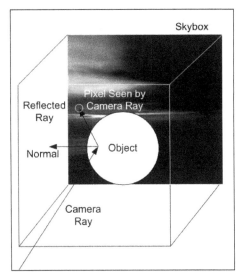

A diagram depicting an apparent reflection being
provided by cube-mapped reflection.

The map is actually projected onto the surface from the point of view of the observer. Highlights which in raytracing would be provided by tracing the ray and determining the angle made with the normal, can be "fudged", if they are manually painted into the texture field (or if they already appear there depending on how the texture map was obtained), from where they will be projected onto the mapped object along with the rest of the texture detail.

Cube mapping and other polyhedron mappings address the severe distortion of sphere maps. If cube maps are made and filtered correctly, they have no visible seams, and can be used independent of the viewpoint of the often-virtual camera acquiring the map. Cube and other polyhedron maps have since superseded sphere maps in most computer graphics applications, with the exception of acquiring image-based lighting. Image-based Lighting can be done with parallax-corrected cube maps.

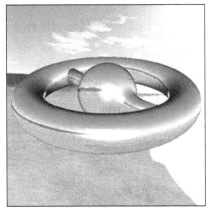

Example of a three-dimensional model
using cube-mapped reflection.

Generally, cube mapping uses the same skybox that is used in outdoor renderings. Cube-mapped reflection is done by determining the vector that the object is being viewed at. This camera ray is reflected about the surface normal of where the camera vector intersects the object. This results in the reflected ray which is then passed to the cube map to get the texel which provides the radiance value used in the lighting calculation. This creates the effect that the object is reflective.

HEALPix Mapping

HEALPix environment mapping is similar to the other polyhedron mappings, but can be hierarchical, thus providing a unified framework for generating polyhedra that better approximate the sphere. This allows lower distortion at the cost of increased computation.

Normal Mapping

In 3D computer graphics, normal mapping, or Dot3 bump mapping, is a technique used for faking the lighting of bumps and dents – an implementation of bump mapping. It is used to add details without using more polygons. A common use of this technique is to greatly enhance the appearance and details of a low polygon model by generating a normal map from a high polygon model or height map.

Normal maps are commonly stored as regular RGB images where the RGB components correspond to the X, Y, and Z coordinates, respectively, of the surface normal.

In 1978 James Blinn described how the normals of a surface could be perturbed to make geometrically flat faces have a detailed appearance. The idea of taking geometric details from a high polygon model was introduced in "Fitting Smooth Surfaces to Dense Polygon Meshes" by Krishnamurthy and Levoy, Proc. SIGGRAPH 1996, where this approach was used for creating displacement maps over nurbs. In 1998, two papers were presented with key ideas for transferring details with normal maps from high to low polygon meshes: "Appearance Preserving Simplification", by Cohen et al. SIGGRAPH 1998, and "A general method for preserving attribute values on simplified meshes" by Cignoni et al. IEEE Visualization '98. The former introduced the idea of storing surface normals directly in a texture, rather than displacements, though it required the low-detail model to be generated by a particular constrained simplification algorithm. The latter presented a simpler approach that decouples the high and low polygonal mesh and allows the recreation of any attributes of the high-detail model (color, texture coordinates, displacements, etc.) in a way that is not dependent on how the low-detail model was created. The combination of storing normals in a texture, with the more general creation process is still used by most currently available tools.

How it Works?

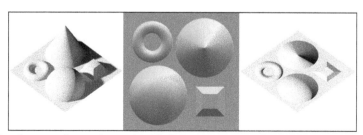

Example of a normal map (center) with the scene it was calculated from (left) and the result when applied to a flat surface (right). This map is encoded in tangent space.

To calculate the Lambertian (diffuse) lighting of a surface, the unit vector from the shading point to the light source is dotted with the unit vector normal to that surface, and the result is the intensity of the light on that surface. Imagine a polygonal model of a sphere - you can only approximate the shape of the surface. By using a 3-channel bitmap textured across the model, more detailed normal vector information can be encoded. Each channel in the bitmap corresponds to a spatial dimension (X, Y and Z). This adds much more detail to the surface of a model, especially in conjunction with advanced lighting techniques.

Spaces

Spatial dimensions differ depending on the space in which the normal map was encoded. A straightforward implementation encodes normals in object-space, so that red, green, and blue components correspond directly with X, Y, and Z coordinates. In object-space the coordinate system is constant. However object-space normal maps cannot be easily reused on multiple models, as the orientation of the surfaces differ. Since color texture maps can be reused freely, and normal maps tend to correspond with a particular texture map, it is desirable for artists that normal maps have the same property.

A texture map (left). The corresponding normal map in
tangent space (center). The normal map in object space (right).

Normal map reuse is made possible by encoding maps in tangent space. The tangent space is a vector space which is tangent to the models surface. The coordinate system varies smoothly (based on the derivatives of position with respect to texture coordinates) across the surface.

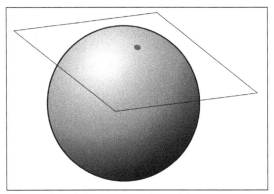

A pictorial representation of the tangent
space of a single point x on a sphere.

Tangent space normal maps can be identified by their dominant purple color, corresponding to a vector facing directly out from the surface.

Calculating Tangent Space

In order to find the perturbation in the normal the tangent space must be correctly calculated. Most often the normal is perturbed in a fragment shader after applying the model and view matrices. Typically the geometry provides a normal and tangent. The tangent is part of the tangent plane and can be transformed simply with the linear part of the matrix (the upper 3x3). However, the normal needs to be transformed by the inverse transpose. Most applications will want cotangent to match the transformed geometry (and associated UVs). So instead of enforcing the cotangent to be perpendicular to the tangent, it is generally preferable to transform the cotangent just like the tangent. Let t be tangent, b be cotangent, n be normal, M_{3x3} be the linear part of model matrix, and V_{3x3} be the linear part of the view matrix.

$$t' = t \times M_{3x3} \times V_{3x3}$$

$$b' = b \times M_{3x3} \times V_{3x3}$$

$$n' = n \times (M_{3x3} \times V_{3x3})^{-1T} = n \times M_{3x3}^{-1T} \times V_{3x3}^{-1T}$$

Interpreting Tangent Space Maps

Unit Normal vectors corresponding to the u,v texture coordinate are mapped onto normal maps. Only vectors pointing towards the viewer (z: 0 to -1 for Left Handed Orientation) are present, since the vectors on geometries pointing away from the viewer are never shown. The mapping is as follows:

```
X: -1 to +1 : Red: 0 to 255

Y: -1 to +1 : Green: 0 to 255

Z: 0 to -1 : Blue: 128 to 255

                light green      light yellow

dark cyan       light blue       light red

dark blue       dark magenta
```

- A normal pointing directly towards the viewer (0,0,-1) is mapped to (128,128,255). Hence the parts of object directly facing the viewer are light blue. The most common color in a normal map.

- A normal pointing to top right corner of the texture (1,1,0) is mapped to (255,255,128). Hence the top-right corner of an object is usually light yellow. The brightest part of a color map.

- A normal pointing to right of the texture (1,0,0) is mapped to (255,128,128). Hence the right edge of an object is usually light red.

- A normal pointing to top of the texture (0,1,0) is mapped to (128,255,128). Hence the top edge of an object is usually light green.

- A normal pointing to left of the texture (-1,0,0) is mapped to (0,128,128). Hence the left edge of an object is usually dark cyan.

- A normal pointing to bottom of the texture (0,-1,0) is mapped to (128,0,128). Hence the bottom edge of an object is usually dark magenta.

- A normal pointing to bottom left corner of the texture (-1,-1,0) is mapped to (0,0,128). Hence the bottom-left corner of an object is usually dark blue. The darkest part of a color map.

Since a normal will be used in the dot product calculation for the diffuse lighting computation, we can see that the $\{0, 0, -1\}$ would be remapped to the $\{128, 128, 255\}$ values, giving that kind of sky blue color seen in normal maps (blue (z) coordinate is perspective (deepness) coordinate and RG-xy flat coordinates on screen). $\{0.3, 0.4, -0.866\}$ would be remapped to the $(\{0.3, 0.4, -0.866\}/2+\{0.5, 0.5, 0.5\})*255=\{0.15+0.5, 0.2+0.5, -0.433+0.5\}*255=\{0.65, 0.7, 0.067\}*255=\{166, 179, 17\}$ values ($0.3^2 + 0.4^2 + (-0.866)^2 = 1$). The sign of the z-coordinate (blue channel) must be flipped to match the normal map's normal vector with that of the eye (the viewpoint or camera) or the light vector. Since negative z values mean that the vertex is in front of the camera (rather than behind the camera) this convention guarantees that the surface shines with maximum strength precisely when the light vector and normal vector are coincident.

Normal Mapping in Video Games

Interactive normal map rendering was originally only possible on PixelFlow, a parallel rendering machine It was later possible to perform normal mapping on high-end SGI workstations using multi-pass rendering and framebuffer operations or on low end PC hardware with some tricks using palletted textures. However, with the advent of shaders in personal computers and game consoles, normal mapping became widely used in commercial video games starting in late 2003. Normal mapping's popularity for real-time rendering is due to its good quality to processing requirements ratio versus other methods of producing similar effects. Much of this efficiency is made possible by distance-indexed detail scaling, a technique which selectively decreases the detail of the normal map of a given texture (cf. mipmapping), meaning that more distant surfaces require less complex lighting simulation. Many authoring pipelines use high resolution models baked into low/medium resolution in game models augmented with normal maps.

Basic normal mapping can be implemented in any hardware that supports palettized textures. The first game console to have specialized normal mapping hardware was the Sega Dreamcast. However, Microsoft's Xbox was the first console to widely use the effect in retail games. Out of the sixth generation consoles, only the PlayStation 2's GPU lacks built-in normal mapping support, though it can be simulated using the PlayStation 2 hardware's vector units. Games for the Xbox 360 and the PlayStation 3 rely heavily on normal mapping and were the first game console generation to make use of parallax mapping.

Bump Mapping

Bump mapping is a technique in computer graphics for simulating bumps and wrinkles on the surface of an object. This is achieved by perturbing the surface normals of the object and using the perturbed normal during lighting calculations. The result is an apparently bumpy surface rather than a smooth surface although the surface of the underlying object is not changed. Bump mapping was introduced by James Blinn in 1978.

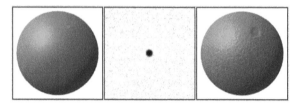

A sphere without bump mapping (left). A bump map to be applied to the sphere (middle). The sphere with the bump map applied (right) appears to have a mottled surface resembling an orange. Bump maps achieve this effect by changing how an illuminated surface reacts to light, without modifying the size or shape of the surface.

Bump mapping is limited in that it does not modify the shape of the underlying object. On the left, a mathematical function defining a bump map simulates a crumbling surface on a sphere, but the object's outline and shadow remain those of a perfect sphere. On the right, the same function is used to modify the surface of a sphere by generating an isosurface. This models a sphere with a bumpy surface with the result that both its outline and its shadow are rendered realistically.

Bump mapping is a technique in computer graphics to make a rendered surface look more realistic by simulating small displacements of the surface. However, unlike displacement mapping, the surface geometry is not modified. Instead only the surface normal is modified *as if* the surface had been displaced. The modified surface normal is then used for lighting calculations (using, for example, the Phong reflection model) giving the appearance of detail instead of a smooth surface.

Bump mapping is much faster and consumes less resources for the same level of detail compared to displacement mapping because the geometry remains unchanged.

There are also extensions which modify other surface features in addition to increasing the sense of depth. Parallax mapping is one such extension.

The primary limitation with bump mapping is that it perturbs only the surface normals without changing the underlying surface itself. Silhouettes and shadows therefore remain unaffected, which is especially noticeable for larger simulated displacements. This limitation can be overcome by techniques including displacement mapping where bumps are applied to the surface or using an isosurface.

There are two primary methods to perform bump mapping. The first uses a height map for simulating the surface displacement yielding the modified normal. This is the method invented by Blinn and is usually what is referred to as bump mapping unless specified. The steps of this method are summarized as follows.

Before a lighting calculation is performed for each visible point (or pixel) on the object's surface:

1. Look up the height in the heightmap that corresponds to the position on the surface.

2. Calculate the surface normal of the heightmap, typically using the finite difference method.

3. Combine the surface normal from step two with the true ("geometric") surface normal so that the combined normal points in a new direction.

4. Calculate the interaction of the new "bumpy" surface with lights in the scene using, for example, the Phong reflection model.

The result is a surface that appears to have real depth. The algorithm also ensures that the surface appearance changes as lights in the scene are moved around.

The other method is to specify a normal map which contains the modified normal for each point on the surface directly. Since the normal is specified directly instead of derived from a height map this method usually leads to more predictable results. This makes it easier for artists to work with, making it the most common method of bump mapping today.

Realtime Bump Mapping Techniques

Realtime 3D graphics programmers often use variations of the technique in order to simulate bump mapping at a lower computational cost.

One typical way was to use a fixed geometry, which allows one to use the heightmap surface normal almost directly. Combined with a precomputed lookup table for the lighting calculations the method could be implemented with a very simple and fast loop, allowing for a full-screen effect. This method was a common visual effect when bump mapping was first introduced.

Texture Mapping

Texture mapping is a graphic design process in which a two-dimensional (2-D) surface, called a texture map, is "wrapped around" a three-dimensional (3-D)object.Thus, the 3-D object acquires a surface texture similar to that of the 2-D surface. Texture mapping is the electronic equivalent of applying wallpaper, paint,or veneer to a real object.

The simplest texture mappings involve processes such as that shown below. Three identical squares, each covered randomly with dots, are directly mapped onto the three visible facets of a 3-D cube. This distorts the size sand shapes of the dots on the top and right-hand facets. In this mapping, the texture map covers the cube with no apparent discontinuities because of the way the dots are arranged on the squares.

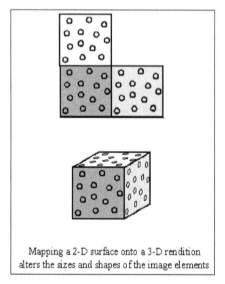

Mapping a 2-D surface onto a 3-D rendition alters the sizes and shapes of the image elements

In some mappings, the correspondence between the 2-D texture map and the 3-D object's surface becomes "messy." An example is the application of a pattern of squares to the surface of a sphere. It is impossible to paste checkered wallpaper onto a sphere without cutting the paper in such a way as to create discontinuities in the pattern. This problem occurs with many texture mappings.

A complex pattern can, in some cases, be seamlessly wedded to the surface of a 3-D object using a sophisticated graphics program.The pattern is generated directly on the 3-D rendition, rather than using a texture map.For example, a sphere can be given a wood-grain finish.The squares-on-a-sphere problem cannot be solved, but it is possible to fit a pattern of triangles onto a sphere by adjusting the sizes of the triangles.

Displacement Mapping

Displacement mapping is a powerful technique for adding detail to three dimensional objects and scenes. While bump mapping gives the appearance of increased surface complexity, displacement mapping actually adds surface complexity resulting in correct silhouettes and no parallax errors.

A major benefit of displacement mapping is the ability to use it for both adding surface detail to a model and for creating the model itself. For example the detail added to the surface of a crocodile's skin could be done with displacement mapping or all the detail required to model a piece of ter-rain can be stored in a displacement map and a flat plane used for the base surface. Displacement mapping can be applied to different base surfaces for example NPatches as used by DirectX 9 and subdivision surfaces.

Displacement mapping was first mentioned by Cook as a technique for adding surface detail to objects in a similar manner to texture mapping. A base surface can be defined by a bivariate vector function $P(u, v)$[1] that defines 3D points (x, y, z) on the surface. A corresponding scalar displacement map for that surface can be represented as d(u, v). As an alternative to the one dimensional scalar displacement vector displacements could also be used. The normals on the base surface can be represented as $\hat{N}$ (u, v). Using this representation the points on the new displaced surface P`(u, v) are defined as:

$$P'(u,v) \ = \ P(u,v) + \ d(u,v)\hat{N}(u,v)$$

Where,

$$\hat{N}(u,v) = \frac{\hat{N}(u,v)}{\left|\hat{N}(u,v)\right|}.$$

A two dimensional example of a displacement map is shown in figure, where $N'(u, v)$ is the normal to the displaced surface.

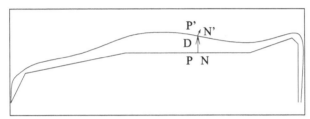

Displacement mapping.

DirectX 9.0 Displacement Mapping

The first API support for displacement mapping appears in DirectX 9.0. DirectX 9.0 supports two styles of displacement mapping, presampled and filtered. The presampled method is supported by ATI RADEON 9700 class hardware and filtered version by MATROX's Parhelia hardware.

Presampled

Presampled displacement mapping allows the user to specify the values that are used at each vertex for displacement. An NPatch surface is used as the base surface. Depending on the level of detail set for NPatch tessellation, the number of vertices will be larger after tessellation. This increase from tessellation must be taken into account when generating the number of per vertex displacement values stored in the presampled set of displacement values. The total number of displacement values used is the sum of the input number of vertices plus the number of introduced vertices from tessellation. The one dimensional displacement map assigned to the vertex shader must contain the same number of presampled displacement values. As each vertex is passed into the vertex shader a displacement value is loaded into a register from the displacement map which has been set as a texture map for sampling. To displace a vertex along the normal the displacement value is loaded into a register and used to compute a new vertex position in the vertex shader.

Filtered

Filtered displacement mapping allows the user to specify a mipmap chain of displacement maps and sample them using tri-linear filtering. Using each vertex's 2D texture coordinate, the appropriate mipmap level of the displacement map mipmap chain is bilinearly sampled based on the requied level of detail. The sampled value is placed in a register for use by the vertex shader to compute the displacement at that vertex in the same manner as that for the presampled case. The displacement map can be stored as 8bit or 16bit values.

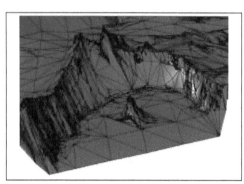

The Crater Lake.

Adaptive Tessellation Algorithms

Fixed tessellation inserts a fixed number of vertices into each triangle in a mesh regardless of whether the new vertices change the shape of the original triangle or are even visible within a particular rendering of the scene. Different schemes for adaptive tessellation for displacement mapping have been presented taking into account the change in the surface represented by the displacement map and screen size.

A scheme using a series of tests for recursive adaptive tessellation was presented by Doggett and Hirche. This scheme uses only edge based tests removing the need for global mesh information and allowing it to be implemented within the per triangle constraints of modern graphics hardware pipelines. Edge based tests also ensure that no cracking occurs when two triangles sharing the same edge introduce different tessellation levels. The edge based tests start by calculating a mid point for each edge. The first two tests are aimed at measuring the change in the curvature defined by the displacement map. Firstly the sum of displacements around the two end points and midpoint are found using a precomputed Summed-Area Table. This detects any major changes in the average height surrounding each vertex. Using the summed heights around the vertex ensures that changes in height that are not located exactly at the vertices are detected. The problem with this test is that it averages the displacement values resulting in high frequency changes in the surface being missed if there is no low frequency change. To detect the low frequency change in surface curvature the normals at the two end points are compared with the new midpoint normal. Together these two simple tests detect the changes in the displacement map. Adapting tessellation level to view point is also important and this is performed by checking the pixel length of the edge in screen space. This test needs to be performed after the points are transformed into screen space. A final test is added to check that recursive tessellation is stopped once the resolution of the displacement map is reached. An example using this adaptive displacement mapping algorithm is shown in figure.

A similar recursive adaptive scheme is presented by Moule and McCool, which improves upon the robustness of the previous algorithm by using interval analysis. By storing the minimum and maximum value in a mipmap chain, an interval that bounds an edge can be found. The naive approach would be to use the level of the interval heirarchy that bounds the desired edge, but this approach produces poor results. Instead they propose to use the union of up to four entries from the heirarchy to construct a tighter bound. This interval is compared against a threshold in screen space and if larger the edge is split. By comparing in screen space a view dependent tessellation is achieved. The combined coverage of the interval bounds on each edge of a triangle cover the entire area of the triangle. This ensures that all displacements across the surface of the triangle are taken into account. The tessellation scheme runs in real time without hardware support and is improved by preserving the results of the oracle between tessellation levels.

Other Algorithms

Doggett, Kugler and Strasser present a rasterization approach to displacement mapping where tessellation is driven by rasterization of the original triangle at an appropriate level of detail. A similar approach to using rasterization is also presented in, including the proposal to use the maximum height for generation of displacement map mipmap chains.

Lee et al. combine subdivision surfaces with displacement maps to create a surface representation that can adaptively select the level of detail by using only subdivision and bump maps, or add increasing amounts of detail by displacement mapping a subdivision surface.

A volume rendering technique presented by Kautz extrudes a volume along the normals of each triangle that contain the maximum extent of the displacement map. The volume is rendered using the typical hardware accelerated algorithm for volume rendering where transparent slices perpendicular to the view point are rendered. This technique requires high fill rates and large texture bandwidths.

References

- A-buffer-method: geeksforgeeks.org, Retrieved 23 June, 2019

- "3dworld: hardware review: caustic series2 r2500 ray-tracing accelerator card". Retrieved april 23, 2013.3d world, april 2013

- Wolf, mark j. P. (15 june 2012). Before the crash: early video game history. Wayne state university press. Isbn 978-0814337226

- System 16 - sega model 3 step 1.0 hardware (sega)". Www.system16.com. Archived from the original on 6 october 2014. Retrieved 7 may 2018

- Volume-rendering, tutorials: byclb.com, Retrieved 13 July, 2019

- Warren, tom (june 8, 2019). "microsoft hints at next-generation xbox 'scarlet' in e3 teasers". The verge. Retrieved october 8, 2019

- Thomas, j.j., and cook, k.a. (eds) (2005). An illuminated path: the research and development agenda for visual analytics, ieee computer society press, isbn 0-7695-2323-4

- Ebert, david s; musgrave, f. Kenton; peachey, darwyn; perlin, ken; worley, steven. Texturing and modeling: a procedural approach. Ap professional. Isbn 0-12-228730-4

5

3D Projection

Any method of mapping three-dimensional points on a two-dimensional plane is known as 3D projection. Some of the most common types of projection are parallel projection, orthographic projection, oblique projection, isometric projections and perspective projection. This chapter closely examines these types of 3D projection to provide an extensive understanding of the subject.

It is the process of converting a 3D object into a 2D object. It is also defined as mapping or transformation of the object in projection plane or view plane. The view plane is displayed surface.

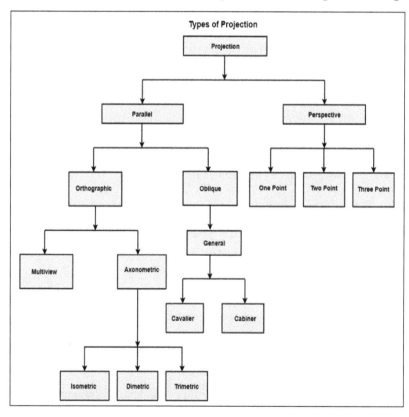

3D projectors are used to map a three dimensional data into 2-dimension surface. 3D projector is a very useful instrument to help out in the graphic work of scientists, engineers as well as designers. The process of 3D projection is used for making models in computer, with pen on paper of three dimensional objects. To make 3D projection image certain scale is used or a technique of perspective is applied. But scaling and perspective lose their characteristics once it transcribes three dimensions into two dimensions. Usually 3D is considered as model of an object it is also named to projection process in movie making.

Types of 3D Projectors

During transferring 3-dimension data into two dimension plane a sacrifice is made to lose something readily. There are two types of 3D projection with individual pros and cons.

Perspective Projection

One way to make 3D projection on to a two dimensional plane is perspective. Perspective creates an impression to the eyes as the object to be seen has three dimensions. However, when the measurements are taken it proves otherwise and do not give equal proportional. The three dimensional effects are created by using eye perspective phenomenon.

Orthographic Projection

It is also the process of projecting three dimensional object on to a two dimensional surface. This technique employs true measurements but object does not show depth. Orthographic projection has many different names as per the nature of object demonstration. These are cross-section, plane, elevation and bird's eye.

Uses of 3D Projectors

3D projectors are used in variety of fields. It is not restricted to science only rather mathematics and art also employ this technique to give practical demonstration:

- Engineers project 3D image into two dimensional surfaces as on the graph paper to show the structural demonstration of a building or house. In the process of 3D projection engineers do drafting by measuring three coordination points.

- Second used of 3D projection is in the field of computer graphics. Using the two dimensional surface of computer a 3D projection is made with the help of graphics software. Computer graphics can project environmental scene or 3 Dimensional objects.

- In the fields of science and mathematics3D projectors are used to make model of natural occurrence or demonstrate an equation.

- 3D projectors are very purposeful and demonstrative as to give effect of real life. It can be seen in movies when impression is made as a three dimensional objects are seen while in actual they are made on two dimensional surfaces.

Depth in the presentation of 3D projection is very important and its origin is traced back in 1920. Since now it has been improved radically yet the mechanism is same. To create depth two images are used to place at the same time on the screen which produce the impact of depth and give three dimensional appearances. Glasses that can filter colors or polarity enable the eyes to see the two distinct images. One's eye is able to see one image and when both eyes coordinate these two images it produces three dimensional effect.

Parallel Projection

A parallel projection is a projection of an object in three-dimensional space onto a fixed plane, known as the projection plane or image plane, where the rays, known as lines of sight or projection lines, are parallel to each other. It is a basic tool in descriptive geometry. The projection is called orthographic if the rays are perpendicular (orthogonal) to the image plane, and oblique or skew if they are not.

A parallel projection is a particular case of *projection* in mathematics and *graphical projection* in technical drawing. Parallel projections can be seen as the limit of a central or perspective projection, in which the rays pass through a fixed point called the *center* or *viewpoint*, as this point is moved towards infinity. Put differently, a parallel projection corresponds to a perspective projection with an infinite focal length (the distance between the lens and the focal point in photography) or "zoom". In parallel projections, lines that are parallel in three-dimensional space remain parallel in the two-dimensional projected image.

A perspective projection of an object is often considered more realistic than a parallel projection, since it more closely resembles human vision and photography. However, parallel projections are popular in technical applications, since the parallelism of an object's lines and faces is preserved, and direct measurements can be taken from the image. Among parallel projections, orthographic projections are the most realistic, and are commonly used by engineers. On the other hand, certain types of oblique projections (for example cavalier projection, military projection) are very simple to implement, and are used to create quick and informal pictorials of objects.

The term parallel projection is used in the literature to describe both the procedure itself (a mathematical mapping function) as well as the resulting image produced by the procedure.

Properties

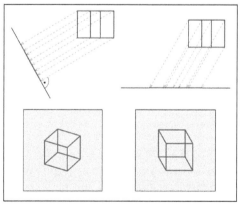

Two parallel projections of a cube. In an orthographic projection (at left), the projection lines are perpendicular to the image plane (pink). In an oblique projection (at right), the projection lines are at a skew angle to the image plane.

Every parallel projection has the following properties:

- It is uniquely defined by its projection plane Π and the direction $\vec{v}$ of the (parallel) projection lines. The direction must not be parallel to the projection plane.

- Any point of the space has a unique image in the projection plane Π, and the points of Π are fixed.

- Any line not parallel to direction $\vec{v}$ is mapped onto a line; any line parallel to $\vec{v}$ is mapped onto a point.

- Parallel lines are mapped on parallel lines, or on a pair of points (if they are parallel to $\vec{v}$).

- The ratio of the length of two line segments on a line stays unchanged. As a special case, midpoints are mapped on midpoints.

- The length of a line segment parallel to the projection plane remains unchanged. The length of any line segment is shortened if the projection is an orthographic one.

- Any circle that lies in a plane parallel to the projection plane is mapped onto a circle with the same radius. Any other circle is mapped onto an ellipse or a line segment (if direction $\vec{v}$ is parallel to the circle's plane).

- Angles in general are not preserved. But right angles with one line parallel to the projection plane remain unchanged.

- Any rectangle is mapped onto a parallelogram or a line segment (if $\vec{v}$ is parallel to the rect-angle's plane).

- Any figure in a plane that is parallel to the image plane is congruent to its image.

Orthographic Projection

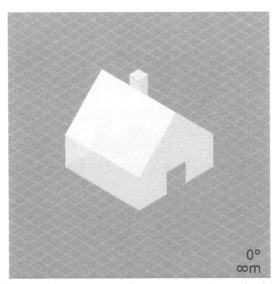

A parallel projection corresponds to a perspective projection with a hypothetical viewpoint; i.e. one where the camera lies an infinite distance away from the object and has an infinite focal length, or "zoom".

Orthographic projection is derived from the principles of descriptive geometry, and is a type of parallel projection where the projection rays are perpendicular to the projection plane. It is the projection type of choice for working drawings.

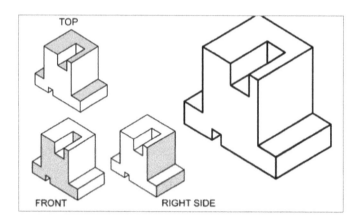

The term orthographic is sometimes reserved specifically for depictions of objects where the principal axes or planes of the object are parallel with the projection plane (or the paper on which the orthographic or parallel projection is drawn). However, the term multiview projection is also used. In multiview projections, up to six pictures of an object are produced, with each projection plane perpendicular to one of the coordinate axes. Sub-types of multiview orthographic projections include plans, elevations and sections.

When the principal planes or axes of an object are not parallel with the projection plane, but are rather tilted to some degree to reveal multiple sides of the object, it is called an axonometric projection. Axonometric projection is further subdivided into three groups: isometric, dimetric and trimetric projection, depending on the exact angle at which the view deviates from the orthogonal. A typical (but not obligatory) characteristic of axonometric pictorials is that one axis of space is usually displayed as vertical.

Oblique Projection

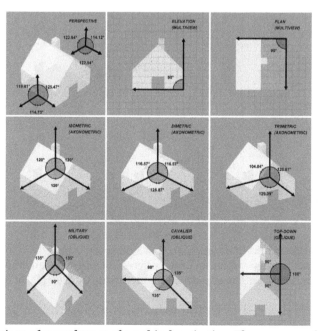

Comparison of several types of graphical projection. The presence of one or more 90° angles is usually a good indication that the perspective is *oblique*.

In an oblique projection, the parallel projection rays are not perpendicular to the viewing plane, but strike the projection plane at an angle other than ninety degrees. In both orthographic and oblique projection, parallel lines in space appear parallel on the projected image. Because of its simplicity, oblique projection is used exclusively for pictorial purposes rather than for formal, working drawings. In an oblique pictorial drawing, the displayed angles among the axes as well as the foreshortening factors (scale) are arbitrary. The distortion created thereby is usually attenuated by aligning one plane of the imaged object to be parallel with the plane of projection thereby creating a true shape, full-size image of the chosen plane. Special types of oblique projections include military, cavalier and cabinet projection.

Analytic Representation

If the image plane is given by equation $\Pi : \vec{n} \cdot \vec{x} - d = 0$ and the direction of projection by $\vec{v}$, then the projection line through the point $P : \vec{p}$ is parametrized by,

$$g : \vec{x} = \vec{p} + t\vec{v} \text{ with } t \in \mathbb{R}..$$

The image P' of P is the intersection of line g with plane Π; it is given by the equation,

$$P' : \vec{p}' = \vec{p} + \frac{d - \vec{p} \cdot \vec{n}}{\vec{n} \cdot \vec{v}} \vec{v}.$$

In several cases, these formulas can be simplified.

(S1) If one can choose the vectors $\vec{n}$ and $\vec{v}$ such that $\vec{n} \cdot \vec{v} = 1$,, the formula for the image simplifies to,

$$\vec{p}' = \vec{p} + (d - \vec{p} \cdot \vec{n}) \vec{v}.$$

(S2) In an orthographic projection, the vectors $\vec{n}$ and $\vec{v}$ are parallel. In this case, one can choose $\vec{v} = \vec{n}, |\vec{n}| = 1$ and one gets,

$$\vec{p}' = \vec{p} + (d - \vec{p} \cdot \vec{n}) \vec{n}.$$

(S3) If one can choose the vectors $\vec{n}$ and $\vec{v}$ such that $\vec{n} \cdot \vec{v} = 1$, and if the image plane contains the origin, one has $d = o$ {\displaystyle d=o} $d=o$ and the parallel projection is a linear mapping:

$$\vec{p}' = \vec{p} - (\vec{p} \cdot \vec{n}) \vec{v} = \vec{p} - (\vec{v} \otimes \vec{n}) \vec{p} = (I_3 - \vec{v} \otimes \vec{n}) \vec{p}.$$

(Here I_3 is the identity matrix and $\otimes$ the outer product.)

Orthographic Projection

Orthographic projection (sometimes orthogonal projection) is a means of representing three-dimensional objects in two dimensions. It is a form of parallel projection, in which all the projection lines are orthogonal to the projection plane, resulting in every plane of the scene appearing in affine transformation on the viewing surface. The obverse of an orthographic projection is an oblique projection, which is a parallel projection in which the projection lines are *not* orthogonal to the projection plane.

The term orthographic is sometimes reserved specifically for depictions of objects where the principal axes or planes of the object are also parallel with the projection plane, but these are better known as multiview projections. Furthermore, when the principal planes or axes of an object in an orthographic projection are not parallel with the projection plane, but are rather tilted to reveal multiple sides of the object, the projection is called an axonometric projection. Sub-types of multiview projection include plans, elevations and sections. Sub-types of axonometric projection include isometric, dimetric and trimetric projections.

A lens providing an orthographic projection is known as an object-space telecentric lens.

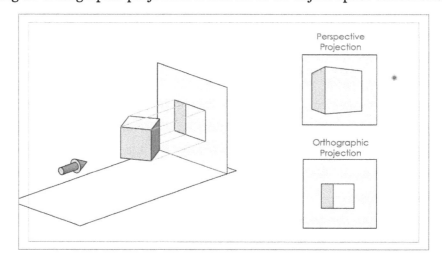

Geometry

A simple orthographic projection onto the plane $z = 0$ can be defined by the following matrix:

$$P = \begin{bmatrix} 1 & 0 & 0 \\ 0 & 1 & 0 \\ 0 & 0 & 0 \end{bmatrix}$$

For each point $v = (v_x, v_y, v_z)$, the transformed point Pv would be

$$Pv = \begin{bmatrix} 1 & 0 & 0 \\ 0 & 1 & 0 \\ 0 & 0 & 0 \end{bmatrix} \begin{bmatrix} v_x \\ v_y \\ v_z \end{bmatrix} = \begin{bmatrix} v_x \\ v_y \\ 0 \end{bmatrix}$$

Often, it is more useful to use homogeneous coordinates. The transformation above can be represented for homogeneous coordinates as

$$P = \begin{bmatrix} 1 & 0 & 0 & 0 \\ 0 & 1 & 0 & 0 \\ 0 & 0 & 0 & 0 \\ 0 & 0 & 0 & 1 \end{bmatrix}$$

For each homogeneous vector $v = (v_x, v_y, v_z, 1)$, the transformed vector Pv would be

$$pv = \begin{bmatrix} 1 & 0 & 0 & 0 \\ 0 & 1 & 0 & 0 \\ 0 & 0 & 0 & 0 \\ 0 & 0 & 0 & 1 \end{bmatrix} \begin{bmatrix} v_x \\ v_y \\ v_z \\ 1 \end{bmatrix} = \begin{bmatrix} v_x \\ v_y \\ 0 \\ 1 \end{bmatrix}$$

In computer graphics, one of the most common matrices used for orthographic projection can be defined by a 6-tuple, (left, right, bottom, top, near, far), which defines the clipping planes. These planes form a box with the minimum corner at (left, bottom, -near) and the maximum corner at (right, top, -far).

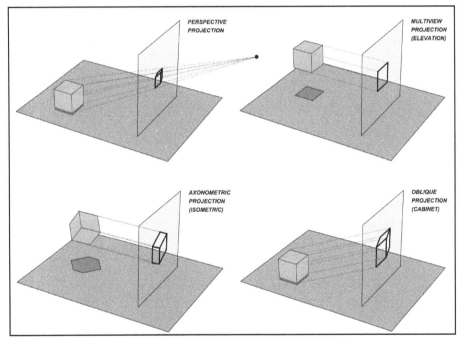

Various projections and how they are produced.

The box is translated so that its center is at the origin, then it is scaled to the unit cube which is defined by having a minimum corner at $(-1,-1,-1)$ and a maximum corner at $(1,1,1)$.

The orthographic transform can be given by the following matrix:

$$P = \begin{bmatrix} \dfrac{2}{right-left} & 0 & 0 & -\dfrac{right+left}{right-left} \\ 0 & \dfrac{2}{top-bottom} & 0 & -\dfrac{top+bottom}{top-bottom} \\ 0 & 0 & \dfrac{-2}{far-near} & -\dfrac{far+near}{far-near} \\ 0 & 0 & 0 & 1 \end{bmatrix}$$

which can be given as a scaling S followed by a translation T of the form,

$$
p = ST = \begin{bmatrix} \dfrac{2}{right-left} & 0 & 0 & 0 \\ 0 & \dfrac{2}{top-bottom} & 0 & 0 \\ 0 & 0 & \dfrac{2}{far-near} & 0 \\ 0 & 0 & 0 & 1 \end{bmatrix} \begin{bmatrix} 1 & 0 & 0 & -\dfrac{left+right}{2} \\ 0 & 1 & 0 & -\dfrac{top+bottom}{2} \\ 0 & 0 & -1 & -\dfrac{far+near}{2} \\ 0 & 0 & 0 & 1 \end{bmatrix}
$$

The inversion of the projection matrix P^{-1}, which can be used as the unprojection matrix is defined:

$$
P^{-1} = \begin{bmatrix} \dfrac{right-left}{2} & 0 & 0 & \dfrac{left+right}{2} \\ 0 & \dfrac{top-bottom}{2} & 0 & \dfrac{top+bottom}{2} \\ 0 & 0 & \dfrac{far-near}{-2} & -\dfrac{far+near}{2} \\ 0 & 0 & 0 & 1 \end{bmatrix}
$$

Sub-Types

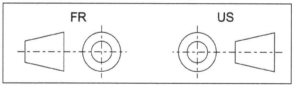

Symbols used to define whether a multiview projection
is either third-angle (right) or first-angle (left).

With multiview projections, up to six pictures of an object are produced, with each projection plane parallel to one of the coordinate axes of the object. The views are positioned relative to each other according to either of two schemes: first-angle or third-angle projection. In each, the appearances of views may be thought of as being projected onto planes that form a six-sided box around the object. Although six different sides can be drawn, usually three views of a drawing give enough information to make a three-dimensional object. These views are known as front view, top view and end view. Other names for these views include plan, elevation and section.

The term axonometric projection is used to describe the type of orthographic projection where the plane or axis of the object depicted is not parallel to the projection plane, and where multiple sides of an object are visible in the same image. It is further subdivided into three groups: isometric, dimetric and trimetric projection, depending on the exact angle at which the view deviates from the orthogonal. A typical characteristic of axonometric projection (and other pictorials) is that one axis of space is usually displayed as vertical.

Cartography

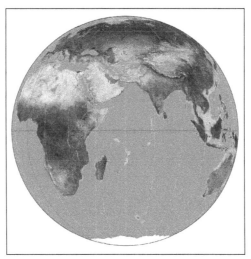

Orthographic projection (equatorial aspect)
of eastern hemisphere 30°W–150°E.

An orthographic projection map is a map projection of cartography. Like the stereographic projection and gnomonic projection, orthographic projection is a perspective (or azimuthal) projection, in which the sphere is projected onto a tangent plane or secant plane. The *point of perspective* for the orthographic projection is at infinite distance. It depicts a hemisphere of the globe as it appears from outer space, where the horizon is a great circle. The shapes and areas are distorted, particularly near the edges.

The orthographic projection has been known since antiquity, with its cartographic uses being well documented. Hipparchus used the projection in the 2nd century BC to determine the places of star-rise and star-set. In about 14 BC, Roman engineer Marcus Vitruvius Pollio used the projection to construct sundials and to compute sun positions.

Vitruvius also seems to have devised the term orthographic for the projection. However, the name *analemma*, which also meant a sundial showing latitude and longitude, was the common name until François d'Aguilon of Antwerp promoted its present name in 1613.

The earliest surviving maps on the projection appear as woodcut drawings of terrestrial globes of 1509 (anonymous), 1533 and 1551 (Johannes Schöner), and 1524 and 1551 (Apian).

Oblique Projection

Oblique projection is a simple type of technical drawing of graphical projection used for producing two-dimensional images of three-dimensional objects. The objects are not in perspective, so they do not correspond to any view of an object that can be obtained in practice, but the technique does yield somewhat convincing and useful images.

Oblique projection is commonly used in technical drawing. The cavalier projection was used by French military artists in the 18th century to depict fortifications. Oblique projection was used almost universally by Chinese artists from the first or second centuries to the 18th century, especially when depicting rectilinear objects such as houses.

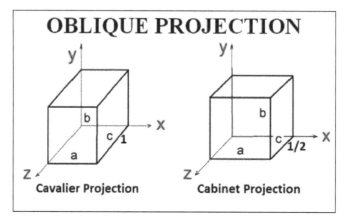

Oblique projection is a type of parallel projection:

- It projects an image by intersecting parallel rays (projectors).

- From the three-dimensional source object with the drawing surface (projection plane).

In both oblique projection and orthographic projection, parallel lines of the source object produce parallel lines in the projected image. The projectors in oblique projection intersect the projection plane at an oblique angle to produce the projected image, as opposed to the perpendicular angle used in orthographic projection.

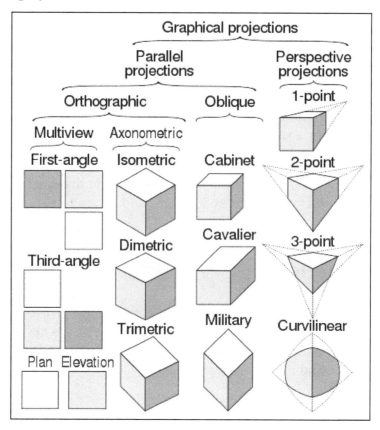

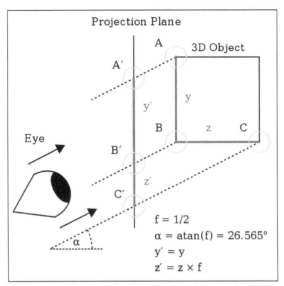

f = 1/2
α = atan(f) = 26.565°
y′ = y
z′ = z × f

Oblique projection of a cube with foreshortening
by half, seen from the side.

Mathematically, the parallel projection of the point (x, y, z) on the xy-plane gives $(x + az, y + bz, 0)$. The constants a and b uniquely specify a parallel projection. When a = b = 0, the projection is said to be "orthographic" or "orthogonal". Otherwise, it is "oblique". The constants a and b are not necessarily less than 1, and as a consequence lengths measured on an oblique projection may be either larger or shorter than they were in space. In a general oblique projection, spheres of the space are projected as ellipses on the drawing plane, and not as circles as you would expect them from an orthogonal projection.

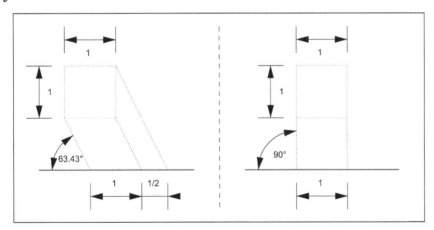

Top view of a comparison of an oblique projection (left) and an orthographic projection (right) of a unit cube (cyan) onto the projection plane (red). The foreshortening factor (1/2 in this example) is inversely proportional to the tangent of the angle (63.43° in this example) between the projection plane (colored brown) and the projection lines (dotted).

Oblique drawing is also the crudest "3D" drawing method but the easiest to master. One way to draw using an oblique view is to draw the side of the object you are looking at in two dimensions, i.e. flat, and then draw the other sides at an angle of 45°, but instead of drawing the sides full size they are only drawn with half the depth creating 'forced depth' – adding an element of realism to the object. Even with this 'forced depth', oblique drawings look very unconvincing to the eye. For this reason oblique is rarely used by professional designers or engineers.

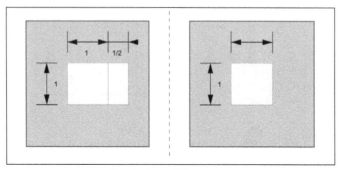

Front view of the same.

Oblique Pictorial

In an oblique pictorial drawing, the angles displayed among the axis, as well as the foreshortening factors (scale) are arbitrary. More precisely, any given set of three coplanar segments originating from the same point may be construed as forming some oblique perspective of three sides of a cube. This result is known as Pohlke's theorem, from the German mathematician Pohlke, who published it in the early 19th century.

The resulting distortions make the technique unsuitable for formal, working drawings. Nevertheless, the distortions are partially overcome by aligning one plane of the image parallel to the plane of projection. Doing so creates a true shape image of the chosen plane. This specific category of oblique projections, whereby lengths along the directions x and y are preserved, but lengths along direction z are drawn at angle using a reduction factor is very much in use for industrial drawings.

- Cavalier projection is the name of such a projection, where the length along the z axis remains unscaled.

- Cabinet projection, popular in furniture illustrations, is an example of such a technique, where in the receding axis is scaled to half-size (sometimes instead two thirds the original).

Cavalier Projection

In cavalier projection (sometimes cavalier perspective or high view point) a point of the object is represented by three coordinates, x, y and z. On the drawing, it is represented by only two coordinates, x'' and y''. On the flat drawing, two axes, x and z on the figure, are perpendicular and the length on these axes are drawn with a 1:1 scale; it is thus similar to the dimetric projections, although it is not an axonometric projection, as the third axis, here y, is drawn in diagonal, making an arbitrary angle with the x'' axis, usually 30 or 45°. The length of the third axis is not scaled.

It is very easy to draw, especially with pen and paper. It is thus often used when a figure must be drawn by hand, e.g. on a black board.

The representation was initially used for military fortifications. In French, the "cavalier" is an artificial hill behind the walls that allows to see the enemy above the walls. The cavalier perspective was the way the things were seen from this high point. Some also explain the name by the fact that it was the way a rider could see a small object on the ground from his horseback.

Cabinet Projection

The term cabinet projection (sometimes cabinet perspective) stems from its use in illustrations by the furniture industry. Like cavalier perspective, one face of the projected object is parallel to the viewing plane, and the third axis is projected as going off at an angle (typically atan(2) or about ~63.4°). Unlike cavalier projection, where the third axis keeps its length, with cabinet projection the length of the receding lines is cut in half.

Mathematical Formula

As a formula, if the plane facing the viewer is xy, and the receding axis is z, then a point P is projected like this:

$$P \begin{pmatrix} x \\ y \\ z \end{pmatrix} = \begin{pmatrix} x + \dfrac{1}{2} z \cos \alpha \\ y + \dfrac{1}{2} z \sin \alpha \\ 0 \end{pmatrix}$$

Where α is the mentioned angle.

The transformation matrix is:

$$p = \begin{bmatrix} 1 & 0 & \dfrac{1}{2} \cos \alpha \\ 0 & 1 & \dfrac{1}{2} \sin \alpha \\ 0 & 0 & 0 \end{bmatrix}$$

Alternatively you could remove one third from the leading arm projected off the starting face, thus giving the same result.

Military Projection

In the military projection, the angles of the x- and z-axes are at 45°, meaning that the angle between the x-axis and the z-axis is 90°. That is, the xz-plane is not skewed. It is rotated over 45°, though.

Examples:

Besides technical drawing and illustrations, video games (especially those preceding the advent of 3D games) also often use a form of oblique projection. Examples include SimCity, Ultima VII, Ultima Online, EarthBound, Paperboy and, more recently, Tibia.

Potting bench drawn in cabinet projection with an angle of 45° and a ratio of 2/3.

18th century plan of Port-Royal-des-Champs drawn in military projection.

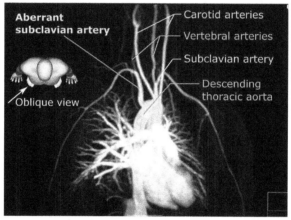

A 3D rendered magnetic resonance angiography, shown in an oblique projection in order to distinguish the aberrant subclavian artery.

Isometric Projections

Isometric projection is a method for visually representing three-dimensional objects in two dimensions in technical and engineering drawings. It is an axonometric projection in which the three coordinate axes appear equally foreshortened and the angle between any two of them is 120 degrees.

An isometric view of an object can be obtained by choosing the viewing direction such that the angles between the projections of the x, y, and z axes are all the same, or 120°. For example, with a cube, this is done by first looking straight towards one face. Next, the cube is rotated ±45° about the vertical axis, followed by a rotation of approximately 35.264° (precisely arcsin $\frac{1}{\sqrt{3}}$ or arctan $\frac{1}{\sqrt{2}}$, which is related to the Magic angle) about the horizontal axis. Note that with the cube the perimeter of the resulting 2D drawing is a perfect regular hexagon: all the black lines have equal length and all the cube's faces are the same area. Isometric graph paper can be placed under a normal piece of drawing paper to help achieve the effect without calculation.

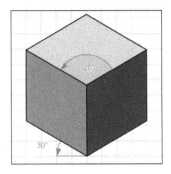

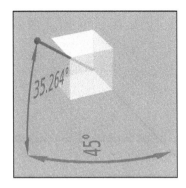

Isometric drawing of a cube.   Camera rotations needed to achieve this perspective.

In a similar way, an *isometric view* can be obtained in a 3D scene. Starting with the camera aligned parallel to the floor and aligned to the coordinate axes, it is first rotated vertically (around the horizontal axis) by about 35.264° as above, then ±45° around the vertical axis.

Another way isometric projection can be visualized is by considering a view within a cubical room starting in an upper corner and looking towards the opposite, lower corner. The x-axis extends diagonally down and right, the y-axis extends diagonally down and left, and the z-axis is straight up. Depth is also shown by height on the image. Lines drawn along the axes are at 120° to one another.

The term "isometric" is often mistakenly used to refer to axonometric projections, generally. There are, however, actually three types of axonometric projections: isometric, dimetric and trimetric.

Rotation Angles

From the two angles needed for an isometric projection, the value of the second may seem counterintuitive and deserves some further explanation. Let's first imagine a cube with sides of length 2, and its center positioned at the axis origin. We can calculate the length of the line from its center to the middle of any edge as $\sqrt{2}$ using Pythagoras' theorem . By rotating the cube by 45° on the x-axis, the point (1, 1, 1) will therefore become (1, 0, $\sqrt{2}$) as depicted in the diagram. The second rotation aims to bring the same point on the positive z-axis and so needs to perform a rotation of value equal to the arctangent of $\frac{1}{\sqrt{2}}$ which is approximately 35.264°.

Mathematics

There are eight different orientations to obtain an isometric view, depending into which octant the viewer looks. The isometric transform from a point $a_{x,y,z}$ in 3D space to a point $b_{x,y}$ in 2D space looking into the first octant can be written mathematically with rotation matrices as:

$$\begin{bmatrix} c_x \\ c_y \\ c_z \end{bmatrix} = \begin{bmatrix} 1 & 0 & 0 \\ 0 & \cos\alpha & \sin\alpha \\ 0 & -\sin\alpha & \cos\alpha \end{bmatrix} \begin{bmatrix} \cos\beta & 0 & -\sin\beta \\ 0 & 1 & 0 \\ \sin\beta & 0 & \cos\beta \end{bmatrix} \begin{bmatrix} a_x \\ a_y \\ a_z \end{bmatrix} = \frac{1}{\sqrt{6}} \begin{bmatrix} \sqrt{3} & 0 & -\sqrt{3} \\ 1 & 2 & 1 \\ \sqrt{2} & -\sqrt{2} & \sqrt{2} \end{bmatrix} \begin{bmatrix} a_x \\ a_y \\ a_z \end{bmatrix}$$

where $\alpha = \arcsin(\tan 30°) \approx 35.264°$ and $\beta = 45°$. As explained above, this is a rotation around the vertical (here y) axis by β, followed by a rotation around the horizontal (here x) axis by α. This is then followed by an orthographic projection to the xy-plane:

$$\begin{bmatrix} b_x \\ b_y \\ 0 \end{bmatrix} = \begin{bmatrix} 1 & 0 & 0 \\ 0 & 1 & 0 \\ 0 & 0 & 0 \end{bmatrix} \begin{bmatrix} c_x \\ c_y \\ c_z \end{bmatrix}$$

The other 7 possibilities are obtained by either rotating to the opposite sides or not, and then inverting the view direction or not.

Usage in Video Games and Pixel Art

Isometric graphics were regularly used in video games during the 1980s and 1990s, as the technique provided a limited 3D effect that could be achieved with the constrained resources of microcomputers of the era. The style is also used for sprites and pixel art, achieving a characteristic style still used in retrogaming.

Perspective Projection

In perspective projection farther away object from the viewer, small it appears. This property of projection gives an idea about depth. The artist use perspective projection from drawing three-dimensional scenes.

Two main characteristics of perspective are vanishing points and perspective foreshortening. Due to foreshortening object and lengths appear smaller from the center of projection. More we increase the distance from the center of projection, smaller will be the object appear.

Vanishing Point

It is the point where all lines will appear to meet. There can be one point, two point, and three point perspectives.

One Point: There is only one vanishing point.

Two Points: There are two vanishing points. One is the x-direction and other in the y -direction.

Three Points: There are three vanishing points. One is x second in y and third in two directions.

In Perspective projection lines of projection do not remain parallel. The lines converge at a single point called a center of projection. The projected image on the screen is obtained by points of intersection of converging lines with the plane of the screen. The image on the screen is seen as of viewer's eye were located at the centre of projection, lines of projection would correspond to path travel by light beam originating from object.

Important terms related to perspective:

1. View plane: It is an area of world coordinate system which is projected into viewing plane.

2. Center of Projection: It is the location of the eye on which projected light rays converge.

3. Projectors: It is also called a projection vector. These are rays start from the object scene and are used to create an image of the object on viewing or view plane.

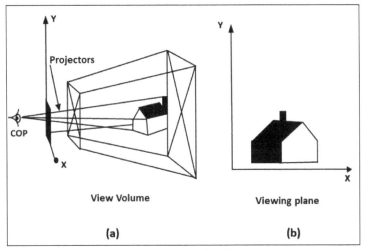

Prespective Projection.

Anomalies in Perspective Projection

It introduces several anomalies due to these object shape and appearance gets affected:

1. Perspective foreshortening: The size of the object will be small of its distance from the center of projection increases.

2. Vanishing Point: All lines appear to meet at some point in the view plane.

3. Distortion of Lines: A range lies in front of the viewer to back of viewer is appearing to six rollers.

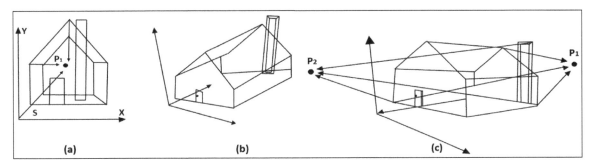

Foreshortening of the z-axis in figure (a) produces one vanishing point, P_1. Foreshortening the x and z-axis results in two vanishing points in figure (b). Adding a y-axis foreshortening in figure (c) adds vanishing point along the negative y-axis.

Translation

A translation process moves every point a constant distance in a specified direction. It can be described as a rigid motion. A translation can also be interpreted as the addition of a constant vector to every point, or as shifting the origin of the coordinate system.

Suppose, If point (X, Y) is to be translated by amount Dx and Dy to a new location (X', Y') then new coordinates can be obtained by adding Dx to X and Dy to Y as:

```
X' = Dx + X

Y' = Dy + Y

or P' = T + P where

P' = (X', Y'),

T = (Dx, Dy ),

P = (X, Y)
```

Here, P(X, Y) is the original point. T(Dx, Dy) is the translation factor, i.e. the amount by which the point will be translated. P'(X', Y') is the coordinates of point P after translation. Examples:

```
Input : P[] = {5, 6}, T = {1, 1}

Output : P'[] = {6, 7}

Input : P[] = {8, 6}, T = {-1, -1}

Output : P'[] = {7, 5}
```

Whenever we perform translation of any object we simply translate its each and every point. Some of basic objects along with their translation can be drawn as:

1. Point Translation P(X, Y) : Here we only translate the x and y coordinates of given point as per given translation factor dx and dy respectively.

   Below is the C++ program to translate a point:

```cpp
// C++ program for translation

// of a single coordinate

#include<bits/stdc++.h>

#include<graphics.h>

using namespace std;

// function to translate point

void translatePoint ( int P[], int T[])

{
    /* init graph and putpixel are used for
        representing coordinates through graphical
```

```
        functions
    */
    int gd = DETECT, gm, errorcode;
    initgraph (&gd, &gm, "c:\\tc\\bgi");


    cout<<"Original Coordinates :"<<P<<","<<P;


    putpixel (P, P, 1);


    // calculating translated coordinates
    P = P + T;
    P = P + T;


    cout<<"\nTranslated Coordinates :"<< P<<","<< P;


    // Draw new coordinatses
    putpixel (P, P, 3);
    closegraph();
}


// driver program
int main()
{
    int P = {5, 8}; // coordinates of point
    int T[] = {2, 1}; // translation factor
    translatePoint (P, T);
    return 0;
}
```

Output:

```
Original Coordinates : 5, 8
Translated Coordinates : 7, 9
```

2. **Line Translation:** The idea to translate a line is to translate both of the end points of the line by the given translation factor(dx, dy) and then draw a new line with inbuilt graphics function.

Below is the C++ implementation of above idea:

```cpp
// cpp program for translation
// of a single line
#include<bits/stdc++.h>
#include<graphics.h>

using namespace std;

// function to translate line
void translateLine ( int P[], int T[])
{
    /* init graph and line() are used for
       representing line through graphical
       functions
    */
    int gd = DETECT, gm, errorcode;
    initgraph (&gd, &gm, "c:\\tc\\bgi");

    // drawing original line using graphics functions
    setcolor (2);
    line(P, P, P, P);

    // calculating translated coordinates
    P = P + T;
    P = P + T;
    P = P + T;
    P = P + T;

    // drawing translated line using graphics functions
    setcolor(3);
    line(P, P, P, P);
    closegraph();
}
```

```
// driver program

int main()

{

    int P = {5, 8, 12, 18}; // coordinates of point

    int T[] = {2, 1}; // translation factor

    translateLine (P, T);

    return 0;

}
```

Output:

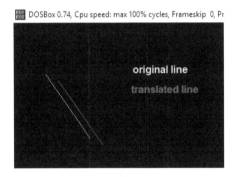

3. Rectangle Translation: Here we translate the x and y coordinates of both given points A(top left) and B(bottom right) as per given translation factor dx and dy respectively and then draw a rectangle with inbuilt graphics function:

```
// C++ program for translation

// of a rectangle

#include<bits/stdc++.h>

#include<graphics.h>

using namespace std;


// function to translate rectangle

void translateRectangle ( int P[], int T[])

{

    /* init graph and rectangle() are used for

    representing rectangle through graphical functions */

    int gd = DETECT, gm, errorcode;

    initgraph (&gd, &gm, "c:\\tc\\bgi");

    setcolor (2);

    // rectangle (Xmin, Ymin, Xmax, Ymax)
```

```
    // original rectangle

    rectangle (P, P, P, P);


    // calculating translated coordinates

    P = P + T;

    P = P + T;

    P = P + T;

    P = P + T;


    // translated rectangle (Xmin, Ymin, Xmax, Ymax)

    // setcolor(3);

    rectangle (P, P, P, P);

    // closegraph();
}


// driver program

int main()

{

    // Xmin, Ymin, Xmax, Ymax as rectangle

    // coordinates of top left and bottom right points

    int P = {5, 8, 12, 18};

    int T[] = {2, 1}; // translation factor

    translateRectangle (P, T);

    return 0;

}
```

Output:

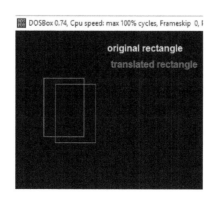

References

- Computer-graphics-projection: javatpoint.com, Retrieved 21 July, 2019

- Cucker, Felix (2013). Manifold Mirrors: The Crossing Paths of the Arts and Mathematics. Cambridge University Press. Pp. 269–278. ISBN 978-0-521-72876-8.

- 3d-projector: freewimaxinfo.com, Retrieved 27 May, 2019

- Maynard, Patric (2005). Drawing distinctions: the varieties of graphic expression. Cornell University Press. P. 22. ISBN 0-8014-7280-6.

- Computer-graphics-perspective-projection: javatpoint.com, Retrieved 18 April, 2019

- Translation-objects-computer-graphics-reference-added-please-review: geeksforgeeks.org, Retrieved 14 July, 2019

Permissions

Index

Printed in the USA
CPSIA information can be obtained
at www.ICGtesting.com
JSHW051416221024
72173JS00006B/1370